Inventing Ties and Bonds in English

Diasporic Literary Consciousness

Inventing Ties and Bonds in English

Diasporic Literary Consciousness

Edited by

Binod Mishra

P.J. Paul Dhanasekaran

AUTHORSPRESS

Worldwide Circulation through Authorspress Global Network
First Published 2008
by
Authorspress
E-35/103, Jawahar Park
Laxmi Nagar, Delhi-110 092
e-mail: authorspress@yahoo.com

Inventing Ties and Bonds in English: Diasporic Literary Consciousness
ISBN 978-81-7273-434-3

Printed in India at Tarun Offset, Delhi.

Foreword

Diaspora has emerged in recent times as a variety of literature that at least deserves to be called literature with a difference. Diasporic literature is a play upon the origins which have been lost to a literary mind. The loss of origin generates forms of memory which torture the creative imagination of the artist in very many ways. Diasporic consciousness, therefore, is an awareness of the other within the nativist's burdens of the creative psyche that oscillates between the two worlds—one lost and the other misbegotten, for it satisfies only the needs of curvatures of the body and its contours. A creative writer's nativity songs are older than the facticity of the country in which he is born for it requires a labour of five thousand years to be there where a creative writer ought to be. Revolution of consciousness is not understandable with the help of syllogistic reasoning. Consciousness is the seed syllable of a particular locale within the cosmic sense of the temporality of time and the spatiality of space. What it means is that a literary consciousness is born as an adjective and not as a noun. Naming is the first act of misplacement which, then, leads to endless displacement in one's literary outlook.

Body-mind binaries are subaltern regions within a creative writer's sublunary consciousness. This is truer of the native and the non-native versions of the identity crisis syndrome. Alienation, displacement, hybridity and acculturation, then become the aetiological forces that drive the pulley—which, in turn, victimises agents who generate them. Indian diaspora is an act of multiculturalism—a tremendous regime of historical consciousness that gets displaced in terms of metaphorical dualities that keep on incubating and exploding at given intervals of time. Migration is the core of diasporic consciousness. In a sense, all literatures the world over are diasporic in character since they are the effect of migrations made by the people from one country to another over endless periodicities of time spread over millenniums.

Thus, the theory holds that the Aryans came from central Asia and entered India via Iran and other neighbouring countries. Dravidians, the original inhabitants, were pushed back to the southern region of the country even though there were wars between *Nagvanshis* and the marauding Aryans. The Greek invasion of India is a well recorded fact of our history. The influence of Greek art and literature has also been noticed upon Indian sculpture and paintings of the times. Nativism is in crisis here. Again, Muslim invasions redefined India once and for all. Their invasion targetted centres of culture, education that belonged to the natives. The burning of the library at Patliputra is a loss India can never overcome, for so many invaluable manuscripts have already been lost. The advent of the British and the East India Company tells its own story of the englishing of India. What then is the native? And who is a native? All of us carry blood—consanguinities too deep for history to unearth. A Babylon or Mohen-jo-daro of Indus Valley Civilisation are but just interludes in the ongoing carnival that God conglomerates and disbands at the christening strokes of His desire.

Given the above burdens of textuality, what, then, is diaspora? Human societies are mixed races; it is the will to rule, to supersede others, even to underscore and overscore that generates illusions of generic necessity resulting in the birth of different species. England, America, countries in Europe and the rest are all part of what in the Indian tradition has long been known as *Vasudhaiva Kutumbakam*—the whole world is our family. When cultures grow materialistic in the outpourings of their creative energy, differences that were marginalised before come to the surface, and the conflicts between the mainstream and the substream begins. *Rig Vedic* India, thus, is not a caste or class conscious India even though later *Vedas* do mention categories that lead to differences in society at various levels. It is only in the era of *Smriti* literatures in India that caste gets the religious sanction. The differences, therefore, are sedimented and the diasporic consciouness has enough space to grow.

Buddha refused to accept the *Vedas* as the ultimate and only sources of knowledge. Krishna also proclaimed the same idea in *The Bhagavad Gita*. The 'other' is born in a culture many times; this configures tropological consciousness within a creative mind. Tropes and metaphors, by their very nature, invite comparisons between two or more objects. The diasporic consciousness can be visualised within a native tradition just as in the case of the evolution of Indian literary consciousness. Sanskrit, for example, is the language in which the major texts of the Indian tradition have been written. But there is another India—India of Malayalam, Kannada, Telugu, Tamil among other languages which, respectively, have a degree of antiquity and historicity with which many literatures in the West would stand only as a second fiddle. Such literatures might view Sanskrit as exercising colonial infiuence upon other Indian literatures. This augurs for the birth of a diasporic consciousness.The folk literatures and the languages might feel the same in relation to the standardised versions of literatures within their own regional access. This is another diaspora. Such diasporas can be multiplied indefinitely, not to speak of the troubles in Northeast India and Punjab, Jammu and Kashmir, which have 'displacement' as the root of their trouble.

Diaspora carries a certain *angst* about itself, very much in the existential sense as Sartre propounded it. All migrations are part of the 'search for gold' myth. Be it the British advent in India or the European or British migration to America—all such migrations grew under a tenacious desire to acquire and multiply material possessions. Indian diaspora now is a reality at least three hundred years old if not more. However, much of the scholarship has considered Indians' migrations to Southeast Asia, America, Britain and Europe, Australia as constituting an Indian diaspora. This is not the whole story of the daispora. Indian diaspora is also shaped, cultured and nourished by the influx of people from different countries. Such influxes and settlements do bring in a change in the native sensibility which begins architecting a different world view altogether after such habitable changes. The Greek, Muslim and the British invasions, as said earlier, did bring about a change in the normative understanding of the culture of India by natives themselves. The settlements of Hebrews,

Christians, Muslims do tell us about the transformed India, different from the *Vedic* or the Buddhist times.

Diaspora, therefore, is a twice–born fiction. There are Indians who are diasporic in consciousness within the domains of the country; there are Indians who have gone abroad for various reasons but India continues to pursue them. There are many sub-groups within a group and categories. Sindhi and Parsi poetry and novel in India, though written by native Indians, are diasporic in nature because it searches for its home elsewhere. The poetry of Nissim Ezekiel and Keki Daruwalla, for example, as poetry written by some other Indian writers, is struggling to be Indian, for such poetry shows no grasp of thousand of years of Indain tradition as manifest in terms of its rituals and dogma and the whole cultural cycle. Even when an attempt is made by such writers to belong to India, the attempt does not seem to be natively bred. This is not so with Aurobindo and Tagore where each image and each symbol smells of the son-of-the-soil theory. Diaspora, thererfore, is less about migration and more about division. A disaporic writer is a disintegrated entity. The differential distances that a creative writer has created for himself—willingly or unwillingly—are distances that marshal centricities of his ego contours. Moreover, it is not only litterateurs who have migrated abroad from India; there are technocrats, doctors, scientists, and others and many do not have any qualms of having left India. Still, the diaspora has taken place at many economic and social levels or caste, class and creed, and the responses have been varying. The diaspora is multi-lingual and not in English alone.

Aurobindo's education at Cambridge did not make him a diasporic writer. He returned to the country as India needed his services. In spite of having close links with W.B. Yeats, Rabindranath Tagore did not go outside India for a habitation and a name. The case of Toru Dutt sisters is the same. India's first generation of diasporic writers migrated to Fiji, Mauritius, Caribbean Islands and the rest of the places in Southeast Asia. Their migratory zeal was grounded in searching for means of better livelihood. These were lower and middle class people whose cries for return to the homeland seem genuine outpourings of languishing souls. But the writers who migrated after the post-independence era, during the modern and the post-modern periods, are writers with a different kind of allegiance to the homeland—the likes of Vikram Seth, Shashi Tharoor, Salman Rushdie, among many others. Even though many of these writers migrated to the West before Indian independence, the flavour and the colour of their writing is that of a city-bred Indian who uses a post-modernist idiom showing no concern with India's problems as a nation. The concern depicted is low-mimetic, derogatory, and denunciatory of India's thousands of years old culture.

Raja Rao and A. K. Ramanujan are the two writers who continue to represent India in a high-mimetic mode—the latter though not always. Raja Rao is our foremost diasporic writer. His diaspora is synthetic and not disintegrated or alienated. His India is an inborn India, inborn within him and his passion for his motherland grows and fulfils itself whatever country Raja Rao might be writing in. He is a diasporic writer who shows scriptural consciousness of India's long past. His novels are patterned upon the *Puranic* structure where the allegorical mode dominates. Allegory is the trans-temporal mode of the way Indian reality is represented. Its power of layering manifests the illusionary *(Maya)* mode only too well. The rest of the Indian writers failed to show this Indianness whle living abroad. The other diasporic writers must learn it from Raja Rao—the way India is lived and expressed abroad—the syncretist's way. Raja Rao once said that India looks much better from abroad. The urgency and imaginative clairvoyance of a creative writer link him inevitably to the object of his desire. A.K.Ramanujan, on the contrary, is not always able to keep the mode of high seriousness so urgently required for expressing the Indian reality. He has recourse to irony, satire and other low–mimetic tools that somewhat configure Indian reality in a Western way. Parthasarthy, the poet, represents yet another variety of Indian diaspora. He began writing in English while in India but his migration abroad made him switch over to his mother tongue.

Mahatma Gandhi, Jawaharlal Nehru, B.R. Ambedkar, among others represent three distinct varieties of the Indian diaspora. Gandhi's collected works have proved to be of lasting influence upon a whole generation of Indian English writers. Gandhi carried an India of his dreams in South Africa and was able to materialise it at a great cost. The grounding notions of Gandhi's textaulity are freedom from all forms of slavery, restoration of dignity to all human beings, removal of poverty and an equitable distribution of powers and responsibilities. Gandhi's speeches and his autobiography and the newspaper journal *Harijan* are of seminal importance for the students of Indian English literature. The novels of Mulk Raj Anand, R.K. Narayan, among others are based upon Gandhian ideology with vital correspondences in Buddhism, Marxism and even Christianity. Gandhi is decidedly a nation whose tale can be variously narrated by the creative writers. Gandhi dose not lose his faith in himself as an Indian even though he encounters great oppositions in terms of foreign cultures and political ideology.

Nehru's *Discovery of India* is a stylistic gem where India is reconstructed on the basis of principles of scientism, objectivity and secularism. Nehru's stint at the Trinity College, Cambridge, helped him evolve the vision of a modern India where science ran parallel to the centuries-old religious cross-currents. The diasporic face in Nehru's life makes him construct a stronger India—economically and socially. B.R. Ambedkar's stint in California made him architect the destiny of a nation. His writings have not received the focus that they need, for his is the best example of protest writing, stylistic mellifluousness not wanting. Gandhi, Nehru Ambedkar thus create a new India while spending their time outside India. They do not long for the sweet home: they come back and create it. Will our diasporic writers learn from this experiment and work accordingly? If the idealogical frontiers of the writings of Nirad C. Choudhary and Rudyard Kipling meet, the purpose of Indian diasporic writing is defeated. Denunciation of national identities by those who belong to that identity circle is the most self-abnegating act, and the tradition of such writing becomes the tradition of the Masters under whose tutelage such kind of writings flourishes. Singapore and Australia are other important destinations for Indian English literature.

The major question, though, is of the canon of Indian diasporic writing. We have to evolve a body of criticism, theory and historical perspective to account for the kind of writing diasporic literature has turned out to be. The normativities of standard have to come from the diasporic writers themselves. Aurobindos and

Raja Rao's are rare breeds and so are Gandhis and Nehrus. There is yet to emerge a significant Indian English dramataist who could organise and sediment the Indian tones, nuances and other flavours of language and character in English. *The Ramayana* and *The Mahabharata* canons no more hold good in a post-modernist era. Sanskrit poetics can only be applied partially, and not always with success. We shall have to evolve an idiom of criticism—interpretation and judgement —for the non-resident Indian English creative writer who shall continue to long for the country without ever coming to the motherland. One could get a clue here from the works of Sir William Jones, Charles Wilkins, N.B. Halhed, J.Z. Helwell, among others, who did provide critical insights that could form a base for evolving critical models in this regard. The comparative methodology is of paramount importance here. This would also involve a study of the acculturation processes that create necessary distances between the native and the foreign and *vice versa.* Diasporic literature, undoubtedly, builds up new ties, and in foreign lands, but in the process also disrupts ties, cultures and histories. The case with second and third generation diasporic writers is still different because the nature and colour of their relationship with the motherland undergoes radical transformations. Such transformations do put in the whole diasporic literary endeavour in crisis.

Binod Mishra and P.J. Paul's anthology of critical articles on the Indian diasporic writing is a praiseworthy attempt. The volume covers considerable range and period and is able to excite the imagination of a layman like me. Diasporic literature can only grow given the existential conditions under which the world has become a global vllage. Literary productions are an act of faith; a creative writer cannot but have his affinities with this or that segment of a cultural set up. To that extent all literary works have destined destinations even though the gamut of their applicability might be very vast. A global literature is a literary impossibility for that would imply the loss of the local. All universals grow in the local— a certain here and a certain there. The universal in itself is an abstraction. Diasporic Indian english fiction can stand comparison to any other kind of fiction the world over; the same might be true of Indian English diasporic poetry. This is, however, not true of Indian English Drama, or for that matter, Indian English literary theory or criticism. The editors deserve congratulations as their work might inspire many more studies to follow in this regard.

Charu Sheel Singh
Professor of English
Mahatma Gandhi Kashi Vidyapeeth
Varanasi

Preface

We are living in an age of cultural exchange and the world has shrunken into a drawing room, thanks to the spawning wings of technology. But man tries to sympathise and offer his helping hand to the problems of the world in a variety of ways. And literature continues to keep the record of all these happenings. Indian writing in English has achieved many milestones. This is not because of the writers living and contributing their mite in India alone but also because of those writers who, though living away from their nation, have kept enriching the literary world with Indian experiences, tastes, customs and cultural affiliations and, of course, the skirmishes and encounters at times. The writers of the Indian diaspora from diverse geographical locations across the globe have been supplementing to the larger palette of literary tradition. Representing an extraordinary diversity of languages, cultures, ethnicities and religious traditions, they have provided us a large canvas of diasporic consciousness blended with historical, cultural and racial connections, in addition to spiritual affinities and anomalies. Sharing with male writers, the women writers also keep enriching the perspective of gender along with the themes of migrancy, ethnicity and post-coloniality.

With a view to familiarise these writers with Indian readers, especially the students and scholars pursuing their studies in Indian colleges and universities, the need to understand and interpret the different keywords related to diaspora and their signifinace in a new world has become imperative. It is a fact that interaction, exchange and distancing do not widen but bridge the gap created by time and clime. The anthology *Inventing Ties and Bonds in English: Diasporic Literary Consciousness* is an outcome of the long felt need and expectations of avid readers endeavouring to accommodate themselves against the odds that have become a reality.

The anthology comprises twenty-two articles both from Indian and foreign scholars working in the field of diasporic literature. The authors discussed are Raja Rao, Nirad C. Chaudhuri, Amitav Ghosh, V.S. Naipaul, Bharati Mukherjee, Kamala Markandaya, Dom Moraes, Kiran Desai, Stephen Gill, Jayant Mahapatra, Chitra Banerjee Divakaruni, G.S. Sharat Chandra, etc. Since diversity is an ingredient of diasporic literature, the essays have not been arranged chronologically. In the present-day world the history and geography commingle to make an exemplary communion.

The anthology opens with a comprehensive yet critical essay by G.S. Jha. Considering Indian diaspora fiction in English, though as an experimental recreation with repetitive content, Dr. Jha does not ignore the third world consciousness that the new term offers. He finds Indian diasporic writers kowtowing to the sickness of mending their walls in a world of amendments, and craving for space in an age of spacelessness.

Laksmisree Banerjee in her incisive paper advocates the importance of the poetic texts of women authors across the world. She discovers in their works a sharp movement from the earlier agonised cries through later war cries to an emancipatory expansion of vision and space, bringing dissolution of earlier imbalances to make it a globalised reality of worlds within and beyond.

Krishna Barua makes an indepth study of Naipaul's two novels in the light of Gandhian idealism. Naipaul's fiction gives a discourse on retrieval of the present through the fabrication of the past, and experiments with the construction of the self and the challenge to cultural and ideological polarities. The tensions created in the mind of his protagonist represent the universal phenomenon of continuous movement and dispossession, and enables them to fight the challenges of the third world, believes Dr. Barua.

Basavaraj Naikar makes a very close examination of Nirad C. Chaudhary's *Three Horsemen of the New Apocalypse.* He is of the view that Chaudhary's views should not be taken only as fulminations but also as the harsh realities of modern civilisation. Though satiric in most of his works, Chaudhary holds the decadence of lifestyle and values responsible for the despair prevalent throughout the world.

P. Gopi Chand and P. Naga Suseela explore an innovative pattern in Raja Rao's *Kanthapura.* They consider the veteran novelist to be the first to introduce the ethno-cultural element, not only at the level of the theme but also at the level of the medium of narration. Rao's excellence, according to them, lies in his courage to take liberties with the grammar of King's English or Queen's English and the super-imposition of the rhythm, cadence, and grammar of the mother tongue, Kannada in particular and Indian ethos in general.

Gur Pyari Jandial makes a comparative study of the works of Bharati Mukherjee and Anjana Appachana. She discovers that though concerned with the questions of feminist ideology, Mukherjee's characters have an edge over Anjana Appachana. The protagonists of both the novelists emerge victoriously by burning in the fire of struggle and discrimination. While Appachana's characters bear trouble in their community, Mukherjee's endure as expatriates. The consciousness of their own existence helps them forge through their fissures to their real bonds.

N. Sharada Iyer in her paper on Dom Moraes traces the theme of loneliness, insecurity, continuous exile and search for redemptive love in his poems. A free-spirited Moraes, according to Dr. Iyer was a figure of paradoxes and to whom belonging was a matter of being at home in a period than a place. She considers Moraes a wandering minstrel haunted and repelled at the same time between the opposing pulls of India and England.

Ms. Shweta Kushal and Prof. Evangeline Manickam in their exhaustive paper make a close observation of Naipaul's *Magic Seeds* and call the inhabitants of a diasporic world a generation of exiles. V.S. Naipaul, according to them, expresses the migrants' dilemma of belonging, of finding their space in a world or surroundings they are not sure of, of wanting to belong to a place. In a diasporic world people belong to nowhere except the deeps within themselves.

Kalpana Purohit records the wake of a new consciousness in the light of Gandhian movement that stirred the thought processes of simple villagers in Raja Rao's *Kanthapura*. Indian diaspora is not restricted to the longings for Indian land and people but also to

Indian ideals, idols and their ideologues, and that is what Raja Rao's seminal book offers.

Naikar views Chaudhuri's *Thy Hand, Great Anarch!* as another frank expression and honest picture of continuous struggle, and of the major historical events of Indian life in general. Despite the disproportionate elements of autobiography and memoir in it, the autobiograpghy, as Naikar opines, is an outstanding repository containing cultural records of India with epic proportions.

Malati Mathur in her innovative paper traces Indian diasporic writers in Singapore. She examines the works of some Indian writers, who despite their originality and craftsmanship could not attain the status they deserved. The works of these writers both in prose and poetry comprise the fractured consciousness and problems of socio-political and cultural transformation in keeping with the theme of diasporic community at large.

Subbulakshmi Sundaram in her incisive paper underlines the importance of connectedness in Amitabh Ghosh's *The Hungry Tide*. She applauds Ghosh for integrating a whole spectrum of perspectives underscoring the unbroken thread that allows the past to possess the future as well as the present.

Shubha Mukherjee portrays identity crisis and conflicting emotions of two generations in Chitra Divakaruni's *Queen of Dreams*. Divakaruni's characters, according to Mukherjee, swing between acceptance and adjustment where the consciousness of one's being threatens one's becoming. The need to balance the two has become a diasporic reality.

Mini Chandran considers Amitav Ghosh's *The Hungry Tide*—a novel all about human language. Though making a dichotomy between the language of the powerful and the language of the subaltern, she feels the novelist having an eye and ear for lots of in-between spaces and ambiguous positions that are often interchanged among the characters.

Sudhir K. Arora in his analysis of Kamala Markandaya's novel *Pleasure City* emphasizes that only a proper synthesis between the East and the West can result in a harmony without affecting the native countries of two. The need to understand and discover each other's native roots can help in mutual existence and respect which has become a diasporic reality and which if ignored can hamper the progress of the two.

The anthology also includes Jaydeep Sarangi's interview with Stephen Gill, an Indian diasporic writer based in Canada. Gill candidly narrates the split existence of diasporic writers and poets who, though are hurt, yet can enrich themselves with the beauty and benediction of accommodating more worlds than one within to widen their scope and experience.

Ashok Kumar discovers in Nirad C. Chaudhuri a straightforward and self-centred intellectual who makes a candid expression of the typical conflict suffered by a middle-class Indian intellectual in the early years of the twentieth century because of his European sensibility acquired in the course of English education and Western influences. Though an autobiography the tone goes beyond the extent of the author's delicate narration and encompasses a decisive interlude of the nationalised history of Bengal in particular, in addition to his views on Hinduism in general.

Beerendra Pandey in his scholarly paper discovers Bharati Mukherjee's attempts to integrate the Indian and American myths in *Jasmine*. He situates this integration as Bhaba's third space—the in-between site of transition—where binary oppositions commingle through conflict. The transformed self of Jasmine, the subaltern to Jase, the empowered, according to Dr. Pandey, is an upward move constitutive of her hybrid space in particular and of subaltern in general.

Jaydeep Sarangi in his comparative study of Stephen Gill and Jayant Mahapatra raises the vital issues of land and identity. These two realities pester and provoke the craft of the two artists.While Gill's poetry is suffused with the emptiness of the people in exile and cross-cultural encounter, Mahapatra's is an unending description of socio-cultural deterioration of the present-day India. Dr.Sarangi believes that while Gill offers world- consciousness by accepting and accommodating in a multicultural world, Mahapatra endeavours to waken the Indian masses to realise the glories of the past to safeguard their true identity.

M. Rizwan Khan in his well researched paper traces the collective consciousness of Indian diasporic communities getting an outlet, and representation of their cultural affinities oscillating amidst the harsh reality of settling in a new world and resurrecting their loyalities to their native roots. Dr. Khan strongly believes that Indian films act not only as a reminder of cultural constructs to the new generation of Indian diasporic communities but also soothe the bruises of the elder generation distanced by the histories and geographies of time.

Priyanka Tripathi in her short paper on Kiran Desai's award-winning novel traces the dissatisfaction of the members of a community shifting and drifting to new horizons in search of a lucrative calling. In a disporic world where these shifts have become a common phenomena, the heart longs back and the mind often militates to accept the new reality.

The anthology comes a full circle with Basavaraj Naikar's article on G.S. Sharat Chandra's poems. His poems record the opposite pulls of longing (for India) and belonging (to America), and striking a balance between physically going away from the native country and emotionally coming home repeatedly. This paradoxical experience of going and coming happens to be an important aspect of diasporic experience.

We extend our thanks to all contributors who not only contributed their scholastic essays to this anthology but also kept enquiring from time to time. The anthology could not have been complete without the constant support, suggestions and blessings of our esteemed teachers, colleagues and friends, especially Prof. Pashupati Jha (IIT, Roorkee), Dr. Bibhu Padhi (Cuttack), Prof. Krishna Mohan (Pilani) Shri Dasho Zangley Dukpa (Vice Chancellor, Royal University of Bhutan) and Prof. Pratap Narayan Jha (LNMU, Darbhanga). We shall be failing in our duty if we do not register our deep sense of gratitude to Prof. Charu Sheel Singh (Kashi Vidyapeeth), who took the pains to read the manuscript and wrote a Foreword to it. We are also indebted to Abhyudaya Anand Mishra who helped us in formatting the manuscript patiently.

We also register our heartfelt thanks to the publisher, Authorspress, New Delhi for taking a keen interest in our proposal and publishing this anthology in less time than expected. Sudarshan Kcherry deserves a special appreciation for his prompt correspondences and subtle suggestion regarding the title of the book. We hope that the responses of the readers will go a long way in invigorating the consciousness of the diasporic world threatening space-time continuum at times. Therein rests the significance of inventing ties and bonds.

Binod Mishra
P.J. Paul Dhanasekaran

List of Contributors

Ashok Kumar, Department of Applied Science and Humanities, IMS Engineering College, Ghaziabad, Uttar Pradesh. Email-write2saini@gmail.com

Prof. Basavaraj Naikar, Professor and Chairman, Department of English, Karnatak University, Dharwad— 580003.

Beerendra Pandey, Lecturer, Central Department of English, Tribhuvan University, Kathmandu, Nepal.

Prof. Evangeline Manickam, Department of Humanities and Social Sciences, Indian Institute of Technology, Madras.

Gur Pyari Jandial, Lecturer, Department of English Studies, Dayalbagh Educational Institute, Dayalbagh, Agra- 282005.

Gauri Shankar Jha, Head, Department of English, RAF. Government College Changlang, Arunachal Pradesh.

Jaydeep Sarangi, Head, Department of English, Seva Bharati Mahavidyalaya (Vidyasagar University), Kapgari-721505, W.B., India. E-mail: sarangij@rediffmail.com

Kalpana Purohit, Associate Professor, Department of English, J N V University, Jodhpur, Rajasthan, India, E-mail: kalpana1410@rediffmail.com

Laksmisree Banerjee, Head, Department of English, JWC of the Ranchi University, Jharkhand, India.

Malati Mathur, Senior Lecturer in English, Government Arts College, Alwar, Rajasthan, India.

M. Rizwan Khan, Reader, Department of English, Aligarh Muslim University, Aligarh, U.P.

Mini Chandran, Department of Humanities & Social Sciences, Indian Institute of Technology, Kanpur, U.P.

N. Sharada Iyer, Head, Department of English, Vasanta College for Women, Rajghat Fort, Varanasi. E-Mail: sharadavns@yahoo.co.in

P. Gopi Chand, Department of English, J.K.C. College, Guntur-522006, Andhra Pradesh, India. E-mail: gopi_paruchuri@yahoo.com

P. Naga Suseela, Department of English, J.K.C. College, Guntur-522006, Andhra Pradesh, India. E-mail: pnsjkc_e@yahoo.com

Priyanka Tripathi, Research Scholar, Department of Humanities & Social Sciences, Indian Institute of Technology, Kharagpur, West Bengal, India.

Krishna Barua, Associate Professor, Department of Humanities and Social Sciences, Indian Institute of Technology, Guwahati. Email: krishnabarua@yahoo.com

Sudhir K. Arora, Department of English, Maharaja Harishchandra P.G. College, Moradabad, Uttar Pradesh. E-mail: sudhirarora_72@yahoo.com

Shubha Mukherjee, Senior Lecturer, Department of English, Sathyabama University Chennai, Tamil Nadu. E mail: shubhagm12@ gmail.com

Subbulakshmi Sundaram, Reader in English, Sourashtra College Madurai-625004, Tamil Nadu. Email: suba_m@yahoo.com

Ms. Shweta Kushal, Research Scholar, Department of Humanities & Social Sciences, Indian Institute of Technology, Madras. E-mail: eva@iitm.ac.in

Contents

1

Dimensions of Indian Diaspora Fiction in English

— Gauri Shankar Jha

Right from its inception Indian English writing has been a thwarted soul thriving on imitation, translation, borrowing, compromise and sometimes encounters: imitation implies that of British style; translation implies that of available texts; borrowing implies that of Western values; compromise implies that with alien norms, and encounter implies that of intrinsic pattern with uncomfortable exigencies. The present scenario is not altogether different and Indian diaspora fiction in English is not an exception that forms the major volume of Indian English writing. While talking of Indian diaspora fiction in English, so many questions crop up in our mind, for instance? Does it have its independent identity, Does it possess some unique characteristics that determine its separate status? Does it reflect Indianness in the true sense? How such writers rule over Indian English writing?

The present paper seeks to examine such writings that appear to me a maze of nothingness repeating the same sort of ideas in every piece of writing, in almost all works of all writers; you may call it a negative procreation, yet my vindication lies in the following proposition; for this purpose I would like to select a few writers only and their works, for the simple reason that this brief paper cannot cover its wide horizon.

Normally diaspora fiction lingers over alienation, loneliness, homelessness, existential rootlessness, nostalgia, questioning, protest and assertions and quest of identity; it also addresses issues related to amalgamation or disintegration of cultures, discrimination, margins of two different social milieus, internalising nostalgia and suffering a forced amnesia—we may call it a literary/cultural phenomenon with a distinct melting pot syndrome or that of *Salad bowl* where identity of each ingredient is under question. Surprisingly, the writer has to relocate himself afresh for which he has to undergo penance such as readjustment, adaptation, participation and fulfilment amidst dilemmas and self-imposed ghettoisation. But what about the Nobel Laureate V.S.Naipaul, my first target: where does he stand now? He associates himself with one stance, the next moment he deviates; his selection for the Nobel Prize is under question—is it for his old-fashioned travelogues, or for his autobiographical novels, or his inconsistent stories or his deciduous articles? He does not possess anything uncommon and so he cannot be taken on par with Raja Rao, Mulk Raj Anand or Shri Aurbindo, the pillars of Indian English writing. Let us analyse his work first.

To his credit, we find a plethora of works: in the name of novels, *The Mystic Masseur, The Suffrage of Elvira, Miguel Street, A House for Mr Biswas, Mr. Stone and The Knght's Companion, The Mimic Men, In a Free State, Guerrillas, A Bend in the River, Half a Life,* etc., in the name of travelogues, *The Middle Passage, An Area of Darkness, India a Wounded Civilisation, etc.*, in the name of short stories, his two books *A Flag on the Island* and *The Loss of El Dorado* and in the name of collection of articles we have *The Overcrowded Barracoon,* Movingly his house is overcrowded as he is a full-time writer and in this regard his dedication cannot be questioned. *The Mystic Masseur (1957), The Suffrage of Elvira (1958)* and *Miguel Street (1959)* deal with the rootlessness of Trinidadian society which resorts to adoption, compromise, submission, etc. for sheer survival. *An Area of Darkness* has frustration and disappointment out of nostalgia for the old land. *A House for Mr Biswas* is concerned with homelessness, as John Thieme explains:

> A complete portrait of Hindu life in colonial Trinidad has been realised through the description of Mr. Biswas' experiences in each of the novels many hours which represent: the passive dependent life of the child; the Hindu's dependent states as a member of the extended family; as abortive attempt at escape through small time

> capitalism (the chase); the construction of plantation system(the Barracks); the impossibility of complete emancipation (the house he builds at green vale and near short hills); unsuccessful parody of phantocracy (Short hills); and finally, the partial freedom possible once one has realised one's limitations (the St. James House).
>
> (Thieme, 1975, 12)

Here my contention is whether Trinidadian Hindu society is real Hindu / Indian society on the basis of which Naipaul draws the whole picture and tries to justify his stand. Not only that, such misleading projections invite erroneous reactions and criticism, too, from what India or Indian society is. *Again,* search for house is not only related to diaspora life, rather it is a common characteristic of the present life, it is a global weakness. On the other hand, Naipaul's assertions of his perfect knowledge of India, its civilisation and culture, of Hindu society and even Muslim culture do not appear to be sound enough to be relied. We do not have any evidence whether he has gone through our ancient scriptures like Eliot and Yeats, but, certainly he pretends to be so, and voice against capitalism is fashion of the day. Besides, it has autobiographical reflection too. The point that I wish to emphasize is that Naipaul does not possess anything that we may call innovative or novel, and such diasporic writing is totally irrelevant. Naipaul's making may be different, as K. Shivarama Karanth puts it:

> Rights and wrongs, dangers and rewards and many similar elements force an individual to avoid or choose courses of action . . . . Creative literature is not a marathon race. If experiences are our urge to writing, bow do we evaluate such experiences? Life consists of so many things that make it a whole. Which part or aspect is important? There are so many individual elements and the totality is life. . . .
>
> (Karanth, 1990, 8-24)

Naipaul's life seems to be betraying totality and his works are consciously carved out with insufficient patterns. It is not an ideologically innocent gesture, rather a conscious exercise revealing conflicts, repressions and contradiction suffered at the personal level. In this context Homi Bhabha seems to be more relevant as he says: "The very idea of pure ethnically cleared national identity can only be achieved through the death, literal and figurative, of the complex interweaving of history, and the culturally contingent borderlines of modem nationhood." (Bhabha., 1994, 5)

Naipaul is in almost abnormal obsession with the idea of India, and disenchanted when confronted with the ground reality and in all his texts keeps on hovering. The same thing happens with Rushdie's egotistic Salim Sinai in 1981 and Professor Malik Solanka in 2001, as 'wounded self', 'energetic fury', 'lightning strings of puppet' and 'helpless nonviolent'. Similar is the case of Vikram Seth, Amit Chaudhari, Rohinton Mistry and others. Graham Huggan explains it more clearly:

> Mediated events (refers to the Barcelona Conference, 'India: Fifty Years After', in Sept. 1997) such as these are characteristic of the current appeal of India and more specifically of Indian Literature in English consumer item."
>
> (Huggan, 2001, 59)

However, Huggan has to accept such trend as specific to diaspora writing as he further suggests:

> The future of Indian literature in English at the millennium seems indisputable, the reputations of its best known writers intact, its commercial success virtually ensured. Yet it remains a cause for concern that nearly all the recognised writers are located in the Diaspora.
>
> (Huggan, 2001, 77-78)

Not only that, diaspora writing displays its postmodern trait, too, as pointed out by Linda Hutcheon:

> Post-modernism has art forms that are fundamentally self-reflexive, in the other word, art that is self-consciously art (or artifice), literature that is openly aware of the fact that it is written and read as part of a particular culture, having as much to do with the literary past as with the social present.
>
> (Hutcheon, 1988, 12)

In fact, it is not subversion of true issue, nor a staggering exercise, rather a deep concern and anguish, the lost identity of the land of exile, in search of (perhaps) some cosmetic remedies. It is the ability to conceive India from outside with premature nationalist sentiments and its rich culture with myopic eyes but never India as it is. The reader is left awestruck — is it an appeal to racial purity, militarism, violence and religious orthodoxy— taking nation as an emotional, spiritual, religious, catholic and missionary identification of a people — a new species with hybrid identities: racial, ethnic, regional and national. The writing falls within the domain of exile, trial and homecoming. Naipaul and other diaspora writers appear to be handicapped, as they do not have a tradition of their own, it may be the particular social, political, philosophical structure of the existing society of England or America or Canada or any other country. Consequently their work remains without a meaningful hero—perhaps a multiracial immigrant, slave (of imposed culture or colonial compulsions)— restless to establish their identity; this anguishing experience of a lack of tradition remains the hallmark of their fiction. Not surprisingly, their search becomes trap as the form / theme they adopt prove to be repetitive of the colonial drive or otherwise; the man here is without a core, running after a mirage with an intense desire to live in the present, with an unanswerable future and a strong pull of the past / the root, as Nietzsche puts it, in *Thus Spoke Zarathustra*:

> In each Now, Being begins; round each. Here turns the sphere of There. The centre is everywhere. But is the path of eternity.
>
> (Marcuse, 1956,122)

Salman Rushdie is right in his observation when he says:

> In the modern age, we have come to understand our own selves as composites, often contradictory, even internally incompatible; we have understood that each of us is many different people. Our younger selves differ from our older selves; we can be bold in the company of our employers, principled when we instruct our children and corrupt when offered some secret temptation, we are serious and frivolous, loud and quiet, aggressive and easily abashed. The nineteenth century concept of the integrated self has been

> replaced by this jostling crowd of I's. And yet unless we are damaged, or deranged, we usually have a relatively clear sense with my many selves to call all of them "me".
>
> (*The Observer*, 10 August. 1997)

Naipaul intends to identify himself with the prevalent reality: social, political or personal, yet his world suffers from certain constraints such as lack of enterprising nationality, despair and anguish, undefined social potential, imperfect empathy, orchestration of perceptions, multiple, metaphorical implications, paradox of ceremonial departures, danger of non-existence and the compulsion to adopt the same beaten path. Consequently, *The Enigma of Arrival* introduces a changed man, disillusioned on arrival in the land of his imagination; *In a Free State* projects a biased protagonist, victim of alienation, loneliness and despair; *Guerrillas* laments the social situation: thoroughly materialistic, without faith, ideas or ideals, exhausted in all ways, 'about the unity of experience and the illusion of pain' (261); *A Bend in the River* presents the structural and psychological balance between the subjective and objective, internal and external, I' and 'We' society and individual, colonial West and colonised third world, ideas and actuality; *'Mr Stone and the Knigh's Companion'* humanises its narrator Mr. Stone; *A House for Mr. Biswas* cites an orphan 'Mr Biswas' maligned by the sense of excessive insecurity coupled with an urge of freedom, self-imprisoned, egoistic, subjective, personal and unfit; *The Mystic Masseur* aspires for power; *The Suffrage of Elvira* necessitates the political awakening; *The Mimic Men* questions the co-existences of politics and simplicity; and *Half a Life*, precisely, delineates an autobiography of diaspora and self. Finally Naipaul admits, in his reception speech to the Nobel Committee and the Swedish Academy in Stockholm on 7 December 2001, "I am the sum of my books." Naipaul's writing confirms Pranjape's observation:

> Since Diaspora writing emanates from identity formation leading to further and more sophisticated articulation of identity, or manifests in community, national hood, and also large global contexts, it is important to remember and perceive Diaspora space as at all time explanatory, fluid and dynamic so that intersections within histories, past and futures do not congeal into rigid boundary laden states.
>
> (Pranjape, 2001, 59)

Perhaps it is a typical twentieth century literary phenomenon, as pointed out in Selected *Writing of Gertrude Stein*:

> So the twentieth century. . . . is a time when everything cracks, where everything is destroyed, everything isolates itself; it is a more splendid thing then a period where everything follows itself.

Bharati Mukherjee, too, can be bracketed under the same category, though she considers herself an American and claims to have overthrown "the smothering tyranny of nostalgia and surmounted the temptation of ghettoisation:" (Mukherjee, 1992, 35). Contrary to her assertion, the cultural references and the intertexts that she uses in her writing defy her own statement establishing something else available in her handling of the theme of individuality, 'outsider/ insider', 'otherness', Indian customs, patriarchal tradition and the shift to American paradigms such as individual expression, autonomy and the pursuit of happiness very distinct in the progression of her writing, the early and the later ones. Her journey from *The Tiger's Daughter* (1971) to *Desirable Daughters* (2001) exhibits her movement away from the 'aloofness of expatriation' to the 'exuberance of immigration' (*Darkness*, 3); Naipaul is her mentor; she confesses:

> In my self I detect a pale and immature reflection of Naipaul; it is he who has written most movingly about the pain and absurdity of art and exile, of 'third world art' and exile among the former colonisers; the tolerant incomprehension of hosts, the absolute impossibility of ever having a home a 'Desh'.
>
> (Clark & Mukherjee, 1977, 287)

Her 'Tara' of *The Tiger's Daughter* is a typical product of Indian society, a victim of Indianness, fails to cope with the American cultural milieu, suffers from the sense of insecurity and instability, and finds herself nowhere; she is very much like Naipaul's Mr. Biswas, O'Neill's Mr. Yank and most of the characters of the twentieth century diaspora writing in search of identity, dignity, belongingness and a place of one's own. It may be construed as a satirical picture of Indian women who resort to the protection of their father or a father-like figure or husband whenever confronted with a crisis, obviously passive and dependent, in firm grip of fear and alienation like Dimple of *Wife*. Dimple's obsession is 'Americanisation' and so she prefers to obliterate her past roots and finally disillusioned, her fantasy world shattered, leading to the killing of her husband as an act of self-assertion. This is the tragic journey of an Indian wife initiating her journey from the model of Sita and culminating in the so-called American progressive society of infidelity, pregnancy, abortion, murder and blackmail. This is a typical theme of diasporic fiction, often called East-West encounter, a psychic-social problem on psycho-analytical approach of expatriate writing. Jasmine's protagonist, too, has the same fate. Analogy with Naipaul is evident as she admits in *Darkness*: "Like Naipaul, in whom I imagined a model, I tried to explore state-of-the-art expatriates. Like Naipaul, I used a mordant and self-protective irony in describing my character's pain"(2).

Another writer who deserves to be cited is Prof. Satendra Nandan who is a Fijian-Indian or Indian Australian having commitment to respect the condition of the Fijian-Indians in his poems and prose pieces such as *Line Across Black Water* (Poems), *Voice in the River* (Poems), *Faces in a Village* (Poem), *The Wounded Sea* (Novel) and *Requiem for a Rainbow.* Once again, Naipaul is a great influence here and so the same theme of nostalgia, displacement and dilemmas, survival and progress, under the hostile sky, pluralistic and symbiotic co-existence of the major ethnic communities, harrowing reality of multiculturalist nation (as Fiji), fragmented and fragmentary selves, ethnic hatred and discrimination, exile and dispossession, peripatetic and multilayered existence, lost homelands and the travails of arriving and departures, belongings and alienations, imaginary homelands and creative continuum, poignancy and pain, aesthetic and political, abduction and coafinement, civilised and civilising world, cultural and spiritual awakening, etc., also true for Meena Abdullah and Christopher Cyrill in *The Time of the Peacock*: (1965) and *The Ganga and its Tributaries* (1993), *Coming to 'Requiem for a Rainbow* of Prof. Nandan, we can very easily trace the autobiographical touches, and he admits, about his writing:

> . . . like my life it is flawed and fragmentary. But it is a story, or a version of it: one's life is, in the final analysis, the ultimate text. It would be pretentious to call it a memoir; it

> is certainly a piece of autobiographical writing. . . . This is one ordinary son's extraordinary experience." (Preface, 12)

It is a story of the marginalised and dispossessed as Naipaul's mimic men: "We were the mimic men so compellingly and lethally explored in Vidia Naipaul's novel of the same name. He had delineated, without sentimentality or compromise, the malaise of our lives. (45) The first two chapters 'Fourteenth May: an Eclipse' and 'Suva: the Twice Banished' have the history of a failed nation-state whereas 'Nadi: The River Between', 'Delhi: A Light Among the Ruins' and 'Canberra: The Goldengrove Unleaving' have diaspora consciousness coping with the inevitable process of displacement and replacement, a true story of thousands of Fijian Indians, going back to the past, in search of their roots, identity and belongingness: "Like India, it's for me a deeply beautiful world, but difficult to live up to its meaning for an individual." (71)

The diaspora self is the eternal wanderer, away from the paradise, their home: "Most of our people have become homeless in their own home country, strangers among familiar faces, lived spaces. They say exiles live in one place and remember the reality of another; one belongs where one cannot be, and one is where one does not belong" (Pie, 12). Prof. Nandan and Naipaul have the same things to say as a common approach of Diaspora fiction:

> Christopher Cyril's 'The Ganga and its Tributaries' carry the same massage: I once wanted you to marry an Indian girl, but now I want you to mix your genes. You are an Anglo Indian born in Australia. You are like a Trinity Marry mix..." (146)

Cyrill's *The Ganga and its Tributaries,* the Australia-born boy dreams of places in India made known to him by his parents; in his day-dreams and thoughts the landscapes are interchangeable:

> It occurred to me one day as I watched the model that India had roughly the same outline as Australia (21), again and, "My uncle and aunt spoke with accents that reminded me of the accents of the men who set on a natures' trip and my father was also talking with an accent."(28)

Cyrill has deliberately marginalised the white Australian figure in his work; the canvas is filled with India and Indians only; his friend Jack finds himself displaced, but the solidarity of his own family remains intact. In Mena Abdullah's *The Time of the Peacock,* Indian food and Punjabi accent (Indian English) dominate and Cyrill's characters who have the same Indian English used in the family. Indian awareness is evident in the conversation. "There is the soul of Brahmin in thee. Thou knowest how to flatter and please. Thou knowest the words that should be true." (Abdullah, 1973, 39)

Though living in a distant land these writers cannot divorce their relationship with their earlier social milieus. Edward Said explains it as a man made historical process:

> Men make their own history, that what they can know is what they have made, and extend it to geography: as both geographical and cultural entities to say nothing of historical entities, such locals, regions, geographical sectors as 'Orient' and 'Occident' are man-made. Therefore as much as the West itself, the Orient is an idea that has a history and a tradition of thought, imagery and vocabulary that have given it reality and presence in and for the West. The two geographical entities thus support and to an extent reflect each other.
>
> (Said, 1978, 5)

This particular action can be explained with Jung's concept too, "The conscious mind is based upon and result from an unconscious psyche which is prior to consciousness and continues to function together with or despite consciousnesses. (Jung, 1940, 13)

My focus, precisely, is on a common ground where different cultures meet, interact, resist and reconcile; such reconciliation does not ignore resistance, rather it is a prerequisite; it is here in the diasporic function that cultures come in contact with each other. They affirm and deny each other, accept and discard, acknowledge and resist, select and reject, and the ambivalence continues endlessly. We may notice in Bharati Mukherkjee in India (or in the Bengali Indian in New York) that gradually hybridisation starts, Americanisation creeps in and cultural indicators have no distinct mark. It becomes 'Christian-Hindu Muslim' self or 'American-English-Indian' self or likewise, and Bharati Mukherjee makes it clear in her interview with Tirthankar Chanda in 1996.

> I wrote *The Tiger's Daughter* when I was a real expatriate. I thought of beginning, middle and end from an omniscient, God-like point of view. I was also ironising the traditional Anglo Indian Fiction, but I still thought of the cosmos like a whole entity and I could step aside and look on the characters as fitting in a certain perspective. By the time, I came to write *Wife* which came out in 1975, I could introduce a limited third person who would not have the gods in his/her toes. 1 was standing just behind the shoulder of one character *Wife* has got a lot more bitterness, more venom, and more energy.
>
> (*Commonwealth*, vol.18, No.2, p. 56)

We can notice the transformation in characterisation and there is a Time when she wants to forget her past and question its being, as we find in *Jasmine*, talking to Danel, in search of a particular word for an Indian equivalent: "You mean Hindi, not Indian, there is no such thing as Indian"(10). Such writings use their diasporic status as a ploy to keep their identity separate. They dislike to recognise in India distinct cultures represented by several Indian languages—a multicultural phenomenon.

Diaspora writing directly reflects the immigrant experience that comes out of immigrant settlement. Uma Parameswaran has defined it very cautiously:

> . . . first is one of nostalgia for the homeland left behind mingled with fear in a strange land. The second is a phase in which one is so busy adjusting to the new environment that there is little creative output. The third phase is the shaping of Diaspora existence by involving themselves in ethno-cultural issues. The fourth is when they have 'arrived' and start participating in the larger world of politics and national issues.
>
> (*ALR*, Vol.1, No.2, p.165)

That is why her work bears involvement with reality, a sense of wonder and fear, acute nostalgia as in *The Door I Shut Behind Me* and *Trishanku and Other Writings*. The pull of past is so strong that throughout her works it appears and reappears and she laments, "When we leave our country we shut many doors behind ourselves though we are not aware of it at the time" and yet "there are many doors ahead of us" (Parmeswaran, 1998, 105). She cannot abandon her past and her diasporic consciousness carries its history, philosophy and vision; she cannot come over Sita, Meera, Savitri, Rama, Lakshman and Jatayu. She sticks to Indian legend and myth and collaborates Indian culture; she cannot compromise with the present, as Sharad says in *Sons Must Die and Other Plays*:

> It upsets me profoundly to find myself in a crowd. All those alien faces staring at or through you. It makes me wonder, makes me ask myself, what am I doing here? Each so self-contained, so complete, looking at me as though I should not be there.
>
> (Parmeswaran, 1998, 82)

And the next moment, the son retorts,

> *Our people, our old country, Dad. There's no 'our people' and no 'gold country' for anyone in the world any more, least of all for us. This is our country and here we shall stay.*
>
> (Parmeshwaran, 1998, 83)

Here lies the clash between the past and the present, the two generations, concern for root and rootlessness, native land and new land, preoccupation and the third space, singular culture and multiculture (cultural synthesis) --- and such trend continues in all diasporic writing.

Meena Alexander is another name who may be mentioned in this regard. Like other diasporic writers she is aware of displacement, homelessness, fragmentation of identity, dislocation, origin, race, culture and nationality too. Her prose works *Manhattan Music*, *Nampally Road*, and *The Shock of Arrival: Reflections on Postcolonial Experience* vindicate her stand whereas *Fault Lines: A Memoir* unfolds her inner self. *Manhattan Music* introduces with characters like Sandhya, Draupadi, Rashid and Jay, situated in different stages of exiles; Sandhya is in voluntary exile who complies to the societal dictates of accompanying her husband to her homeland; Draupadi inherits the complex from her parents; Rashid battles constantly with his memories of home; and, Jay, a permanent nomad for whom home or motherland is a meaningless entity. Though in exile, Sandhya never recovers from the ongoings of her motherland; the repercussions of Indian politics influences her, sketches her own image placed in her hometown. The racial tauntings are disturbing to her and she gathers the sense of insecurity; horrifying memories disturb her; and her life becomes terrible nightmares reluctantly resigning to fate. To Sandhya, New York does not provide soothing experience, in her loveliness, she is 'afloat in the city' (3), her 'memory swelling like black water threatened to drown her' (4). She has to face hyphenated identities, divided loyalties and fragmented dreams, rushes to her Egyptian lover for solace and strive hard to save her father. To Draupadi, these things matter least, she is of a different make, "born in America... epitome of newness "(3). She is aware of her family history, class disorientation, colour discriminations, multiple dislocations and homelessness. *Manhattan Music* raises all these problems, fails to solve them and finally compromises, providing no solutions at all. *Nompally Road* has a young woman as its protagonist, Mira whose homeland does not help her to translate her Romantic philosophy to become a writer and falsify the concept of nationalism, where Gandhi becomes meaningless and the rape of a poor Muslium woman Razneiza by a group of policemen is the stark reality. Now the question is that of ideology, of socialism, of commitment, of nationalism, of culture and of utopian framework, of colonial discomfort and postcolonial achievements *Fault Lines* is an autobiographical sketch that centres on the question of identity, home, culture and the postcolonial constructions. She pronounces:

> I always felt that what I really was being left out as an Indian woman. I felt that I had to go back to India (25). I carry that world around with me — writing poems that are rooted in this soil and this landscape, in a village in South India. It is as if by doing this I can reconstitute what is critical for me and nourish myself (23). My grandfather was a great idealist who really believed that there was a new India waiting, a new world based on issues like land reform and equality for all people. I had this extraordinary world available to me, (23-24).

Later on she finds my voice imprecise, my ignorance that of a perpetual immigrant, a woman with nowhere to lay her head."(32).

Shock of Arrival is yet another autobiographical narrative which furnishes gateways into Meena's psyche presented in fictional characters, the grief of homelessness. She puts together cultures, languages as well as genres to highlight her experience of diasporic self.

Jhumpa Lahiri, yet another name, though from a distant land, voices diasporic sensibility very truly. Her *Interpreter of Maladies* has bagged several prizes, at the same time, it has also invited bitter criticism from a few corners too, such as 'poverty-stricken material', 'absence of depth', 'no amount of craft and skill in language or descriptive details'; 'void at the heart of original conception'; a misfit for 'greatening of life'. 'lacking in high seriousness', 'no graph of life', 'excess of value of form over value of content ,' etc. It is a collection of nine stories, of 'mini India' settled abroad, battling with the same complex as we find in other diasporic writings: nuances of cultural interactions, native consciousness, imposed lifestyle, human despair, psychic dilemma, marital discord, loneliness, seclusion unsolved crisis, emotional frigidity, etc. Marital discord of New England forms the gist of *A Temporary Matter* which rests for a while with the birth of a new child and ends with his death; modernity takes away the lustre of value-based life and the mother remains a relic of the past. Maladjustment continues in *The Interpreter of Maladies* accompanied by infidelity.

When Mr. Rizada came to Dine is a passive political report, valuable for its characterisation. *A Real Durwan* exposes the vanity and escapist tendency ingrained in human nature, ridicules the residents of the flat who kick out Boori Ma (the symbol of maternal love and care, though incapacitated by senility), looking for a real durwan. Lahiri's derision and approbation go together. The story *Sexy* is display of sexual behaviour of women at different levels, perhaps the desire and passion of human being with unlimited frontiers, based on Freudian explanation. *Mrs. Sen's* tells us about the snobbery of the New Englanders, loneliness of Indian woman and the uncomfortable transplantation of alien culture. *The Blessed House* is a centre of compromises, sacrifices and adjustments, necessary for a sweet home. We find social satire in *The Treatment of Bibi Haldar*, human life defined in a new way. Human relationship an its different modes have been explained in the *Third and Final Continent*. Precisely these stories are an attempt to negotiate the two cultures with varying degrees of success, their attitudes, their concerns, and their lifestyles; centring on social preoccupations such as love, marriage, marital discord, extramarital affairs, old age, illness, poverty and death. Like most of the diasporic fiction, Jhumpa engages herself in exposing the conflict of culture, maladjustment, loneliness uncomfortable relationships, sexual adventures and urgency of a home with final resolution, "Now, I am *free to* discover life as *I* please," (as Bibi says in *The Treatment of Bibi Haldar*. As usual dilemmas remain unresolved, conflicts unsettled, complexities unread and questions unanswered.

Rohinton Mistry also follows the same pattern and his *Tales from Firozsha Baag* presents the smiles and tears, bickerings and blessings of a whole line of Parsi Indians in Canada. Instances of 'otherness' steeped in India is present in *The Ghost of Firozsha Baag; Squatter* deals with maladjustment leading to misadventure; *Lend M e Your Light* talks of displacement, contradictions and ambiguities—and all of them constitute a multicultural saga of great importance. The protagonist of *Swimming Lessons* and *Squatter* shuttles between Bombay and Toronto and the nation of 'otherness' and 'outsiders' haunts them. In *Lend Me Your Light* Persi never loses his identity as he belongs to the middle class whereas the upper class Jamshed adopts the American dream and develops a distaste for India; Percy remains consistent. Kersi reveals his inner self, *My entire* burden of ridden and puzzles, unsolved. . . . I, Tiresias, throbbing between two lives, humbled by the ambiguities and dichotomies confronting me —s" (*TFB*, 192). Jamshed lives in 'confusion, disdain, arrogance'. All characters of the stones reflect the diasporic anxiety in one way or the other. My proposition is to ratiocinate the repetitive trend of Indian diasporic fiction.

Now the question is whether such diasporic writers (we may call them postcolonial) intend to rewrite nationalism (in some other way) to empower indigenous traditions and cultures, depreciated by a colonial past, as a voice of the subalterns (the doubly displaced) or it is simply be an outburst of challenges of displaced mass regarding identity formation, class-conflict, nationalism and cultural dissemblance. Yes, expatriate Indians write with a sense of shared culture and shared history. In fact, the "diaspora" is a theoretical formulation that explains questions regarding cultural identity and literary representations. If we calculate truly, we find in these diasporic writers accepted oneness of culture, sought to be pronounced, from A.K. Ramanujan to Meena Alexander, from Salman Rushdie to Bharati Mukherjee and from Gayatri Spivak to Homi Bhabha. This exile has been defined variously. Edward Said calls it "one of the saddest fates "(*Reflections*, 47) 'dislocation' or an 'in-betweenness' (*Representations*, 52-58), "away from family and familiar places but also meant being a sort of permanent outcast, some one who never felt at home, and was always at odds with environment, inconsolable about the past, bitter about the present and the future" (Said, *Reflections*, 47). In this definition we have answers of the particular trend of diaspora writings. About the autobiographical tool, Leigh Gilmor points out, "Autobiography demonstrates that we can never recover the past, only represent it (86). These writers have to face the dominant feeling of 'otherness' and 'outsider' in a "state of being fully adjusted" (Said, 53); they fail to "take up life and become a citizen of just anywhere" (Said, 62), yet Said is not of the view that being exiled "is to be totally cut off, isolated hopelessly, separated from your place of origin" (*Reflections*, 48); the immigrants live, "neither completely at one with the new setting nor fully disencumbered of the old, beset with half-involvements and half detachments, nostalgic and sentimental on one level, an adept mimic or a secret outcast on another." (Said, *Reflections*, 49). In *Imaginary Homelands* Salman Rushdie says "exiles or emigrants or expatriates are haunted by some sense of loss, some urge to reclaim, to look back —we will not be capable of reclaiming precisely the thug that was lost" (10); he discovers himself and other expatriates not as "gods but wounded creatures, cracked lenses, capable only of fractured perceptions"(12). If we provide the diasporic writings the safe shelter of postcolonialism, once again, it may be read as "a free floating metaphor for cultural embattlement and as an almost obsolete signifier for the histriocity of race". (Suleri, 247). It is not surprising, to explain in simple words, one of the most complex formations of space, in human history is the emergence of the multicultural space and under this scenario, a writer has to accept it, as M.G. Vassanji tells S.C. Bill in an interview:

> We lived through a period of transitions and big change moments across continents, from India to Africa and within Africa and so on, plus the personal changes within your lives—the political changes, colonialism, wars, independence, revolution—and you had to find out why you were, what you were what happened to you. It's like coming out of a state of shock, trying to remember what happened during the lost hundred years.

In this horrible new crisis a writer cannot afford to do or discard his identity.

In my study I have tried to establish that Indian diaspora fiction in English coming out of writers settled in different countries focus the same pattern of content, which appears to be repetitive, monotonous and, at times, insignificant though they expose their genuine experience. That is why I call it a labyrinth of nihility and tautology, though I felt and lived in true sense of term. I have cited writers living in America, Australia. Fiji, Canada and England to prove my point. I have, deliberately, dropped a few names, like Salman Rushdie, who for me, is a class apart, though his writing also have those ingredients, Amitav Ghosh who believes in 'Chutnifications' of history, and a lot more. However, my observation should not be taken as a negative approach as I still feel Indian diaspora fiction in English as an experimental recreation of the third world consciousness and a valuable tradition in itself.

Bibliography

Thieme, J., "V.S Naipaul' Third World", *The Journal of Commonwealth Literature*, August 1975.

Karanth, K.S. *My Concern for Life and Literature*, Sahitya Academy, 1990.

Bhabha, H.K. *The Location of Culture*, London, New York Routledge, 1994.

Huggan, G., *The Postcolonial Exotic: Marketing the Margins*, London: Routledge; 2001.

Hutcheon, L., *The Canadian Postmodern*, Toronto: Oxford UP, 1988.

Marcuse H., *Eros and Civilisation*, London: Routledge and Kegan Paul, 1956.

Naipaul ,V,S., *Guerrillas*, Harmonworth, Penguin, 1977.

Paranjape, M., ed., *I am Diaspora": Theories, Histories, Texts*, New Delhi, Indian Pub, 2001.

Mukherjee, B. "A Four hundred years Old Woman", in Janet Sternburg ed. *The Writer on Her Work*, New York, Norton, 1992.

_______________ , *Darkness*, Toronto, Penguin, 1985.

Clark & Mukherjee, *Days and Nights in Calcutta*, New York, Dobleday, 1977.

Nandan, S., *Requiem for a Rainbow*, Canberra, Pacific Indian Publication, 2001.

Cyrill, C., *The Ganga and its Tributaries*, Victoria: Mcphee Gribble, 1993.

Said, E.W., *Orientalism*, London: Penguin Books, 1978.

Jung, C.G., *The Integration of the Personality*, Translated by Standey Dell, Lowe and Brydone Printers Ltd. London 1940.

Mukherjee, B., *Jasmine*, Harmondsworth, Penguin, 1990.

Parmeswaran, U., *Trishanku and Other Writings*, New Delhi; Prestige Books, 1998.

_______________ , *Sons Must Die &. Other Plays*, New Delhi Prestige Books, 1998.

Lahiri, J. "Interpreter of Maladies," New York, Houghton Mifflin & Co. 1999.

Mistry, Rohinton, *Tales from Firozsha Baag*, Penguin, 1987.

BIll, J.C., *Taboos : M.G. Vasanji, The Power to Bend Spoons; Interviews with Canadian Novelists*, at Beverly Damio, Toronto Mercury Press, 1988.

Suleri, S., "Woman Skin Deep; Feminism and the Postcolonial Condition", *Critical Inquiry*, 18.2 (1992).

Said, E., Intellectual Exile. Expatriates and Marginais, *"Representations of the Intellectual: The 1993 Reith Lectures*, New York, Pantheon 1994.

_______________ , "Reflections on Exile". *Out There; Marginalisations and Contempony Culteres*. ed. R. Fergusan et al. Cambridge Mass; M I T Press1990.

Rushdie, S, "Imaginary Homelands", *Essays and Criticism 1981- 1991*, London; Gretna, 1992.

Leigh, G. *Autobiographies; A Feminist Theory of Self Representation*; Ithaca; Cornell U.P. 1993.

Abdullah M. & Ray Matthew. *The Time of the Peacock*, Angus & Rob. 1973.

2

Nations of the Soul: A Global Poetic Fraternity

— Laksmisree Banerjee

In the aftermath of the Imperial Era, with the birth of independent postcolonial societies, female poetic writings have assumed a new literary significance of a novel brand of nationhood, liberalisation and democratisation. These poetic compositions cutting across barriers and wide extensions of Time and Space, in both indigenous and diasporic realms, manifest a positive, aggressive identity, which may well be defined as a socio-psychological, ethnic, cultural and literary configuration or space designated here as 'Nations of the Soul'.

The Poetic Texts of Women Authors across the Commonwealth and Eurocentric World evince a certain specific and innovative way of defining the meanings of nation, nationhood and the narrativisation of the intersecting points of gender, identity and race. Hence, it is a fruitful, critical exercise to interpret and analyse the singular coalescence of vision, perspectives and creative delineations of this new, emerging theory of 'Nation' in the context of evolving feminist and post-feminist historiography.

Within the ambit of essays on imaginary homelands and of feminist interpretations of 'Subaltern' texts in postcolonial discourse, this differentiated category of a women-specific nationhood, unifying varied segments of aesthetic sisterhood across the globe, becomes a significant area of study. This interesting genre as well as counter-canon situates as well as problematises these 'Nations of the Soul' as an extended metaphor and conceptualised space of women's experiences, issues, struggles, perceptions, projections of truths and the creative expressions of suppressed feminist histories and trajectories. This paper reflects upon the quintessential questions of homogeneity versus heterogeneity, spirit versus body, nature versus culture, multi-culturalism versus isolationism, centre versus periphery, etc.' Though reactionary and resistant to a certain extent, in the prioritisation of the female consciousness, these nations of the soul defy temporal and territorial borderlines in their formidable integrations of poetic artistry. Further, they display a certain wholeness of vision etched out of the depths of female creativity and identifiable in the harmonious resonance of women's poetic voices and activism sustaining their state of universal sisterhood.

In the course of the study, many paradoxical positions are arrived at, while the epistemological status of this dialectic naturally reinforces the problematic determination that all female creativity and narrativity in varied temporal and geospatial territories is monolithic. These debatable viewpoints could well be investigated and questioned through the critical framework of such postcolonial critique as that of R. Radhakrishnan's *Nationalism, Gender and the Narrative of Identity*, Aijaz Ahmad's reinterpretations in *Jameson's Rhetoric of Otherness and the National Allegory*, Rajeshwari Sunder Rajan's *Representing Sati : Continuities and Discontinuities* and such other critical focus on the de-colonising of the mind along with the positivist complicity with 'subaltern' insurgency and 'feminist' radicalism. The compositions of such varied world women poets as Toru Dutt, Sarojini Naidu, Kamala Das, Emily Dickinson, Christina Rosseti, Elizabeth Barret Browning, Margaret Atwood, Sylvia Plath, Gillian Clarke, Elizabeth Bartlett, Adrienne Rich, Stevie Smith, Elaine Feinstein, Edith Sitwell, Sujata Bhatt, Shanta Acharya, Chitra Divakaruni, Meena Alexander, Imtiaz Dharker, Tara Patel, Eunice De Souza, Rukmini Bhaya Nair, etc., from diverse temporal and spatial regions, could well be examined and re-evaluated as composite creators of a resurgent poetic activism lending credence and permanent validity to their 'Nations of the Soul'.

In the postulation of this new nation of womanhood, one notices a definite centralisation of women's emancipatory struggles and issues, which run parallel to and often in conflict with the earlier nationalist movements, which gave birth to postcolonial independent states. While recognising the fluidity of divergent cultural and poetic constructions, one must also keep in mind the absolute definitions used in the framing of any specific genre or canon. Says Aijaz Ahmad in his essay on the representation of women in a postmodern situation:

> The axiomatic fact about any canon formation, even when it takes shape as a counter-canon, is that when the desired literary typology is constructed, the canonising agency selects certain kinds of authors, texts and styles, privileging them over others..[1].

In this connection, one would have to accentuate and focus upon only those poetic texts, which project the selfhood and identity of women as explicit and unambiguous statements of their 'Nations of the Soul', born out of the palimpsestic, hitherto suppressed histories of women. While reading these symptomatic women's poetic compositions, one would definitely arrive at an ideological location of a representative universalism and a central poetic alliance despite cultural and historical differences. The earlier fragmentations, alienations, identity crisis and divisive forces of victimisation, easily dissolve into a newly enhanced fabric of unity and a resonant harmony. One may, in this context, re-examine Muriel Rukeyser's lines: "When I wrote of the women in their dances and wildness, it was a mask / — when I wrote of the god, / fragmented —in exile form myself / —There is no mountain, there is no god — / No more masks! / Now, for the first time, — / the fragments join in me with their own music".[2]

Maitrayee Choudhary's[3] socio-scientific etching of a liberal state based on the role of women as agents, recipients and equal participators in the formation of a nation as well as her perspective of women as the emblems of a specific culture and ethos, complete only half the picture. The other half could well be garnered through the psychoanalytic properties and symbolical elements that Julia Kristeva[4] attributes to poetic language. Our starting point could be obtained from affecting a balance of these two perspectives of a socio-culturally liberated state and the use of a revolutionary poetic language for re-defining the limitless limits of this new category. The earlier imbalances of gender, race and class being washed off, we derive new tools of creative vision, symbolism and expression in the strong and powerful 'We' of Sylvia Plath's *Mushrooms:* "Overnight, very / Whitely, discreetly —Our toes, our noses / Take hold on the loam, / Acquire the air — So many of us! So many of us! —Nudgers and shovers / Inspite of ourselves, / Our kind multiplies; / We shall by morning / Inherit the earth, / Our foot's in the door" [5]. Beyond the political and socio-scientific gamut of definitions and beyond the fallacy of the existence of a theoretical, determinate and unitary locale for a so-called 'Nation', we have an entire corpus of such metaphorical and symbolical poetic language and reconstructions of woman power, laden with the signification for asserting the truth of these conceptualised 'Nations of the Soul' as embodiments and representations of an entire female community of poets and artists across the globe. The Indian woman-poet Rajlukshmee Debee Bhattacharya, though far away from Sylvia Plath and worlds apart in both temporal and spatial terms, creates effusively a similar allegory of female power through her poem *Punarnava,* the ever renewing "velvet-green medicinal creeper" climbing up the "lichened wall —sprouting leaves, / growing in greenness / eternal companion on the rooftop." [6]

In cutting across political, cultural, geographic and time-bound barriers, these world women poets could now be assessed and acknowledged as a major aesthetic group impacting global transformations through their poetic activism and ratification of the truth, the beauty and the intensity of the woman's world as an integral part of the larger realms of human affairs. In this sense, these 'Nations of the Soul' carved out from the depths of authentic women-poetry, are formidable zones of progressive human thinking and democratisation born out of mighty women-pens, which have dissolved and dissipated the agonies, marginalisation and brutalisation of the *Wretched of the Earth.*[7] R. Radhakrishnan, in extending the line and scope of Partho Chatterjee's adverse critique of 'Indian nationalism' as a problem of male and feudal conservatism, advocates an innovative and radical feminist historiography:

"Feminist historiography is representational in the sense that it speaks for those questions and concerns that stem from women's issues initially, but in doing so, it understands (and expands) 'gender' as a category that is much more comprehensive in its scope and goes beyond its initial commitment to merely one specific constituency".[8]

This propagation of a non-totalising and non-teleological feminist historiography holds true in the perception of these 'Nations of the Soul' as relevant indices for understanding the female-specific issues as larger issues of the human world around. In this holistic framework, dealing with the representational questions and concerns of women, the politicisation of 'gender' does not hold any water. The well-defined, articulated and designated space of women-poetry, taking its birth and growth from the female artistic consciousness and socio-psychological experiences, transcends regional and local categories to be smoothly blended in a homogeneous poetic space. When Emily Dickinson speaks of the supremacy of the domain of her soul in her Poem No. 303: "The Soul selects her own Society —/ Then shuts the Door —/ Then closes the Valves of her attention" or about the sanctity of her individual Nation of the human spirit in her Poem No. 214: "I taste a liquor never brewed - / From Tankards scooped in Pearl / Not all the Vats upon the Rhine / Yield such an Alcohol! / Inebriate of Air am I / And Debauchee of Dew / Reeling through endless summer days / From Inns of Molten Blue," [9] one can almost hear Sarojini Naidu's ode to her 'Invincible Flowering Soul' in its myriad colours 'reblossoming like a grove' though strengthened 'in the flame of sorrow'. Naidu's *Indian Dancers* 'now silent, now singing and swaying and swinging — / Now wantonly winding, they flash' [10] are as strong, as stable and vibrant as Christina Rossetti's 'Earth' written in another frame of Time and Space: "Earth grown old, yet still so green, / Deep beneath her crust of cold / Nurses fire unfelt, unseen."[11]

A common alliance of poetic souls among women writers of the world becomes an undeniable catalyst in impacting the progression of contemporary society towards more balanced, modernised and equalised goals. The defiance of patriarchy in an identifiably purified and exclusive space often strikes through undertones rather than overtones, transcreating and merging subtly with the connotations and composites of womanhood and nationhood. Though one might argue that Rossetti, Dickinson and Naidu write in the conventional idiom, diction and metaphor of a bygone age, when female poetry was seeped in traditional romanticism, more in complicity with than interrogation of patriarchy, the synergies, synonymities and parallels are often deeply submerged. One may easily connect Naidu's Indian Gypsy "tameless with the bold falcon's agile grace and the lithe tiger's sinuous majesty" with Elizabeth Bartlett's "cataclysmic love" leading into "landscapes and inscapes too, sometimes tracts of unknown counties, most often the one great hill" in a single spanning thought. The all encompassing, self-assured and belligerent stance of Kamala Das asserting *"It is I who laugh, it is I who make love / — I am sinner, I am saint. I am the beloved and the / Betrayed. I have no joys which are not yours, no / Aches which are not yours. I too call myself I,"*[12] finally connects the woman with the world. It is more than evident here that feministic poetic compositions have traversed through great distances to achieve a total integration with humanistic themes. However, the predominance of the female artistic premise continues to invigorate and illuminate the wider zones of human thought and activity. Consider lines from Gillian Clarke's *Red Poppy*: "So she walks out of the rectangles / Of hard, crowded America / And floods the skies —/ You can put out the sun with poppy, / —she paints out language, land, sky, / So we can only look and drown in deeps / Of poppy under a thundering sun".[13] The unmistakable nuances, subtext and meta-text of female nationhood resonates with almost similar lines in Laksmisree Banerjee's 'Sky': "When the storm broke in, / she looked through / at the outside jettying in —/ No walls, only a heap / of dry, incinerated hopes / — She started building / once more / This time, not a home but a sky."[14] Hence, 'Nation' is no longer a traumatised space for segregation of the oppressed victim but a proclaimed arena of female fortitude and spiritual beauty, as wide as the sky, as deep as the ocean and as diversely ornate and multi-hued as a garden.

In investigating the varied linguistic, mythic, historical, cultural and symbolic dimensions and precincts of these 'Nations of the Soul', one discovers a happy interlink between every temporal and spatial category of women-poets from grandmothers, through mothers to daughters. One notices a sharp movement from the earlier agonised cries, through later war cries to a final emancipatory enlargement of vision and space with an imaginative dissolution of earlier imbalances. As Adrienne Rich expostulates in 'Frame': "Her body is different now, / It is holding together with more than a hint of fury / and more than a hint of fear,"[15] the Commonwealth and Fellowship of Poet-sisters, has finally arrived at a point of meaningful convergence. Feminism, with its backlash and a new era of Post-feminist Humanism, refocuses and redefines imaginative, conceptual and cultural parameters for the understanding of these female 'Nations of the Soul' in a broader, deeper and a more holistic category. These are no longer ghettoised, gendered spaces but significant spheres of human issues and experiences grounded in a globalised reality of worlds within and beyond worlds. Though, today's *Draupadi* is "Once more / stripped to the raw nerves and / bared in books and case studies" feeling the weight of "an anachronistic civilisation", she is now an epitome and a spokesperson of the entire human race with "the global features on her face" and "her heart arrested at a still point in history".[16] The earlier struggles, subversions, desperate battlelines and oppressive silences have given way to a new, radical tranquillity of an unconquerable nationhood of women across the world.

Notes and References

1. Aijaz Ahmad, "Salman Rushdie's Shame: Postmodern Migrancy and the Representation of Women", *In Theory*, OUP, 1992, p.123.
2. Ed. Florence Howe, "The Poem as Mask" by Muriel Rukeyser, *No More Masks*, Harper Perennial, 1973, p. xxvii.
3. Maitrayee Choudhary, "Gender in the Making of the Indian Nation-State", *Nation and National Identity in South Asia*, Orient Longman, 2000, p. 113-114.
4. John Lechte, "Introduction", *Julia Kristeva*, Routledge, 1990, pp. 5-6.
5. Ed. Fleur Adcock, "Mushrooms" by Sylvia Plath, *The Faber Book of 20th Century Women's Poetry*, Faber & Faber, 1987, p. 233.
6. Ed. H.K. Kaul, "Punarnava" by Rajlukshmee Debee Bhattacharya, *Poetry India : Emerging Voices*, Hind Pocket Books, 1992, pp. 21-22.
7. Ed. Gregory Castle, "The Wretched of the Earth" by Frantz Fanon, *Postcolonial Discourses*, Blackwell Publishers, 2001, pp. 4-5.
8. Ed. Gregory Castle, "Nationalism, Gender and the Narrative of Identity" by R. Radhakrishnan, *Postcolonial Discourses*, Blackwell Publishers, p. 193.
9. Ed. Helen McNeil, Poem Nos. 214 & 303, *Emily Dickinson : Selected Poems*, Phoenix Poetry, 2003, pp. 5 & 17.

10. Ed. K.C. Lahiri, "Indian Dancers" & "Indian Gypsy" by Sarojini Naidu, *Indo-English Poetry in Bengal,* Writers Workshop, 1974, pp. 130-135.
11. Ed. Jan Marsh, "Advent", *Christina Rossetti: Selected Poems,* Phoenix Poetry, 1996, p. 3.
12. Ed. Arlene Zide, "Introduction" by Kamala Das, *In Their Own Voice,* Penguin, 1993, p. 46.
13. Ed. Linda France, "Red Poppy" by Gillian Clarke, *Sixty Women Poets,* Bloodaxe Books, 1993, p. 85.
14. Laksmisree Banerjee, "Sky", *I am the Woman: I am the World,* UBSPD, 2004.
15. Ed. Florence Howe, "Frame" by Adrienne Rich, *No More Masks,* Harper Perennial, 1973, p. 204.
16. Ed. Arlene Zide, "Draupadi" by Lakshmi Kannan, *In Their Own Voice,* Penguin, 1993, p. 97.

3

Experiments with Truth: Restructuring of Gandhian Experiences in Naipaul's *Half a Life* and *Magic Seeds*

— *Krishna Barua*

Perhaps no life in any period has been so closely documented as that of Mahatma Gandhi, which still continues to inspire and move the masses. There may be many reservations about the way Nobel Laureate V.S. Naipaul analyses the postcolonial dilemma arising out of Gandhi's principles of non-violence and satyagraha. Probably Naipaul wants to make sure that his readers should understand Gandhi and his ideology, without building a halo around him.

The analogy between an interpretation of historical ideas and the break-up of the congealed meanings in a work of fiction is always helpful. Naipaul's attempts to understand Gandhi in his literary works have been more on the variations in structuring of identity in a dominant cultural praxis. It is of no surprise how faithfully Naipaul could produce fictional depictions of shifts in identity crisis that had inspired many such resistances, and how he could reflect that the contemporary experiences constantly demanded a redefinition of identity under Gandhian terms.

The aim of the paper is to reconsider the disenchanted paradox of the Gandhian experiments with Truth in Naipaul's *Half a Life* and *Magic Seeds*. What drove the transformation in Gandhi was his capacity for self-creation or, as he termed it, his fascination with "experiments" (Gandhi 3) in living. By tracing the central philosophical and ethical concerns that drive the desire for self-speculation, the paper shall attempt to discuss the tensions thematized in these novels, the interplay between the multiplicity of allusions to Gandhi that can investigate the history of absence or presence of memories and the success of his strategies; of encounters between the West and the East and the ambiguities that question construction of the self and the challenge to cultural and ideological polarities. Both *Half a Life* and *Magic Seeds* begin with high ideals, and end with crippling realities, which test the strength of character in times of great stress, exploring various happenings and anarchism through assorted anecdotes, drama and bawdy episodes.

A few years back on his visit to India, Naipaul had said that Mahatma Gandhi was still relevant as a "subject of study" (*The Hindu*, Feb. 29,2004) as many of his letters and other documents are still unexplored by writers. Naipaul's attempt to understand Gandhi has been more on the differences of cultural encounters. Paradoxically, it was a record more of a lacerated sensibility in his first book on India *An Area of Darkness* that Naipaul gave us his controversial radical interpretation of the early Gandhi that really disturbed. Drawing freely from the famous autobiography, Naipaul declared that Gandhi was nothing, if not self-obsessed, on his first arrival in England.

Again in *India: A Wounded Civilisation*, Naipaul had disapproved of the Indian way of life and the early Gandhi's severity of experiments of self abnegation in England and South Africa. The vow of celibacy and the non-violence he adopted, were for Naipaul, external symbolisms of the Hindu way of denying the self and its demands. However, the rise of long-suppressed identities under years of drift and aimlessness, that had radically altered Indian society in this decade remained to him a valuable record of an India in transition.

In another paradigm shift of demythologising Gandhi stands Ved Mehta, who pushes beyond history to enquire into Gandhi's ideas and successfully captures something of the nature of his influence on his followers. Naipaul had been accused of "cultural insensitivity" (Review, Jan. 2002) and likewise his observations on Gandhi are acerbic, objective and astute. Whereas Ved Mehta's *Mahatma Gandhi and his Apostles* is a refreshing portrayal of a more personalised experience of a historically accurate Gandhi, where he sought "to discover and truthfully portray the heroic but human pilgrim amid the myths" (Mehta ix). It is here that Mehta traces "the mastery of all human needs and functions, mental and bodily" (ibid) and the way the twin Gandhian concepts of "celibacy and cleanliness" *(ibid.)* was upheld through Gandhi's insistence on personal hygiene and public awareness.

Virtually all of Naipaul's writings deal with the predicament of "unanchored souls" (Nanda 2000), and over the years we can see Naipaul's reaction not just confined to Gandhi, but developing a special way of citing new kinds of knowledge about himself and India and of the half-made societies that would become his subject later.

If one looks at how Gandhi structured his weekly reflections, especially in the earlier chapters of his autobiography, several features emerge. From the perspective of his retreat into an ascetic's existence at his ashramas, Gandhi looks back upon his life as a child, his years in London and South Africa as almost reminiscent of his past selves: "They are linked to the present self, but distant from it. They are in effect, selves he had to progress through to get to where he is today" (Sharma, 52).

We can observe certain ironic parallelisms of Gandhi's autobiographical material and ideas in the journey towards self-realisation of Willie Chandran, the protagonist in the two novels selected for the study. If one is required to make a choice between the complexity of human nature, and the contradictory qualities that can co-exist in a single person, a truth emerges that is borne out by one's experience of life outside as well as inside novels. A travel through time and language, each portrayal, directly or indirectly, is leading Gandhi's life in England, Africa and returning back to India, yet there is a feeling that these countries are observed from Naipaul's personal experiences.

However, *Half a Life* has been hailed as a novel of psychological reductionism. Willie Chandran, in re-treading the survival of Naipaul's magnificent losers, shifts between reversible consciousness of unscrupulous truth on the one hand and the structuring of the rhetorics of lying and hiding on the other. It is a psychotherapic network from the interface of provincial identity to the zeitgeist of multiculturalism and its accompanying socio-centric tensions.

If we consider *Half a Life* as a means of self-expression of personal and social growth, juxtaposed with Gandhi's idealism in *My Experiments of Truth,* it is a series of probing reflections striving to invent a partial Truth under an expatriate's role, however dispassionate and inauthentic.

Willie's adventures in *Half a Life* are the subject of fictional self-parody of the complex structure of Gandhian myth of renunciation. Like Gandhi, Willie's is a sojourn of racial intersections through the triad of the "half & half" (*Half a Life,* 160) expatriate world of India, London and the Portuguese colony of Africa. Though at the end of the novel there is a deliberate shutting off in Germany, Willie comes back again to India and back again to London in *Magic Seeds.* In *Half a Life* Naipaul portrays how Willie's Brahmin father had the courage to break out of the system around the time that Gandhi had written his autobiography. This is Naipaul's perception of the abuse of Gandhian ethos of self-denial and non-violence, an ethos that scorned individual enterprise as an effective moral strategy of aggrandisement. We better understand the situation when questioning the true necessity of Gandhi's champion of the underdog when he acted as an "apologist for the caste system" (Nanda, 18) seeing through the inconsistencies between the practice and the myths that he had read as a child.

The demystification starts early when Willie's father, who remains nameless, makes a declaration to live a " life of sacrifice" (*Half a Life,* 12). When he names his son, William Somerset Chandran after the great writer, he suffers a crisis of identity of a man with self-conscious desires and split subjectivity. This art of dissimulation reaches its peak when, to emulate renunciation chosen voluntarily, and to escape the bondage of birth, he marries an untouchable woman, who is physically and mentally repulsive. The shame lingers, engulfing him in wretchedness and self-disgust. As a confessor or analyst wearing a mask, he plays a role for others and for himself. It is a caricaturing of a life of sacrifice, in short, a charade, withdrawing from "voices loud and rasping ... you have to hide somewhere, until things calm down" (ibid., 16). Ironically, his approach to life as an exacting father and husband is one of deception, of an ascetic in borrowed time.

This may have been Naipaul's narrative strategy of using the psychological substratum as an essence of identity to conquer the key motifs of Gandhism, oppression and slavery. In retrospect, it would be pertinent to comment on the "few escapades" (Nanda, 10), which Gandhi wrote of himself in his autobiography as a boy bridegroom and his practice of *brahmacharya* (self-control) in later life. Literally Gandhi's struggles were marked by battles with his conscience in a never-ending fight to uphold the truth. Naipaul may have seen a narcissistic Gandhi in adopting and living these methods towards a purer, larger ideal, but admitted that it was this self-involvement and truthfulness that permitted Gandhi to become a charismatic leader.

Again we come closer to the real praxis. If Naipaul's intention in some way was in crafting fiction in the light of life narratives, his interpretation of the narrative self of the protagonist's tensions of resistance between verisimilitude and deep secrets shows an interplay between self, mind and inner experiences as that in Mahatma Gandhi's *My Experiments with Truth*, which is in itself a persuasive confession of his subjection to the most rigorous ethical discipline. A victim of hypersensitive conscience, Gandhi had considered it a gross hypocrisy and a violation of Truth not to implement his principles in the smallest actions of daily life. He possessed extraordinary conviction in his beliefs, and went to any physical lengths to uphold them. Even though Willie tries to mask his identity in a myriad of ways, his lack of context can be a reverse engineering metonymy. On the contrary, he tries to shield himself by hiding from the truth because it confronts him with his inner wounds.

When Gandhi had said in his autobiography that "I simply want to tell the story of my numerous experiments with Truth" (Gandhi, 3), so in Willie, there is constant hazard and self-consciousness, where the self gropes for freedom, or rather an illusion of it. Willie is himself "a hybrid" (Champeon, 1), entrapped in a destiny that waver and zigzag amid a triangle of opposing and counterbalancing factors. In his hollow London experience, everything frightened. It was close to Gandhi's purely internal adventure of anxieties in his first encounter of the great city of London in 1890, which Ved Mehta recalls:

> To be an Indian student in London in the late Victorian period was to move on the fringes of English society... Gandhi seemed to have developed an early taste for eccentrics of all kinds—Indian as well as English. (Mehta, 91)

In *Magic Seeds* Naipaul makes Sarojini say: "In London he was like a sleepwalker. He had no means of understanding the great city. He hardly knew what he was looking at..all he could think of was his law studies and his vegetarian food and cutting his own hair" (*Magic Seeds,* 16). Correspondingly, Willie's sojourn on the razor edge of inarticulation becomes "loveless, brutal, a failed rite of passage of masculinity..and almost always inadequate" (Arunima, 54). The reason behind self-absorption is not necessarily self-love, and he continuously resists truth, avoiding facing problems by hiding from them. Guilt and inadequacies need camouflage, developing a series of masks to cover up inherent weaknesses. Identity becomes subjugation to the mechanics of the body, when Willie becomes like "a sexual athlete" (*Half a Life,* 121). "Sex, lies and betrayal are always intertwined" ((Arunima, 54), leading to oppressive and reactionary situations where those who hate being judged are the very people who tend to be judgemental themselves. The parallel between sex and cities is powerful and goes to the heart of Naipaul's preoccupation with individuals as "private cells" (Naipaul, *The Mimic Men,* 22).

Consequently, when Willie arrives with Ana in the new Portuguese territory, he at once decides to leave: "I don't know where I am. I don't think I can pick my way back. I don't ever want this view to become familiar. I must not unpack" (*Half a Life,* 135). This leads Willie to a series of destructive sexual transgressions with no remnants of re-examination and series of betrayals removed from the tangible world of realities. Willie in his frequent excursions to town suffers the pleasures of the wilderness with the suffering people in permanent bondage. For Freud the unconscious was primarily if not exclusively a sexual unconscious. Michael V. Adams asserts that in addition to the sexuality of the unconscious, there is the "raciality" (Vanmoy Adams, 1) of the unconscious. For Naipaul, racial consciousness could never be transcended as a kind of liberation into a bi-cultural experience, and the attempt to have a "global belonging" (*The Hindu,* Feb. 29, 2004) was impossible to attain.

Throughout the novel, there are the processes of transference and counter- transference, projection and translation of unsettling patterns of unresolved conflicts and chronic splits of trapped silence of the Body, which is used as the source of hiding instinct and premature death of inner sensations. Gandhi saw human beings as "four dimensional" (Iyer, ed.16-48) in nature. The body was "self-enclosed, distinct, clearly separated from others" (Parekh, 54) and capable of maintaining its integrity only by preserving its separateness. The body was "the seat of the senses, and thus of the wants and desires associated with them" (ibid.). In *My Experiments with Truth,* Gandhi recalls his voluntary vow of celibacy to get rid of the carnal desires, which he felt were nothing but an impediment to his spiritual development. He successfully implemented which no one in history had ever considered practically possible. Erikson, the eminent Harvard psychoanalyst in probing the ambivalence in Gandhi calls it "a moral absolutism", which Gandhi used "as a weapon against his own instinctuality" (Erickson, 250). Even this fastidiousness in practising what he preached and the advocacy of the simple life led to constant frictions and strains within his family. It was a continuous struggle to reconcile the demands of a public and private life. Although he thought that he had eliminated all traces of violence, he was aware of another form of aggression, "the presence of unconscious sexuality" (Parekh, 28). Accordingly he decided to put his celibacy to the

> severest test by embarking on the extraordinary experiment of sleeping naked with carefully chosen female associates, partly to flush out such residues of sexuality as might remain, and partly to generate the immense energy he thought he needed to subdue the evil raging around him (ibid 28-29).

Willie's fall on slippery substance in Africa, could have been a probable metaphor of Gandhi's Pretoria experience which leads to a break from one hiding-to another, the problematic relations of history, memory and forgetting. The "bruises and cuts" (*Half a Life,* 136) of his long stay of eighteen years brings shame. Shame, though painful, can be an important first step toward self-awareness. "I have risked nothing.... and now the best part of my life is over"(ibid., 138). What the novel attempts to change is not the centring or decentring of time. But a decentrement of subjectivity, a displacement of irony, through a methodical forgetfulness of time that erases, constructs and deconstructs again. The constant shifts between the past, the present, and the future may also reflect preoccupation with social and psychological inconsistencies. This is what Paul Ricoeur meant when he said that forgetting "remains the disturbing threat that lurks in the background of the phenomenology of memory and the epistemology of history" (Ricoeur, 412).

Within days of coming to Berlin, Willie had begun to lean on the strength of his sister. Becoming a survivor, the idea of an alternative world of absence does not bother him. It is the possibility of a complete nothingness and apparent nihilism that Homi Bhabha examines. He literally "loses a feeling of place, or his sense of identification with a place, and he equates placelessness with loss and disorder" (Bhabha, 154). He looks at some Tamil boys raising funds for a great Tamil war-

> I am not like them. They have proclaimed who they are and they are risking everything for it. I have been hiding from myself. I have risked nothing and now the best part of my life is over (ibid., 138).

There is no slippage, but a sense of disjunction and immobility leading to a suspension of judgement where suffering is likewise immobilised. This is because in Willie "Decay and disappearance are a fundamental theme in Naipaul's writing-but without grief, rather as something that makes existence bearable" (Engdahl, 3).

Probably Naipual could understand another side of Gandhi. The Gandhi that could outgrow his idea was not a "cloistered virtue" (Nanda, 143), for he lived and acted according to the challenges of social and political life. Willie Chandran, similarly outgrowing his ideas, however was alone and disengaged throughout, with no trace of any inward questioning. Naipaul asserts that this is "colonial shame and fantasy ..about how the powerless lie about themselves, and lie to themselves, since it is their only resource" (Naipaul, *Two Worlds*, 8). This made Willie reach a point of stasis where neither any country could hide him, nor was he able to go back to his birthplace. Willie's displacement does not necessarily trace the usual "post -colonial predicament" (Arunima, 54), but history, in its diverse portrayal itself becomes "a special case of an all embracing permanent present, waiting to be interpreted and reinterpreted" (Nandy, 57).

However, in Naipaul's *Magic Seeds* through the reconceptualisation of the changing Gandhian concepts of subjectivity

and freedom, Willie continues his disenchanted wanderings, listlessly looking for a meaning to his life. Throughout *Magic Seeds*, we are shifted between Willie's point of view and that of an omniscient voice narrating in a vocabulary that is starkly sanitised and stripped.

In the start of the novel, Willie attempts to find that elusive centre of his world, the centre that lay not in any particular place but in the many areas of darkness of his own inchoate diverse past. When he comments "I was always someone on the outside" (*Magic Seeds*, 2), his sister Sarojini tells him, "You were on the outside because you wanted to be. You've always preferred to hide. It's the colonial psychosis" (ibid). Willie's experiments of captivity and shame were structured somewhat around the postcolonial dilemma of

> ambivalence of splitting, denial, repetition - strategies of defense that mobilize culture as an opentextured, warlike strategy whose aim is rather a continued agony than a total disappearance of the pre-existing culture (Bhabha 102-122).

Willie takes shelter once again to escape from the shame of his past "half life" (*Magic Seeds*, 10) of detached observation and objective analysis towards a return to authenticity and a "regenerative process" (ibid., 12). When Sarojini tells Willie, "I know now that you were no different from Mahatma Gandhi, and couldn't help being what you were" (ibid., 16). She tells him about the dilemma of the early Gandhi in London:

> At the end of this half –life or quarter –life he became dreadfully depressed. He felt he needed help. He wanted practical help. He didn't want to be told to read a history book. Don't you feel you can see yourself a little bit in that young Gandhi? (ibid., 17).

She convinces him to go back to India and makes him read the Mahatma's autobiography: "a remarkable book. Very simple, very fast, very honest." (ibid., 17). Reading the autobiography, Willie wished that "this healing book" (ibid., 19) had come his way many years earlier: "I would have aimed at another life..what darkness, what self-deception, what waste" (ibid.).

The autobiography opened up to Willie truths about memory and history, and how through tremendous odds in experiments of overcoming passions that Gandhi came to confront and finally face Truth. To Willie, the autobiography was of

> shame, ignorance, incompetence...a whole chain of memories that would have darkened or twisted another life: memories that Willie himself would have wished to take to the grave, but which the courage of this simple confession, arrived at by heaven knows what painful ways, made harmless, almost part of folk memory, in which every man of the country might see himself (ibid., 19).

Naipaul starts the book with Gandhi and his obsessions and the search for virtues such as honesty and directness sound simple but are hardest to achieve. In this context, Horace Alexander's remark about Gandhi, of being "a very matter-of-fact mystic" (Alexander, 75) is relevant. Over the past two decades, the simple paradigms of Gandhism and its applicability itself has come under suspicion, generally taken by many as a pose and masquerade for power. Naipaul centres on the level-headed experiments, which were directed towards arriving at truth and developing a practical working system. Gandhi's autobiography, which appealed to Naipaul, was not just the retelling of his life under certain conditions and with certain purposes that shaped his presentation of himself. If one looks at the way Gandhi had structured his autobiography, one notices, "it is a story of how he has evolved into a Mahatma" (Parekh, 262). It is quite evident, therefore that the qualities that seem to pose the most difficulties—"the painful self-revelations, the confessional tone, the demythologising orientations are the very qualities" (Sharma, 42) of Gandhi's autobiography that challenges Naipaul the most.

Willie strove sincerely to give up everything, and fit into a new-found idealism of "the great Guerrilla war" (*Magic Seeds*, 4) to free the lower castes from their immediate physical and social environment. Sarojini emphasized the necessity of the Gandhian ideologies and approach towards life for practical action, "the need to act. 'What can I do?'" (ibid., 20). She told Willie that Gandhi was a wonderful "mixture of thought and intuition. Thought above all..He was a true revolutionary" (ibid., 21). Willie decides to come back to India to follow undemonstratively the Gandhian self -discipline as an insider in a revolutionary system. Inspired by Gandhi's will for experiments, Willie considered that "he felt no shame. He could acknowledge everything" (ibid., 23). Like the Tamils selling roses in Berlin, who "had a look of a man with a cause, the look of a man apart."(ibid., 6), Willie at last, even if momentarily experienced "true pride" (ibid., 22). But Willie's capacity of rational judgement did not allow the right choices to be made which in a way is an enquiry of Naipaul's long-standing obsessions of self-purification in his narratives. Despite Willie's almost immediate realisation that he had "fallen among the wrong people..I think something terrible has happened. I am not with the people we talked about. I don't know how it's happened" (Ibid., 51). To put all of this in a slightly different way, Naipaul saw that these future events of "useless striving and needless pain" (ibid., 139) which determined and controlled the meaning of the "purposeless years" (155) in the past, was a fighting for "semi-comic"(155) causes which could "see no pattern, no thread" (ibid.) rather reversing the conditions the other way around.

Naipaul has frequently written about his impatience with third-world revolutionaries and ill-defined guerrilla groups with their borrowed ideologies. He felt that the revolutionary's stories were more or else of individual ego boosters and had virtually nothing to do with a larger moral or social vision of the world. Naipaul's continuous intolerance of the charade of revolution, even for the people being in the march for years, and the deceptive mimicry of their progressive ideals bears the brunt here. Einstein, one of the revolutionaries says, "No revolution can be a movement of Love" (ibid., 105). Probably, in Naipaul's eyes, this goes against Gandhi's principles of non-violence as the guiding force for all his actions and his extraordinary conviction and total commitment to the cause. As Gandhi had written in his autobiography:

> To see the universal and all-pervading Spirit of Truth face to face one must be able to love the meanest of creation as oneself. And a man who aspires after that cannot afford to keep out of any field of life. Identification with everything that lives is impossible without self-purification. But the path of self-purification is hard and steep. To attain to perfect purity one has to become absolutely passion-free in thought, speech and action; to rise above the opposing currents of love and hatred, attachment and repulsion..(Gandhi, 382-83)

For Naipaul, on the contrary, even though movements have a singular face to conquer all oppression and slavery, the development of independent thought process was missing. The revolutionaries condescendingly describe the peasants as "cricket people, matchstick people.... whose minds have gone after the centuries of malnourishment" (*Magic Seeds*, 41). Gandhi had redefined history, with personal struggle and hardship, ironically similar to the boredom of self-denial in the training camp, "I suppose it is a kind of training, a kind ascetism, but for what I am not sure"(ibid., 51). In the regimented confined world of the jail there are camouflaged Gandhian registers that Willie sees from the prison van

> HATE SIN NOT THE SINNER..was it Gandhian, this expression of a difficult kind of forgiveness, or was it Christian? it could have been both, since many of the Mahatma's ideas were also Christian (ibid., 157).

Gandhian clichés are liberally scattered as signs: "Truth always wins..To do good is the greatest religion..work is worship..Non violence is the greatest of all religions" (ibid., 160).

The Gandhian concern of enslavement recurs "The Greek philosophers never had to deal with the problems of work. They had slaves. Today we are all our own slaves."(ibid., 200).

At the end of it all, Gandhi became a Mahatma while ironically Willie returns disillusioned to England. Willie remains "passive and adrift" (Kakutani) as if the author's sympathetic understanding of "Willie's crippling sense of alienation has been replaced by ill-tempered disdain (ibid.).

However, in the changed role of strategies and narrative structure in representing the self, the Gandhian metamorphosis may not have occurred, but allusions to the inner restlessness, ceaseless striving, not being a slave to conditioned ideas in transparent series of reflections, encountering subjective self-revelation captures the fragile innuendos of that special time and place. Gandhi's allegorical interpretation of the *Bhagavad Gita*, "That man was a battlefield for good and evil" (Mehta, 172) was fundamental to his view on morals and life. These shifting "shut in and shutting out life" (Naipaul, *Two Worlds*, 5) constantly reveal negation of the facts and misrecognition of the most immediate experiences "The world is always in movement. People have everywhere at sometime been dispossessed" (ibid, 4).

The subversions of reality undermine the illusion of enclosed freedom. Across a slow progression of a seemingly ruined circular dilemma of loss, Willie moves amongst those who are unable to peel off the outer masks. Willie can plainly say,"All of us from the subcontinent have trouble with sex. If I had been easier about sex, if I had known how to go out and get it, I would have been another kind of man" (*Magic Seeds*, 111). At times there is the practice of restraint and balance and "not to overdo the personal drama..talked of failure and humiliation and hiding" (ibid., 110). When Naipaul speaks of the sexuality of the unconscious, it is essentially not just euphemizing the past, but also a tale of an exorcism and rejection of the hidden guilt experiences, as in Gandhi:

> Whilst my hands were busy massaging my father's legs, my mind was hovering about the bed-room-and that too at a time when religion, medical science and common sense alike forbade sexual intercourse. This shame of my carnal desire... is a blot I have never been able to efface or forget, It took me long to get free from the shackles of lust, and I had to pass through many ordeals before I could overcome it. (Gandhi, 20-22)

Naipaul's use of the Gandhian method of the self-narrative, as an act of self-construction and self-purification is noticeably felt. Sometimes it is the honesty and humaneness of Gandhi's autobiography that is most challenging. When a direct and accessible route to meaning is blocked, we turn to the frequent allusions to Gandhi as a metaphor to reconstruct meaning by circling around the definition and explanation of our realities. It is as Ved Mehta sees "how Gandhi affected and animated others, how his ideas are now understood and applied" (Mehta, xi). Perhaps this mixed suspicion of a continuing "nostalgia" for Gandhi in Naipaul's works, is like of all the variant ways of using history "the most general, looks the most innocent, and is perhaps the most dangerous" (Chase & Shaw, 1). But nostalgia by itself cannot be a replacement for memory or history or forgetting as it evades the truth and the authentic voice. In a very different context and domain, Naipaul's fictive waverers undergo identical psychological tensions of the transition from servitude to freedom on the crucible of experiments. As Sarojini writes later, "perhaps in the end one way of life is as good as any other..." (*Magic Seeds*, 159). Naipaul still retains a realistic way of looking at India, and perhaps in tracing Willie's pursuits he was looking for his own answers. He has Willie think at the end of the novel, "It is wrong to have an ideal view of the world... That's where the mischief starts. That's where everything starts unravelling" (*Magic Seeds*, 294).

Bhiku Parekh had shown how Gandhi had bypassed the traditional Western debate on the Theory of Man that *"human beings were naturally good or evil"* (Parekh, 62). He had revealed that human beings had "tendency towards good"(ibid.) and self-development was "a right because each individual was unique and should be free to evolve a way of life suited to his psychological and moral constitution" (ibid., 63). In fact, Willie is interesting to us because of how "Naipaul uses him. Otherwise, he is a mental and moral wraith, a man of poses and petty wisdom pitiably won" (Khilnani). If we see Gandhi as a scientist, his laboratory was the entire field of ethics and morals and the guinea pig recurrently was himself. As Gandhi had said:

> Far be it from me to claim any degree of perfection for these experiments. I claim for them nothing more than does a scientist who, though he conducts his experiments with the utmost accuracy, forethought and minuteness, never claims any finality about his conclusions. I have gone through deep self-introspection, searched myself through and through..Yet I am far from claiming any finality or infallibility about my conclusions. (Gandhi, x)

This offering of multiple layers of meaning interwoven into the life story Naipaul seeks to narrate was transference of "that regime of self purification..the project rooted in a vision of personal and collective self-transformation" (Sharma, 43). However, considering the high moral standards he set upon himself for self-evaluation, "even the smallest error of judgment required penace" (Parekh, 125). It may have been that Naipaul's tacit approval of Gandhi's brand of purity which could sometimes become "circumstantial, obtained not by conscious effort but by default" (ibid., 74). Gandhi's purity was "an acquired purity" (ibid., 74) from his journey towards Truth. Search for Truth is " a scientific enquiry. Scientific inquiry is based on causal relations" (ibid.). But Gandhi thought that all phenomena could not be explained in terms of causal relations. In My Experiments with Truth Gandhi relates that incident in the brothel when he was "saved" by mysterious forces: How all this happens-how far a man is free and how far a creature of circumstances—how far free will comes into play and where fate enters on the scene—all this is a mystery and will remain a mystery (Gandhi, 207).

Naipaul perhaps sees that Gandhi's redefinition of the concept of freedom and his mode of resistance, which was always open to dialogues, could bring in a great awakening in the cultural amnesia of our times.

Taking up a cultural and political phenomenon of the figure of Gandhi, Naipaul examines the relation of various ways of retrieving an ineffable memory and re-tells the exercise of gaining fleeting glimpses to Truth. Ved Mehta, concentrating on the humaneness of Gandhi's ideas and principles states that "Certainly it was an extraordinary life, fusing as, as it did, ancient Hindu religion and culture and modern revolutionary ideas about politics and society—from any viewpoint, a strange combination of perceptions and values" (Mehta, ix).

In Naipaul's fiction, it is a discourse on retrieval of the present through the fabrication of the past. It may not serve as a reaction of certain historical changes but provokes us to question the relationships between cultures, which go beyond the superficial resemblances of geography. Truly Naipaul's overriding achievement has been always

> to have imagined and described a new world—the third world—into existence, with ruthless clarity but also with instinctive compassion, as fiction and also as his truth.
>
> (Trivedi, 55)

Works Cited

Alexander, Horace. *Consider India.* Bombay: Asia Publishing House, 1969.

Arunima, G. "Beyond the novel." *The Book Review,* Vol XXVI, No: 1, New Delhi: The Book Review Literary Trust, January 2002.

Bhabha, Homi K. "Signs Taken for Wonders: Questions of Ambivalence and Authority under a tree outside Delhi, May 1817". *The Location of Culture,* Routledge 1994.

Champeon, Kenneth. *Review on Half A Life,* Bookpage. com/ 0111bp/ fiction/ half_a _life. html, 2/20/02: 1

Chase, Malcolm, and Christopher Shaw. "The Dimensions of Nostalgia." *The Imagined Past: History and Nostalgia*. Ed. Chase and Shaw. Manchester: Manchester University Press, 1989. 1-7.

Erickson, Erik, *Gandhi's Truth*. London: Faber & Faber, 1970

Engdahl, Horace. *Presentation Speech Nobel Lecture*, http:// www. Nobel. se/ literature/laureates/2001/presentation-speech.html), 2002.

Gandhi, M.K. *An Autobiography: The Story of My Experiments With Truth*. Ahmedabad: Navajivan Publishing House, 1922.

Iyer, Raghavan. ed. *The Moral and Political writings of Mahatma Gandhi*. Oxford: Clarendon Press, 1986.

Khilnani.http://goldenrulejones.blogspot.com/2004_09_01_goldenrulejones_archive.html, Tuesday, September 14, 2004.

Kakutani, M. *New York Times Review*. November 30, Tuesday 2004.

Mehta, Ved. *Mahatma Gandhi and His Apostles*. New Haven & London: Yale University Press, 1976.

Naipaul, V. S. *Half a Life*, India: Picador, 2001.

________, *The Mimic Men*. London: Penguin Books Limited, 1967.

________, *Two Worlds*, http://www.nobel.se/literature/laureates/2001/naipul-lecture-e.html) Dec 12,2001.

________, *Magic Seeds*, London: Picador, 2004.

Nanda, B.R. *Gandhi and His Critics*. Delhi: Oxford University Press, 1985.

Nandy, Ashish. *The Intimate Enemy*. Delhi: Oxford University Press, 1983.

Parekh, Bhiku. *Gandhi: A Very Short Introduction*. New York: Oxford, 2001.

_______, *Industrialization of autobiography, colonialism, traditionalism and Reform: An analysis of Gandhi's Political Discourse*, New Delhi: Sage Publications, 1989.

Ricoeur, Paul. *Memory, History, Forgetting*. Trans. Kathleen Blamey and David Pellauer. Chicago: Chicago UP, 2004.

Review, *Naipaul, V.S Nobel Prize in Literature 2001* http://www.the-south-asian.com/Jan2002/Naipaul-Introduction.htm.

Sharma, Rashmi. *Autobiographical Writings of Mahatma Gandhi*. New Delhi: Deep & Deep Publications, 2004.

Trivedi, Harish. "Delivering the Truth," *The Book Review*, Vol XXVI, No: 1, Jan'2002. The Hindu, Online edition of India's National Newspaper, Sunday, Feb 29, 2004.

Vanmoy Adams, Michael. "Reimagining ourselves: What does it mean to be "multicultural,' *The C.G.Jung Page*, Http://www.cgjungpage.org/articles/adams1.html 3/18/02

4

Chaudhuri's Prophetic Vision in Three Horsemen of the New Apocalypse

— *Basavaraj Naikar*

A writer who can produce an important book even at the age of ninety-nine is someone very rare and remarkable in the literary world. Nirad Chaudhuri's *Three Horsemen of the New Apocalypse* (1997) happens to be a semi-philosophical treatise on the life of the twentieth-century man. It contains the quintessence of his life-long thinking on human life expressed in a crystal-clear style without getting himself lost in the labyrinth of details. Being an extraordinarily serious scholar of interdisciplinary kind, he has followed similar gigantic scholars of the world for a model of his own writing. As he has put it clearly in his Preface:

> But I shall at least lay my cards on the table. In choosing the form of the book I have taken Machiavelli, Thomas Hobbes and Alex de Toqueville as my models. These great thinkers and writers were not given to looseness of thinking or imprecision in writing. Of these qualities I shall try to give an imitative display. But that is also likely to create mental resistance to what I shall say... (Preface).

He forestalls the critical opinion about his so-called prejudices by saying: I have never allowed my likes and dislikes, my predilections and prepossessions to influence my presentation of my subjects. I have so to speak, tried to keep the lens of my mind free from chromatic aberrations. (Preface). He goes further to confess that it is the expression of his vision of life. "It consists in thinking that I am not the real creator of my books but only the medium or amanuensis for the self-revelation of the subjects I deal with"(Preface). Chaudhuri quotes from the 27th Canto of Dante's *Purgatorio* to illustrate the relation between reason and faith. Virgil, who conducts Dante through the first two post-mortem regions, tells him that, being a Pagan, he cannot take Dante further. Dante, therefore, takes the guidance of Beatrice. Whereas Virgil represents reason, Beatrice represents faith.

Chaudhuri believes in the close connection between the earthly or human life and the larger cosmos. He clearly states that he accepts the theories of contemporary scientists about the nature of the universe and rejects their views about its duration. He believes in the cosmological view that the universe is not a material body or has a material structure and that it is a process and a flow of energy in different directions. But nobody can define the cosmic energy, which may be comparable to a T.V. He describes the spiritual/dynamic power or energy through a scientific, especially a technological metaphor of television, "..the universe is really cosmic TV show run by some power who designed it for some purpose known only to itself"(p.12). Chaudhuri's belief in the cosmos as a process is easily comparable to Whitehead's philosophy of process and becoming. He explains the human happiness in terms of illusions or of Vedantic concept of *maya*: "Man's happiness lies in living on the strength of his illusions. It is the maya of the Hindu philosophy of Vedanta."(p.12).

Chaudhuri rejects the modern scientists' postulate about the end of the universe according to thermodynamics, as he considers it as an expression of scientific nihilism Chaudhuri rejects the futility, meaninglessness and purposelessness of human life propounded by these theories. These theories imply that "Everything that man does becomes a tale told by an idiot signifying nothing"(p.13). He, therefore, emphasizes the importance and necessity of faith in human effort. Faith need not be connected with religion. "Faith in human endeavour is enough"(p.13).

Although Chaudhuri is dismissed in India as a controversial writer, he does not accept this view, as he has never indulged in any controversy with any scholar. Any indulgence in such a controversy is deleterious to his writing career. As every writer follows his own method to arrive at his conclusions about life, Chaudhuri makes it clear that he has followed his own method and expatiates on it in the first chapter entitled "The Reason for this Methodological Prologomena." If there is no meeting between two methodologies, there cannot be any alignment in the views expressed by two scholars. Hence, Chaudhuri warns the reader to note the particular methodology followed by him. He further clarifies in his second chapter, "On the Method", that he does not believe in the statistical method of understanding truth, but prefers to dwell on the essential aspects of truth: I reject the statistical method of finding the truth and refuse to accept the average as any kind of truth. I follow Sherlock Holmes in this. He said the first step in deletion is to find the essential fact among a whole number of them, which might all be connected with the crime. But this calls for an extremely perceptive and keen nose (p. 9).

Chaudhuri makes it very clear that his views on the 'Decline and Fall of Western Civilisation' are not a mere extension of Spengler's views, but are the products of his lifelong observation of the world. He makes a very insightful observation when he says that "Western civilisation today is no longer exclusively Western" (p.10), and that it can be divided into two divisions: "There is an inner circle, which is fully lighted and is occupied by peoples of European origins; around it is a very much larger circle, which is the penumbra of the central sun and is occupied by diverse non-European peoples"(p.10). It is in this faith in the continuity of the world that has given him the will and energy to pursue his vocation of a writer till his centenarian year.

Although Chaudhuri disbelieved in the purposefulness of the world or its evolution in his childhood, in his later years, he accepted the purposefulness of evolution: one restricted to better adaptation to the circumstances of existence of all species; and the other extended to the creation of new forms of animal existence. He firmly believes that the purposelessness of evolution is absurd. He believes that the purposefulness is not complete, but is in the process and therefore incomplete.

He believes that man is united zoologically and in the next stage, he has to be united socially and culturally also. But how is that possible? For this question, Chaudhuri has his own answer. According to him, the zoological evolution has almost been complete as there has not been any emergence of new species. But the zoological evolution is replaced by psychological evolution. This idea of Chaudhuri may not be easily accepted by people as any new view is not accepted immediately by some people.

He firmly believes that the individual's lifecycle is more or less clearly repeated in the lifespan of nations. Birth, growth, static stability, deterioration and death are common to individuals and nations. A distinct genetic group or an ethnic group of different genetic origins united by a common culture, with a common language; development of political power and cultural achievement; acquisition of group consciousness with self-assertiveness; political and cultural expansion, stable staticity, loss of vitality and decline or metaphorical death, happen to be a common pattern of human life according to Chaudhuri. Nations in their old age can have either a golden augustianism or an ignoble existence in a figurative brothel.

Chaudhuri makes it very clear that all opinions are made to obey the historical trends and change the society in turn. For example, he illustrates this formula by citing the example of how a portion of India was effected by the British government in spite of the opposition to it by the Indian leaders, and how the opinion changed suddenly within a short span of seven days. Thus opinions are determined by historical trends and not vice versa. Chaudhuri does not deny free will by preaching mere determinism. He calls it "a very special and restricted kind of determinism," a determinism operating "in a part of the process of evolution, not in the whole." He further clarifies that the end or goal of man is determined, but the course of his action or growth is irregular. He explains it through a geographical simile; "This process is very much like a river flowing down to the sea with many windings, never in a straight course" (p.20). He supports his argument with the examples of the Ganga and Thames Rivers.

Chaudhuri offers the example of costumes. Although costumes are broadly determined by climate, they have a sexual motivation behind them and cannot be explained very rationally as fashion is always sub-rational. Even the evocation of sexual desire is determined by historical trends. "An age of elegance creates elegant clothing. But vulgar age will not only create vulgarity, but even persecutes everything that is not vulgar" (p.21). Fashions, motivated by sexual desire, can be sophisticated (a rapier of sensuality) or shabby (a bludgeon) and are next only to the greed for money. Chaudhuri makes a bold statement that there is no 'taste' in the contemporary world.

Chaudhuri brings in a personal note by saying that he had not seen the death of his parents or in-laws and prepared himself to see the inevitable death of his wife in 1994 at the age of eighty-five. He accepts the inevitability of death or 'The Night of Time' (in Thomas Browne's words) and says how the death of his wife made him lose all his interest in life.

Chaudhuri has selected the three horsemen to represent three ideals of the modern world. The first one is a white horse symbolising individualism; the second one is a red horse symbolising nationalism and known for murderousness. The third one is a black horse symbolising democracy and known for its balancing capacity.

He begins to discuss the subject by giving a history of the word 'individualism'. He opines that the concept of individualism (symbolised by the white horse) was given currency in the nineteenth century and pleads for the beliefs in the individual's supreme worth and importance as well as in his right to act as he pleases. Chaudhuri points out the mistakes made by the American professor in the *Encyclopaedia Britannica* by saying that Toqueville is not the man who used the word 'individualism' for the first time (p.28). He succinctly summarises Toqueville's idea of individualism in the United States as "the right to pursue self-interest in the form of acquisition of money and fulfilment of all desires, good or bad, also amenities of life, without external constraints"(p.28). He further points out how in America this is slightly modified in the sense that while the individual's self-interest is pursued liberally, it should also recognise the right of other individuals to pursue their self-interest. The American Declaration of Independence recognises the inalienable rights of man like "Life, Liberty and the pursuit of Happiness" (p.29).

Then Chaudhuri quotes five meanings of individualism from two famous dictionaries: (1) The *Oxford English Dictionary* differs from Toqueville in so far as it makes a distinction between individualism and egoism (p.30). (2) The second meaning of individualism, according to *OED* is the social theory advocating the free and independent action of the individual as opposed to communistic method of organic action and State interference (p.30). The third meaning, according to *OED* is 'metaphysical' in nature recognising the individual as 'a self-determined whole.' Likewise Chaudhuri examines the other meanings of individualism offered by the two dictionaries (*OED* and *Webster International*) and opines that none of these meanings is adequate to throw light upon the individual's own life and activities (p.31). Herzon also does not clarify as to why an individual wants liberty. Chaudhuri attributes Herzon's apparently irresponsible assertion of liberty to the background of authoritarianism in Europe from 1815 to 1870 (p.32). Individual freedom was not encouraged in Russia. Chaudhuri opines that the doctrine of liberation was challenged in France also. For him, individualism is closely connected not with equality but with liberty (p.34).

Chaudhuri points out the ubiquity of authoritarianism in the world. According to him, authoritarianism, especially papal infallibility was practised in the Second Empire in France. The Catholics had no right to private opinion on Christian beliefs. The Anglican Church in England also practised the same kind of religious authoritarianism. Chaudhuri comments that all religions remain intolerant and heresy hunting is natural to them. Even Protestantism was limited in its liberation. Islam remains more intolerant of other religions. Every Muslim is a Fundamentalist or no Muslim at all. Hinduism is also intolerant in its own way. It has no creed and hence no doctrinal heresy in it.

Then Chaudhuri examines authoritarianism in Europe. He points out how political authoritarianism was practised in France. The French were anti-democratic as late as 1910. Writers like Charles Maurras and Maurice Barres preached royalism and nationalism. Maurras shows that the French government in India is authoritarian. Chaudhuri applies this principle to the British government in India who succeeded in controlling the country through their authoritarianism. Even the French writers supported the French authoritarianism as against the Paris Commune. In the First World War, the Soviet Regime in Russia, the Fascists in Italy and the Nazi in Germany were all authoritarian. In the Second World War, there was a fight between freedom and authority. Chaudhuri makes an insightful observation when he says that "The degradation of the individual was an extreme reaction to the evil authoritarianism that brought about the War"(p.43). He deplored the degeneration of individualism into unrestrained self-indulgence, especially in regard to money and sex. He calls it primarily an American product spreading over to other countries relentlessly. He believes that he is only a particle of the universe—intellectually, morally, spiritually and physically. The Ambassador of Switzerland in India, a theologist, said that Nirad cannot be a Christian.

The basic assumptions of Chaudhuri's individualism are as follows: Man is part of the universe. "In short, man is a microcosm in a macrocosm, comparable to an electrical battery" (p.44). Man is only limited in quality and duration of his existence. But the relationship between man and the universe is not direct, but indirect, i.e., through the earth. The relation is qualitative. The smaller the quality, the greater the power. Man is an agent of the universe for a cosmic purpose. Man's primary functioning is zoological, like any other animal's. Sex is the means of procreation cosmically. Sexual intercourse as an end in itself is a modern perversion and irrationality. The use of contraception is a revolt against biology and a repudiation of ethics. The religious view is totally opposed to biological view of individualism.

Then Chaudhuri examines the religious views about life and death. Religion views death as unimportant and that man is only a sojourner in life. Religion, especially Christianity considers the world as full of evils in which man can be protected only by the grace of God. The world is a wicked one in religion. Man is supposed to renounce the wicked world. Chaudhuri's question is: If the world is wicked, why did God send man into it? If death is certain, what about life? Isn't life uncertain according to religion? Chaudhuri concludes by saying that the religious view of life is anti-biological. He further examines the difference between the biological view and the religious view of life. The individual's lifecycle is biologically determined and the observable lifecycle of human life has an obverse and a reverse. But the biological lifecycle of human life is dismissed by all religions. But although death puts an end to all the human vanity, man emerges as a victor finally. He is not rendered a superfluity on account of his mortality. "He is a necessity like the leaves in a tree which maintain photosynthesis. The Cosmos is the everlasting deciduous tree which is kept alive by its leaves, growing anew and falling seasonally in turns"(p.50).

After commenting upon the various aspects of individualism, he goes on to discuss nationalism (symbolised by the red horse). He quotes six meanings of 'nation' from three famous dictionaries and points out how the earliest use of 'nation' was in A.D. 1300 and how its derived abstract word appeared only in 1836. 'Nation' is primarily a political term, which is different from 'state.' Whereas nation is real, state is accidental. 'People' is preferred to 'nation' in historical and sociological terminology.

Chaudhuri points out how earlier wars were monarchical and dynastic or state-conducted. According to him, national wars began only in the eighteenth century, like the American War of Independence (1775-83), the Second War of American Independence and the French Revolution from 1792 onwards. He points out how nationalism and militarism were combined in the Russian War of Liberation. Similarly he shows how there took place three wars of national liberation in the nineteenth century (1) in Germany, (2) Peninsula War in Spain and (3) Liberation of northern Italy from Austria in 1859.

Chaudhuri shows that the general American notion is that nationalism is opposed to imperialism. But he clarifies that "In reality, nationalism and imperialism are of the same political urge, the first being its defensive aspect and the second its assertive. Nationalism becomes imperialism when a nation becomes so powerful that it seeks to bring other nations under its domination" (p.56). He further defines an empire as a conglomeration of different nationalities—with the hegemony of one of them over the rest—with a hierarchical order within it.

Chaudhuri warns that imperialism and colonialism should not be confused with each other. There is no 'decolonisation'. All colonialism has become permanent. He offers the examples of America and India as instances of permanent colonisation. He offers the historical examples to show how the Europeans were colonists in North America and South America, East Africa, South Africa, Australia and New Zealand, but they were imperialistic in West Africa, India, Burma, Malaya, Indonesia and Indo-China.

Chaudhuri points out that imperialism and nationalism have disappeared from the world, but a new 'Nationalism' has emerged. He highlights the characteristic features of the new 'Nationalism' as follows: (1) It is a self-sufficient and disinterested passion. (2) It is a strong sense of identity or we-ness and is accompanied by xenophobia (which is quite aggressive). (3) It is the political passion of the 'freed-nations' from European imperialism. A national pride and nationalistic inferiority complex are associated with it. (4) A sense of grievance leading to impotent hatred. Then Chaudhuri points out the four ethnic conflicts: (1) Hindus and Muslims in India, (2) Arabs and Jews in the Middle East, (3) Roman Catholics of Ireland and Protestants in the British Isles and (4) Whites and Blacks in South Africa. He generalises in his typical way," ..friendship between nations is fragile, while hatred is ineradicable. In respect of strength, love can never be equal to hatred"(p.61). He further shows how this hatred has increased the military preparation and expenditure and terrorism in Asia and Africa.

Then Chaudhuri discusses democracy symbolised by the black horse. He defines democracy as the domination of the Demos or majority. Talking about the history of democracy over 2,500 years, he says that democracy is a form of government taught by the Athenian philosophers like Plato and Aristotle, and that Greek democracy was formed by the citizens belonging to old families. He rightly points out that modern democracy is really American democracy and cites Lincoln's definition of democracy as a government of the people, by the people and for the people. Once Lincoln said, "You can fool all the people some of the time and some people all the time, but you cannot fool all the people all the time"(p.63). But Chaudhuri adds satirically, "Lincoln could not foresee the power of television to fool all the people all the time"(p.64). Then he shows that Britain and America accepted political democracy after World War I. He opines that total democracy has become assertive and aggressive today, and that it is elitist and a champion among the English people.

Modern governments want to adopt the policy of egalitarianism and create a classless society. Chaudhuri points out how the French egalitarianism is different from the American one, and how the real egalitarianism is accepted in respect of mental powers and not in physical powers. He also points out rightly that the creative function of man is exercised by the mind and that all creation is creation of inequality. According to him, there is inequality in modern egalitarianism.

Chaudhuri opines that there has been a decline and fall of not only Western civilisation but also of Eastern civilisation in general. "I shall only assert that the decline and fall of civilisations is real historical phenomenon, which has again and again been seen in history"(p.71). He shows how the great civilisations of ancient Egypt, Mesopotamia, Iran, Greece, Rome and China fell. Likewise Chaudhuri believes that the ancient Indian civilisation also declined and disappeared although it is not accepted by the present Hindus.

The most accurate definition of 'decadence' is that it presupposes a previous maturity and a high degree of excellence reaching the high peak of its development, and then declining gradually by losing its political and economic as well as cultural creativeness. Then Chaudhuri rightly points out that there can be a national or collective decadence as in the late Hellenistic stage of Greek civilisation and the last stage of the Rom an Empire. "I might add flippantly that I consider Mrs. Thatcher (defined post-premierly as the Baroness Thatcher) as the British Diocletian in a female incarnation"(p.73). He further points out how decadence after the peak of achievement or golden age is a natural order of evolution of human life in recorded history. 'Golden age' always belongs to the past. Even our epics show (according to Chaudhuri) the story of a great victory followed by a disconcerting defeat.

Chaudhuri noticed in his first visit to England in 1955 that the English people were so thoughtless about their future. His later visits to England in 1967-68 and his permanent domicile in England in 1970 confirmed his view about the onset decadence in England. He opines that the decadence has spread to all aspects of English life – like national personality, politics, social, economic, academic and cultural aspects. He sees the English decadence in the Englishman's attitude to expenditure of money. Although this is a trivial matter in the national life, it provides an important clue to the English character and personality. Chaudhuri comments on the English people's preference for cheap items. Likewise, he sees 'decadence' in the English attitude to beauty. According to him, Princess Diana is not as beautiful as she is said to be by the English people. His reading of English history has made him disappointed with the decline in the character of the Spencer family of Althorp. "Certainly, Princess Diana has neither the looks nor the air of Georgiana, Countess of Spencer, nor of her young daughter, as represented in the painting by Reynolds, which is at Althorp"(p.77).

Chaudhuri gives a detailed picture of the decadence of the Spencer family at Althorp from the past grandeur to the present economic compromise. His reading about the past glory of the family and his observation of the present situation creates a blatant contrast between the past and the present. Earl Spencer, the Princess of Wales' brother, hiring the palace to hoteliers to meet the expenditure of 400,000 pounds a year for its upkeep, shows the economic decadence of the royal family.

According to Chaudhuri, the English decadence is of two kinds: one, general; two, malignant. The general decadence is like a chronic disease, not frightening on the surface or in symptoms, but very fatal in effect. The malignant decadence is alarming like the sudden outbreak of a plague, smallpox or cholera.

Chaudhuri is very critical of British life. According to him, the English people do not live naturally, sincerely and unselfconsciously. On the contrary, they believe in false behaviour and become poseurs. "It has become posing, men and women appearing as actors and actresses"(p.79). Posturing and advertising has become the order of the day. Names, labels and titles are more important than substances. Among women, becoming a model has become the supreme ambition of their life. Chaudhuri is stunned and irritated by the artificiality of this posturing in England. The examples of posturing can be seen in 'stills' in statues in shops and 'movies' through TV and video. The "transformation of experience of life into vicarious experience is one of the most noticeable features of contemporary decadence" (p.80).

Chaudhuri points out further how the English women, especially the young, have fallen for the Oriental habit of overloading themselves with jewellery even in their daily life-like synthetic pearls and fake gold – absurdly with jeans pants. Likewise, decadence may be seen in the English women's (especially young ones) treatment of hair. Use of a variety of wigs and colouring the hair differently on different days according to their whims is also part of decadence.

According to Chaudhuri, the government has also grown decadent in three aspects: (1) bureaucracy, (2) high taxation and (3) debasement of money. Such decadence may be seen in the Roman Empire, Czarist Russia and England. The behaviour of bureaucrats in England was not dignified. Chaudhuri, therefore, was depressed by the sight of it, "..to all politically minded Indians the House of Commons was like the political Mecca with its stone of Kaaba"(p.85). Chaudhuri comments that the English people have lost not only their political ambition, but their zest also in politics. The catchwords were used in inverse proportion to their truth. The British parliamentarians' behaving in a false manner –actors and poseurs—shows the decadence of the government. Chaudhuri's honesty and courage may be seen in his remark that the British Prime Minister Mrs. Thatcher or Mr. Major behave like a dictator.

Chaudhuri remarks that in modern England, people practise their religion according to their whims and fancies instead of conforming to the strict injunctions of religion. This is religious decadence according to him. He further remarks that those of the Anglican Church have started obeying the voice of the people instead of the voice of God. In England people have lost their faith in Christianity but have become more superstitious. With the loss of faith in Christianity, the English people have liberated themselves from morality also—from moral inhibitions—in respect of sexual life, stealing and homicide. Chaudhuri describes the English decadence in Biblical style, "Decadence crieth without; she uttereth her voice in the streets; she crieth in the chief places of concourse"(p.88). He offers further details of decadence in England. Decadence may be seen in the increase of adultery and homosexuality, which are considered to be natural. Abortion, which is a revolt against biology and morality, has become very common. The English people reject morality under the pretext of rejecting Victorian morality. Chaudhuri's anger may be seen in his metaphorical attack: "This is like giving a dog a bad name in order to hang it"(p.88). Then he summarises it epigrammatically, "Corruption of the best is the worst corruption"(p.88).

Chaudhuri proceeds to comment on the decadence of the English social life. The social life of the English people has been brought under the power of the state. People have been made helpless against the power of the state. The absolutism of the English state is equal to monarchical absolutism. Instead of people taking care of the government, it is the government, which has to take care of the people. Chaudhuri is really puzzled by this reverse phenomenon.

Family is consubstantial with society, but such family is threatened in England. Hindu society has survived today though political regimes have disappeared. In England, family is in shambles today. Marriage has lost its sanctity and status. Illegal living together of a man and a woman or divorce has replaced the marriage. He points out how men and women live together outside the religious and legal tie in England, and how 'partner' has replaced 'wife'. A new type of family – 'one parent family' i.e., a young woman, especially unmarried mothers—has become common in England and such mothers given special privileges by the government. These women cannot assert who the real father of their child is. Words like 'lover' and 'mistresses' have been replaced by 'boyfriend' and girlfriend'. Chaudhuri is really amused by the elderly people's reference to their 'girlfriends'. He, therefore, remarks rightly, "Decadence, however, degrades words and phrases as well as living"(p.91).

Chaudhuri has noticed decadence in family and education also. According to him, in the past, home was a seat of education and school was an adjunct or extension of home. But now the happy relationship between home and school has been destroyed. The school can give only technical skills and never bothers about the cultivation of character of the student.

Chaudhuri has noticed decadence in the modern language also. It has shrunk from the widest to its narrowest compass. In the past, aristocratic ladies appointed lectrices to read aloud literature to them thereby improving their literary taste and influencing the writers. But nowadays these ladies have themselves become writers without influencing the taste of others. The salon has disappeared now. This is linguistic decadence according to Chaudhuri.

In his view, decadence may be seen in the disappearance of parental authority over children. The misadventure of children is due to the lack of parental authority and responsibility. He offers an example of a child who admitted robbers into the house and helped them carry the money. This is an example of too much of freedom given to children. Sometimes this freedom of children has led to juvenile mafias, which murder and rob in a professional manner. Sometimes the exercise of freedom approaches criminality. For example, sometimes young boys murder children out of curiosity. The least harmful exercise of freedom by young people results in vandalism, i.e., in breaking glass or damaging seats in buses and trains.

Chaudhuri then goes on to comment on cultural decadence in England. Nowadays 'culture' has been replaced by 'civilisation'. The decadence of the British government may be seen in Thatcher's conversion of the Socialist Welfare State into a Capitalist Welfare State. Chaudhuri considers the Welfare State as a decadent state. Mere economic prosperity of a nation cannot enrich their culture. According to him, culture has to be animated by a great passion.

Chaudhuri deplores the decadence of British literary culture. The decadence of the English mind is expressed in the careless and penurious use of language – without precision, adequacy and elegance. Decadence may be seen in the shrinkage of vocabulary, absence of colour in diction, monotony of rhythm and ungrammaticality. Chaudhuri is sorry to notice that "the English mind, too, is losing its depth, its intensity and its capacity for making distinctions" (p.95).

He sees decadence in the changes in the religious diction by the American church. He believes in the view that the "popularisation of diction will not save English Christianity" (p.95) and that all religions have remained staunch, conservative in regard to language. If a man is religious, he will understand the conservative language of religion. "No one understands religious diction unless he is religious"(p.96). Chaudhuri, therefore, concludes, "Popularisation of religious diction then indicates the religious decadence" (p.96).

According to him even the 'secular' employment of English language has become decadent these days. The new English has been vulgar English, which has not developed a homogeneous style. "There have appeared styles as varied as are the fashions in women's dresses" (p.96). Politicians, preachers, and teachers especially journalists have vulgarised the English. Today's journalese is an extraordinary mixture of colloquialism, slang, figurative diction, recondite allusions, figures of speech and bad puns and of the use of French and Spanish in wrong places or contexts. Chaudhuri offers examples of degradation of words like 'sex' and 'gay' and employment of sensational titles in newspapers to redeem the dullness that follows. He comments on this phenomenon in his typical manner, "But I say wickedly that those who need such headlines to be induced to read the news are exactly like those who need aphrodisiacs to perform the sexual act naturally" (p.97).

Then he shows the impact of decadence on the English personality also. It is seen in the following habits and practices: race and colour consciousness. The Englishmen were and are notorious for their contempt for the Indian 'niggers' and black men. They called even a fair man, an M.P., Dadabhai Naoroji, a 'black'.

But nowadays, the British do not mind the black people in their country, as they want to make it multi-cultural and enrich their life. Chaudhuri, therefore, quips, "Today, apparently, the distinction between words adulteration and enrichment has ceased to be recognised"(p.98). He comments on the special prize of 3000 pounds instituted to be given to any black writer born in Britain or Ireland. He refuses to be considered as an Indian writer and holds the view that "Writers should be classified only by the language they write in and not by country, race or complexion"(p.98).

Chaudhuri points out how decadence expresses itself in the hard core of racial and colour prejudice in England. "Both remain in the marrow of their bones"(p.98). All the Indian administrators, individuals and especially university teachers in England feel this. "I can say in a general way that an Indian has to possess at least twice the competence of an Englishman in order to have equality of recognition with his or her English colleagues"(p.98). Then he generalises, "Our general rule about the effect of decadence on any people is that it always weakens their good qualities, but leaves the bad ones as they were"(p.98).

In Chaudhuri's view, modern decadence may be seen in not praising our great men. In other words, scandalmongering has become a common habit, especially in writing biographies and exposing the private (or public) weaknesses of great men. He shows how Empress Theodora was exposed as the "most shameless harlot in her young days as a dancer" by the historian Procopius. The modern English biographers are interested in finding out if a great man is a 'bastard' or a 'bugger' forgetting the fact that the most illustrious William the Conqueror and founder of the English State was a 'bastard'. This is the decadent habit of writers, their views being coloured by rancour and malice.

Erosion of delicate sensibility is the last kind of expression of decadence brought about by audio-visual providers of entertainment like TV and electronic devices. Chaudhuri opines that audio-visual exploitation of literature has destroyed the literary culture. BBC is the worst villain guilty of this. TVs distort and misinterpret literature. Chaudhuri offers an example of Jane Austen's *Pride and Prejudice* to illustrate this kind of distortion. In it, Darcy kissing Elizabeth on the mouth in the TV film is not warranted by the novel. He therefore, says that in "an age of decadence even respect for delicacy disappears"(p.102).

Then he expatiates on the malignant features of English decadence. Large majorities of any nation are passive and thoughtless and submit to the active minority in power. He deplores the criminality of the English masses. There is a good deal of sympathy for criminals in the modern society. The masses have a criminal 'libido' in them which makes them sympathetic to criminals. They, therefore, become vicarious criminals. The sympathy for criminals shows the loss of vitality of a nation. Criminality becomes a norm and acquires the cancerous malignity.

Drug addiction is another form of decadence, according to Chaudhuri. The crimes of the English people are (1) armed robbery on banks and post offices; (2) robberies on private homes accompanied by murder, especially of lone elder women; (3) murders of wives by husbands or vice versa, caused by extra-marital affairs or ill treatment etc; (4) murders committed from homicidal mania; (5) rape on very young girls below sixteen or on old women followed by murder; (6) juvenile crimes committed out of curiosity; (7) stealing babies or murdering babies by unmarried mothers and massacre of young children. Such crimes are irrational and cannot be explained satisfactorily. The Christian

Church parading the murderers of children (Mr. Hamilton), i.e., Christian charity, puzzles Chaudhuri who feels like running away from England.

He has been aware of decadence in India from his childhood itself. He states that there have been two decadences in Indian history. The first decadence for two hundred years before the Muslim conquest at the end of the twelfth century brought about the extinction of the ancient Hindu civilisation. The second decadence in the sixteenth century, after the death of the last Mughal emperor Aurangzeb brought about the extinction of the Indo-Islamic civilisation. Again he noticed decadence in India in 1947 when the national life was 'devoid of colour and changed with tedium'. It had become stagnant and died like a lagoon. He noticed 'unadulterated decadence' in the spiritual, moral and material life of India in 1947. His view of Indian decadence culminates in the recognition of *Thy Hand, Great Anarch*. The descent of India is endless. The Indian decadence does not exhibit the British kind of 'malignity' but seems to be in a 'comatose senility' (p.111). He sees aspects of decadence in India in (1) the complete ineffectiveness of the State in preventing the foreign invasion in spite of its suppression of Hindu-Muslim riots; (2) expediency and opportunism and dishonesty in giving concession to people; (3) exhaustion of Muslim political power and the process of Indianisation in giving power to Hindus (especially Banias) and Indianised Muslims; (4) promotion of private interests under the garb of political life and service; (5) the Marathas and the Congress having similar characteristics like (Marathas) negative xenophobia (especially Muslimophobia) of the Hindus and the mercenary motive of plunder and exaction; (6) the effect of the decline of the state on the masses resulting in the mass's loot, murder, robbing and Pindari; and (7) tolerance of anarchy and corruption or resignation to them.

Commenting on the aspects and stages of political decadence in India, Chaudhuri says categorically that "The most striking aspect of the Government of India after the gift of independence by the British people was its total falsity. Nothing was authentic, nothing sincere, nothing disinterested in it"(p.113). He opines that Nehru was not a scoundrel or a counterfeit but that he was a dictator without dictatorial will and that he was imprisoned in the bureaucracy. "He was wholly genuine, as an Englishman of radical views. But he was not endowed with practical political capacity. As soon as with independence he abandoned his former role of demagogue, he became an ineffable ideologue, flapping his wings against the bars of the cage in which he was put by the bureaucracy"(p.113). He makes a very hard comment on Nehru when he says that Nehru was neither a dictator nor a practical democratic statesman, but took refuge in escapism. The large dams and buildings got constructed by Nehru are described by him as "the pyramids alas! Not as lasting as those of Gizah"(p.114). He further comments that Nehru passed on the task of governing and legislating to the officials and the Congress politicians notorious for their opportunism and adventurism.

Chaudhuri comments that Nehru encouraged only the foreign (especially Cambridge) educated people around him and that they were great opportunists. "Thus India under Nehru government was like castles in Spain resting on kitchens if not sewers"(p.114). Nehru was an Anglicised Indian. Chaudhuri offers a musical metaphor for the dictatorship of Nehru family. "The dictatorship of the Nehru family continued with short interruptions, which were like the 'accidentals' in a musical composition. The normal key was quickly restored"(p.115). He comments on Indira Gandhi's power mongering and unscrupulous behaviour. "The position brought about a transformation in Mrs. Gandhi's character paralleled only by the promising Ivan Romonov's becoming Ivan the Terrible"(p.115). She was, therefore, murdered by the agents of the fanatical Akali Sikhs.

Then Chaudhuri comments upon the present regime of the Indian government. According to him, personal rule has been replaced in India by rule by a fraction or an opportunistic combination of many factions. Further he points out how the present Indian government remains British in spirit, though the British personnel had left India in 1947. He rightly shows that the Indian government is in the hands of bureaucrats – from highest officials like IAS to the lowest clerks and that India is caught in the 'net of Babuism'. Babu means a Bengali clerk. Government by such bureaucracy is a decisive sign of decadence. The 'dealing clerk' is the motive force of all action by the government. The dealing clerk can stop the governmental action by playing truant or going on leave.

Commenting on the social and cultural decadence in India Chaudhuri says that there has been a decadence of mental life also in India. The Hindus did not have a picture of ancient India until the European Orientalists presented it to them. He points out that the British rule in India established a close relationship between the political regime and the Indian people (social order) by creating a Hindu official class and a Hindu professional class.

According to him, the American influence on Indian decadence has been greater than the English. In India there is a popular and lowest expression of Americanism. Many Indians want to migrate to America and settle there which is their cultural home composed of its 'sansculottes'. He offers details of social and cultural decadence in India. Single-minded pursuit of money by Indians is a mark of their decadence. There is a rise of the upstart class of new rich. Licentiousness is practised openly in India and not secretly as in the past. Yet it is less than seen in England. Chaudhuri discerns two reasons for such an open practice of licentiousness: one, disappearance of purdah system and unrestrained meeting of men and women and, two, the Hindu law of divorce, especially the husband's friend being the cause of it. He sees a change in the mores of India. According to him, decadence in India may be seen in the absence of strictness in speech, dressing habit and eating habits. Indians reject their regional dress and accept the Western ones. Abandonment of conservatism in respect of eating is a mark of decadence.

Then Chaudhuri highlights a special Bengali feature of decadence. Being himself a Bengali, he has observed the decadence in Bengali life also. According to him, the disintegration of 'bhadralok' (equivalent of English 'gentlefolk') is a feature of decadence. The Bengali bhadralok believed in blue blood and not in money and therefore a rich man married a poor girl. But now this habit has disappeared. They had massive solidarity of the class, which ignored money. But this process of disintegration began in the 1920s and expedited by three events like the provincial self-government, the World War and the Indian Independence in 1947, which gave an opportunity to people to become rich through political power. This division has created class hatred between the rich and the poor, especially in Bengal.

Turning his attention to America, Chaudhuri confesses that he does not have as close knowledge of America as of England, but sees decadence in America also. Rape and murder are not very common in U.S. as the bond of marriage is very loose there. General permissiveness does not necessitate rape and murder. Young people in U.S. hire jewellery for their engagement rather than invest huge amount of money. Divorce has been very common. After divorce, the couple lives as mere 'friends'. This is a mark of decadence in America according to him. Until the third quarter of the nineteenth century, marriage was indissoluble in America, but now many marriages and divorces are common there.

According to Chaudhuri, Henry James's *Portrait of a Lady* (1881) provides a true picture of traditional American marriage. Even an intelligent woman like Isabel Archer is deceived by an expatriate with self-interest. The Europeans is also a great novel. Americans have abandoned old values especially about man-woman relationship. Chaudhuri believes that the progress of American technology has added up to their decadence. He points out how the word 'techne' is a Greek one meaning craft and how 'technology' is a neologism and a discourse or treatise on the practical or industrial arts and on the handling of matter. He further points out how in America there a greater importance is given to practical application of science than to theory. There is no divine love of truth as in an aristocratic society. Americans care a lot for material welfare. The American obsession with the 'material enjoyments' and comforts may be seen in their use of electric lighting and incandescent bulb especially in the kitchen, vacuum cleaner, sewing machine, refrigerator, telephone, gramophone, typewriter in the office and air-travel.

According to Chaudhuri, technological achievements coexist with decadence. The U.S. has become the centre of diffusion of decadence all over the world. He then offers a historical picture of decadence in the world. Till the eighteenth century, the economic basis of all civilisation in the world was agriculture accompanied by handicraft. Decadence happened within that economic world. But the present decadence happens in the machine age. The Hindu and Islamic fundamentalism is the resistance of the old Hindu and Islamic cultures both to modernisation of human life and to Western decadence. "So decadence may now be said to be triumphant, no longer militant"(p.135). Chaudhuri further points out how the application of nuclear power in America is very great and how it is used for military power, i.e., war and how even space research is used as a means of competition of power. But he is also aware of the fact that space research has given unprecedented knowledge of the cosmos. Nuclear weapons are used as deterrents rather than for positive employment. Nuclear power belongs to the latest industrial basis of human existence, whereas civilisation belongs to the old agricultural basis. Finally, he points out how nowadays decadence is regarded as the normal condition of human life, though not as the most desirable one. There is a fanaticism behind decadence, a form of hubris never seen before. The world has become a continent of Circe and there has been a note of despair in the world.

Chaudhuri has thus discussed at length how decadence has grown all-pervasive in the modern world. Although his views seem to be pessimistic and nihilistic, they express the harsh realities of modern civilisation. His apocalyptic vision, which is negative and satirical, happens to be an extension of his earlier vision articulated in all his works.

Cited Work

Nirad C. Chaudhuri, *Three Horsemen of the New Apocalypse*, Delhi: Oxford University Press, 1997. All the page references are to this edition.

5

Dravidian Rhythms in Raja Rao's *Kanthapura*

— P. Gopi Chand & P. Naga Suseela

Of all the Indian novelists in English, Raja Rao is the only one who experimented with the English language in a way that reminds us of James Joyce's attempt to refashion English by investing it with the rhythms of Irish brogue. Raja Rao in his *Kanthapura* for the first time introduces the ethno-cultural element, not only at the level of the theme but also at the level of the medium of narration. He tells his story in the Indian way. It implies taking a good deal of liberties with the grammar of King's English or Queen's English and the super imposition of the rhythm, cadence, and grammar of the mother tongue, Kannada in particular. He gives us the impression that this is how English would have been spoken if it had been the language of the uneducated rural masses in India.

Being essentially literary critics, many writers approach Raja Rao's *Kanthapura* basically from the perspectives of literary style. They make general statements and express impressionistic opinions about the possible sources of such style and its impact upon sensible readers. We should not expect a literary critic, who is preoccupied with the themes and the artistry of the novel, to speak about its style from the stylistic viewpoint. The present paper is an attempt to examine the nature of style in *Kanthapura* from the stylistic standpoint.

Raja Rao's *Kanthapura* is a very complex work in which the potentialities of the English language are adroitly exploited for narrating an Indian experience in Indian idiom and rhythm. In the foreword to the novel, Raja Rao concedes: The telling has not been easy. One has to convey in a language that is not one's own, the spirit that is one's own.

Indian in experience, spirit and in the style of narration, and alien in form and medium, *Kanthapura* is a unique experiment in fiction. The narrative experience is sought to be communicated in the form of the novel, the grammar, idiom and the rhythm of a native language are inextricably woven into the alien language. Out of the interaction between the native and the alien, emerge interesting intricate patterns of rhythm and syntax. Rama Chandra Rao observes: "Raja Rao's penchant for the vernacular, its rhythm and spirit, interpolating themselves into the English idiom, creates a unique literary style which claims some distinctiveness and international appeal."

Kanthapura is an attempt in fiction to recapture the ethos of resurgent India. The story of the epic struggle is told in the mesmeric rhythms of a ruminative grandmother on whom events and memories impinge in such a rapid sequence, as she has neither time nor need to sort out and select. She talks endlessly about the freedom movement in which she was an active participant. She now talks intermittently from the memory of events, which come to her like a stream. She knows that if she stops talking to organise her recollections into a pattern, the chain of memories may break and other memories may crowd into her agile mind. Once a participant in the theatre of the freedom movement, she now acts as a commentator or a narrator. So her style of narration is fluid and slippery, heavily mannered, over-elaborated and highly involuted. Raja Rao himself says in the Foreword, "We in India think quickly, talk quickly, and, when we move, we move quickly."[3]

In a hurried despair, the narrator of the story tells us everything in one concentrated effort. So each sentence is a record of an endless series. Again to quote from Raja Rao's Foreword, "We tell one interminable tale. Episode follows episode and when our thoughts stop, our breath stops and we move on to other part."[4] Many of the sentences in the novel are interminably long with a number of phrases and clauses dangling from one another in an endless concatenation. The voice of the narrator drones on lavishly, lyrically discursively as she elaborates on the legend of the Gandhian movement for freedom.In experimenting with a new style of story-telling, Raja Rao becomes involved in his own technical virtuosity. He uses certain stylistic devices to communicate the Indianness of human experience and sensibility. Kantak observes: "Kanthapura is Raja Rao's first attempt in full-scale fiction that a whole new dialect seems to emerge fully responsive to the intricate task of narrative structure."[5]

Kanthapura is a triumph of a new dialectic English which is so artistically used in the narration that it does not strike us as an innovative device. It is wholly absorbed in and is congruous with the folk epic purpose of the narration. The pace of narration is alien to English and is evocative of colloquial Dravidian languages like Telugu and Kannada. That accounts for the power and appeal of this style of narrative in which the tempo of the Indian life is infused into the English expressions of the novel. It is the result of bilingualism of the novelist. Raja Rao himself observes:

> We are instinctively bilingual—we cannot write like the English. We should not. We cannot write like only as Indians. Our method of expression, therefore, has to be a dialect which will someday prove to be as distinctive and colourful as the Irish or the American.[6]

Raja Rao's concern to make English echo the English speech tones is of special relevance to the present study. The Dravidian Kannada speech tones are made recognisable in the English of the novel through the aural imagination —a technique that is constantly used in the novel. In the following analysis the sound and morphological aspects of the language are analysed. The phonetic aspect of creative style is known as phono-stylistics. It primarily deals with the analysis of the writer's manipulation of sounds in individual words and in larger utterances. The following phono-stylistics aspects are very striking in the novel:

1. *Vowel-ending Proper Nouns:* The Dravidian languages in general, Kannada and Telugu in particular, are phonetically different from the Aryan languages in their distinctive characteristic. Most of the words in these languages are vowel-ending. Raja Rao makes use of vowel-ending proper nouns. Their distribution and reiteration in the novel lend to the narration peculiarly Dravidian Rhythms. The following are examples:

a) *Vowel-ending Place Names : Kanthapura, Talasanna, etc.* Place names like *Maddur, Tippur, Santur,* and *Bebbur,* although they end with *'r'* in spelling, have the vowel 'u' at the end in pronunciation. The frequency of their occurrence in a language that is known for their consonant-endings makes it peculiarly Dravidian in rhythm.

b) *Vowel-ending Personal Names:* Many native Dravidian personal names have a typical characteristic of ending with vowels. Further, preceding the final vowel is a double consonant which is typical in Telugu, Kannada and Tamil, and to a lesser extent in Malayalam. Raja Rao's choice of personal names and their frequency and distribution in the narrative lend Indianness, more precisely Dravidianness, to the rhythm. The following personal names have three syllables each, and in each name there are one or two double consonants, and each name ends with a vowel:

  — *Female Personal Names:* Kenchamma, Santamma, Akkamma, Rangamma, Venkamma, Narasamma, Nanjamma, Ramamma.

  — *Male Personal Names:* Dheerappa, Ramayya, Subbanna, Timmayya, Rangappa, Chandrayya, Lingayya.

c) There are personal names, though less frequent, in which the final vowel is preceded by a consonant cluster. For example: Rangi, Ratna, Moorthy

d) Polysyllabic personal names of Sanskrit origin but with Dravidian suffixes are found in lesser frequency: Chandrasekharyya, Venkateswarayya, Savitramma, Kamalamma, Ramakrishnayya.

Dravidian or Kannada speech tones serve as marks of individuation and are perceived by the ear. These speech tones are noticed in the pace of the rhythm of speech, in the tendency to repetition, in the quality of diction and phrasing and in the peculiar intonation and speech mannerisms. Many of the morphological and syntactical structures mentioned below are given as representatives of phono-stylistic rhythms. They can also be studied separately under morphology and syntax without reference to the rhythm of constructions.

Rhythmically the following expressions add to the Dravidian melody of Raja Rao's English, whatever may be their structural variations. The attributes of personal names followed by nouns are essentially a morphological or syntactic subject. But their repetition in the body of the narrative lends a special charm to the way of story-telling. Some of them are: Front- house Akkamma, Husking-Rangi, Corner-house Narasamma, Gap-tooth Siddaiah, Left-handed Madanna. The other morphological and syntactic constructions which contribute to the Dravidian rhythms of the English novel are briefly mentioned below:

e) *Functional Address where a person is addressed by name:* No,no Bhattare, Learned Bhattare.

f) *Non-Functional Address where a person is addressed in terms of kinship, real or social:* Yes, sister; Tell brother.

g) Invocation to Gods as in:

   Oh! Goddess destroy this government!
   But Rama, Rama, really if we have to
   hang the sacred thread over the
   shoulders of the Paraiah! [7]

h) *Repetition or Reiteration of a Syntactic Structure:* This is used in various contexts and assumes various shapes. For example, in the following sentence a structure is repeated for intensification:

   Do not drink, do not drink in the name of the Mahatma.

Sometimes a structure or a sentence is repeated under the pressure of anticipation:

> Now we are safe , we are safe.

When a word is repeated under an emotional stress, it gathers incantatory force, as in

> He is gone he is gone he is gone Moorthayya.[8]

i) *Reiteration Interlaced with Alteration:* In some sentences reiteration, instead of coming in a sequence, alternates with other structures. For example:

   — He slips between this personality and that, he slips here and he slips there.

— A child wakes up here and begins to cry, and a cough is heard there—— who is there?

— A sense of looming crisis is beautifully built up through this lilting music sustained through extended descriptions.

j) *Inventive Sobriquets:* Persons are labelled with evocative attributes. The attribute and the person become almost inseparable so much so that when the person is spoken of the attribute is always with him. Examples:

— One-eyed Paraiah, Fig-tree house Rama, Waterfall Venkamma

k) *Condensed Phrasing:* This is again typical of the Dravidian languages in which two or three concepts are condensed into one phrase. More than the structural peculiarity, the rhythm is important here. For Example:

— This is Gandhi Vagabondage, Rag-wide field, Palm space,

l) *Novelty in Verbal Shift:* Some aphoristic proverb-like English English expressions are given unexpected twists which add to the rhythm of the language. Example:

— English 'cock and bull story' is substituted by 'crow-and-sparrow story.'

— English 'Every dog has his day' is substituted with 'Every squirrel has his day.'

— 'A cock does not make a morning' is substituted for English 'One swallow does not make a summer.'

The variety of structures given represents the phonology of style characterised by Dravidian or Kannada speech tones. These rhythms are perceived and enjoyed well only when the morphological and syntactic structures in the narrative are read loudly at a pace of reading which the Dravidian languages, especially Telugu and Kannada, demand.

Morphology

The morphology of style addresses itself to the ways in which the creative writer makes words to suit his creative purpose. Ordinarily the writer does not make experiments with making words. James Joyce is one of the very few novelists who have made experiments of far-reaching consequences with words. Bilingual writers who write in the second language are greatly influenced by mother tongue, its idiom, its formation of words and such other processes. Mulk Raj Anand often makes literal translations of Punjabi and Hindi words and phrases, giving his style an imitable Indian touch. R.K. Narayan plays it safe as far as word formations are concerned. But Raja Rao makes a bold experiment in compounding words in a way in which it is done in Telugu and Kannada. The words that give Indianness to his language are mostly compound words. But they can also be regarded as short syntactic constructions. Semantically they remind us of the Anglo-Saxon Kennings or self-explanatory compounds available in Old English. We tried to focus the Dravidian rhythms in the novel by giving their equivalents in the source languages, Kannada and Telugu. The following structures are strewn all over the narrative:

i) *Noun + Noun:* It cannot be claimed that this is something peculiar to all the Indian languages, much less to the Dravidian languages. In modern English we come across phrases like *London Correspondent, University student* in which the first noun functions as an attribute qualifying the noun that follows. The following are some such expressions.

Expression	*Telugu*	*Kannada*
Trumpet Lingayya	Baakaa Lingayya	Baka Lingayya
Pipe Ramayya	Sannayi Ramayya	Sannayi Ramayya
Temple Lakshmamma	Gudi Lakshmamma	Gudi Lakshmamma
Bell People	Ganta Vaaru	Ganto Prajo
Snuff Satry	Mukkupodum Sastry	Mukkupodu Sastry

The first noun in the construction is descriptive and individualises the person as the surname (family name) does in Telugu or Kannada.

ii) *Noun + Noun: (Appositional):* In the following words the first element which semantically signifies the profession is in pre-opposition to the proper noun that follows it.

Expression	*Telugu*	*Kannada*
Postmaster Suryanarayana Suryanarayana	Postmaster Suryanarayana	Tapalmastru
Patwari Nanjundayya	Karanam Nanjundayya	Shambagha Nanjundayya
Barber Chennayya	Mangali Chennayya	Hojama Chennayya

iii) Agent Noun + Proper Noun: The agent noun in this construction is derivative from a verb and functions as an adjective qualifying the noun that follows it.

Expression	*Telugu*	*Kannada*
Drunkard Dheerappa	Tragubothu Veerappa	Kudaga Veerappa

iv) Compound Noun + Proper Noun: In the following words the first component is a compound word qualifying the personal name that follows it. For example:

Expression	*Telugu*	*Kannada*
Waterfall Venkamma	Jalapatam Venkamma	Tarou Tarou Venkamma
Jack-tree Tippa	Panasa Chettu Tippadu	Halasina Mara Tippa
Front-house Akkamma	Mundinti Akkamma	Yaduru Mane Akkamma
Gap-tooth Siddayya	Torripanti Siddayya	Hallu Mourida Siddayya
Corner-house Narasamma	Molinti Narasamma	Moole Mane Narasamma
Coffee-planter Rangayya	Coffee Thota Rangayya	Coffee Thota Rangayya

v) Caste Name+ Common Noun: Kanthapura falls into natural traditional divisions; each division is predominantly occupied by the families of a particular caste. These caste colonies are named in the following compound words:

Expression	*Telugu*	*Kannada*
Brahmin quarter	Brahmana peta	Brahmana vattara
Pariah quarter	Velivada	Holegiri
Potters quarter	Kummaripeta	Kumbara galli
Weavers quarter	Salepeta	Nayegevera galli
Sudra quarter	Soodrapeta	Sudra galli

vi) Common Noun + Common Noun

Expression	*Telugu*	*Kannada*
Elephant valley	Eenugu loya	Annegudda/ Anne knneve
Eagle tower	Garuda gopuram	Haddu gopura
Devil field	Pisaachi polam	Psaachi hola

vii) Present Participle + Proper Noun: The present participle in the following compound indicates the occupation of the person:

Expression	*Telugu*	*Kannada*
Huasking-Rangi	Vadlu Danche Rangi	Bhatta Kutto Rangi

viii) Noun + Present Participle + Proper Noun: The first component in the structure is made of a two-word unit (Noun + present participle) which serves as an adjective. Semantically the first component indicates either an occupation or a physical habit. For example:

Expression	*Telugu*	*Kannada*
Rice-pounding Rajamma	Biyyam danche Rajammma	Akki buso Rajamma
Nose-scratching keroko	Mukkugeere Nanjammma	Mugu Nanjammma Nanjammma

xi) Numerical Adjective + Participle + Noun: The first component of this three-word compound is itself a compound word consisting of numerical adjective and a past participle. For example:

Expression	*Telugu*	*Kannada*
One-eyed Linga	Ontikanti Lingadu	Vokanna Linga
Nine-pillared house	Tommidi Stambhala Illu	Vambatu Khambada mane

x) *Noun + Participle + Noun:* This closely resembles the earlier group. The difference, however, is the initial elemental first compound is a noun. For example:

Expression	*Telugu*	*Kannada*
Pock-marked Sidda	Masuchi Machala Siddadu	Sidabu Hoduda Sidda
Left-handed Madanna	Parracheti Madanna	Yadcha Madanna

There are longer compounds in which a possessive noun with the apostrophe mark becomes one of the components such as:

Expression	*Telugu*	*Kannada*
The black-serpent's ant-hill	Kalanaagu Putta	Karihavu Ireve gudda

This kind of formation is also used for kinship expressions such as: Barber Chennava's wife's brother, Drunkard Dheerappa's brother's son, etc.

It is possible to dispute the description of the above formation in the morphological terms. In other words they can be described as syntactic constructions. But as we have mentioned in the earlier part of this article these constructions are viewed as rhythmical segments. Each of them may be treated as macro-segment with intonation pitch levels and terminal contours peculiar to such Dravidian formations. Dravidian rhythms are also seen in larger constructions and at sentence levels. In fact, the grandmother's narration has the sing-song Dravidian tones. The inverted constructions like 'clever fellow this Bhattare' is typical of a grand-mother's bedtime stories to her grand children. The following sentences peculiarly Kannada in construction and rhythm: "I tell you, he was not a bad man, was Bhatta."[8]

The rhythms of a native language are also found in larger units of narration like paragraphs. Raja Rao often makes use of proper nouns to create such rhythms. In the following passage the mere sequence of proper nouns rapidly uttered gives a peculiar melody to the narration, while giving an impression of the numerical strength of people who gathered at the ceremonial discarding of foreign-spun clothes:

> He went to Dore and Sastry's son Puttu, and Dore and Sastry's son Puttu went to Post-master Suryanarayana's son's Chandru and Ramu, and then came Pandit Venkatesayya and Front-house Sami's son Srinivas and Kittu, and so Kittu and Srinivas and Puttu and Ramu and Chandru and Srinu, threw away their foreign clothes and became Gandhi's men.[9]

The frequency with which such rhythms get repeated in the narration gives haunting melody to the story. Repletion of phrases, short sentences embedded in large sentences is one of the techniques Raja Rao used in imparting Indian or Dravidian rhythms to the narration. Such sentences are far too many to be quoted here. The following may serve as illustration:

> She told us too, about the stars that are so far that some have poured their light into the blue space long before you were born, long before you were born or your father was born or your grandfather was born; and just as a day of Brahma is a million million years of ours, the day of the stars is a million million times our day, and each star has a sun and each sun has a moon, and each moon has an earth, and some there are that have two moons, and some three, and out there between the folds of the milky way she told us, out there, there is just a chink, and you put your eyes to a great tube and see another world with sun and moon and the stars, all bright and floating in the diamond dust of God.[10]

The repetitive rhythms in songs of mass prayers are translations from Indian languages and as such echo Indian melodies. For example:

> Siva, Siva of the Meru Mount,
> Siva, Siva of the Ganges-head,
> Siva, Siva of the Crescent-moon,
> Siva, Siva of the Crematorium-dance,
> Siva, Siva of the unillusioned heart,
> Siva, Siva, Siva. . . .[11]

This technique of repetition of the phrases and sentences is also found in the spontaneous song of lamentation when Moorthy is arrested: "He'll never come again, he'll never come again, he'll never come again, Moorthappa."[12]

In the prayer songs of Kenchamma or the song of welcome to the king of Heaven or the songs of folk-myths are all full of such familiar Indian rhythms. A loud reading of the novel makes the story more enjoyable than a mere story of the freedom movement can do. The Dravidian rhythms introduced in the novel seem to be spontaneous and effortless. They are not belaboured exercises. The tunes and rhythms are composed in the mind of the writer and given vent in the form of a grandmother's story.

References

1. Raja Rao, Kanthapura, *Orient Paper Back,* 1971; Foreword.
2. K.R. Rao, Raja Rao's, 'Kanthapura', *in* the 'Two Fold Voice' ed. by D.V.K. Raghavacharyulu, Navodaya Publishers, Vijayawada, 1971, p.106.
3. Raja Rao, *Kanthapura,* Foreword.
4. Ibid.
5. V. Y. Kantak, *Raja Rao's Kanthapura,* Chandrabhaga, 1985, p. 35.
6. Raja Rao, *Kanthapura,* Foreword.
7. Raja Rao, *Kanthapura,* Orient Paper Back, 1971; p. 135.
8. Ibid., 211.
9. Ibid., 23.
10. Ibid., p. 46.
11. Ibid., p. 220.
12. Ibid., p. 211.

6

An Exploration of the Feminist Ideology in the Novels of Bharati Mukherjee and Anjana Appachana

— *Gur Pyari Jandial*

The Indian English novel is deeply intertwined with the socio-political and philosophical milieu in which it was born and in which it developed. While the novel of the thirties and forties focused more on social problems, the distress of the oppressed classes and the national movement for political independence, the post-sixties novel is more concerned with the individual and his quest for identity. Changes in family organisation, industrialisation and urbanisation have led to conflict between tradition and modernity. The old beliefs and customs are now being challenged, more so in the context of women. Consciousness of her own individuality coupled with the awareness of issues like social justice has led to an awakening in the Indian woman. She is no longer satisfied with the established roles of a wife, daughter, sister and mother. Education and financial independence have also helped to some extent in this regard.

Women writers writing in English have attempted to project woman as the central figure, and have succeeded to a very large extent in presenting her predicament most effectively. The recent works of women writers have given a new dimension to the image of women in the family and society. One reason for this can be the instinctive perception and insight, which a woman writer has into a woman's problems, responses, anxieties, disturbances and emotional involvement.

A shift from the external world to the internal is a chief characteristic of these novels. Through deep insight and with acute perception, the emotional world of the woman is explored. The writer attempts to portray the deep anguish of a sensitive soul unable to bridge the gulf between expectation and reality. The woman protagonist in the modern Indian English novel is no longer passive and resigned to her fate. She struggles and fights against the circumstances of her life and searches for ways to define herself and find a voice. Contemporary women writers no longer want to portray stereotyped images of women.

In the last twenty years, an increasing number of third world writers have migrated to the West and have chosen to write in the English language. Writers like V. S. Naipaul, Salman Rushdie, Farrukh Dhondy, Jhumpa Lahiri, Ved Mehta, Haneif Kureishi and Shashi Tharoor have sought to record the manner in which they have chosen and adopted their new environment and how they experienced nostalgia, feeling of rootlessness and then a growing identification with the new land. This expatriate sensibility comes through in the writings of Bharati Mukherjee, a non-resident Indian who has emerged as an important Indian English novelist and short story writer. Mukherjee depicts problems faced by Indian and other third world immigrants who attempt to assimilate into North American lifestyles. She concentrates on sensitive, female protagonists who lack a stable sense of personal and cultural identity and are victimised by racism, sexism and other forms of social oppression.

Much of Mukherjee's fiction is informed by her personal experiences. Born to wealthy parents in Calcutta, she earned graduate and postgraduate degrees in English at universities in India before enrolling in the Iowa writing workshop where she met and later married the Canadian novelist, Clark Blaise. Mukherjee's first novel *The Tiger's Daughter* is about Tara, born in Calcutta, schooled in New York and married to an American. Mukherjee seems to be working out her old country from her psyche and so she takes a metaphorical trip back to Calcutta through her protagonist, Tara. The setting of the novel is the Naxalite Calcutta of the 60's and the 70's, filled with riots and protests. In Tara, we see an alienation from the mother country as well as the new one. When she returns to Calcutta she is seen as an admired curiosity for daring to choose an American husband

and rejecting the "arranged marriage". Tara is intelligent, elegant and alert. Unable to adjust to the contradictions between the cultures of the East and the West Tara stands confused. One area in which her confusion lies is the status of women as she finds it in the West and in the East. Tara's husband writes to her, "I miss you very much but you have to work this out." Tara has to work out her own identity and where she belongs. In America, she is racially an outsider and in India she was married "not to a person but to a foreigner and this foreignness was a burden." In the end, the alienation from the mother country works out to be stronger and Tara returns to David and to America. Though she is still at crossroads, she seems to be a step closer towards finding an identity.

Wife, Mukherjee's second novel is a psychological study of Dimple, a young woman from Calcutta who settles in New York with her husband. Raised to be passive and dependent and the idea of marriage as the only goal in life, firmly ingrained in her mind according to the Indian ideals of feminity, Dimple lacks the inner resources to cope with the fear and alienation that she experiences in New York. Her husband Amit, who is preoccupied with economic difficulties, is of little comfort. Dimple's friends try to encourage her to attempt various activities but she cannot adjust. Ultimately, she starts suffering from insomnia. Dimple is a victim of the tradition of passivity. She is shocked by the violence, which is her fundamental experience in New York. Newspapers, car radios, and casual conversations announce murders in alleys and ice-cream parlours. But when the fun of parties and new friends wears off, she finds herself stranded in a fully furnished, fully applianced apartment in Greenwich Village, terrified of the city outside. Television introduces her to the American lifestyle. Amit now seems weak and powerless to her. Gradually Dimple descends into psychotic madness. The novel ends with Dimple murdering Amit. Dimple is a woman trapped between two cultures. She lives in a vacuum, unable to adjust to her situation. Through Dimple, Mukherjee depicts the disorienting and dehumanising effects of urban American society and indicts Indian cultural values that discourage self-reliance in women. Dimple's vision of Sita's docility, sacrifice and responsibility is a flag with many messages. She wants to break through the traditional taboos of a wife. She aspires for freedom and love in marriage. But this aim brings its share of indignation, frustration, grief, resentment, spite and a sterile anger. She therefore moves from a state of mute resentment to disgust and intolerance, which finally culminates in violence and disaster. Dimple's deterioration can also be viewed as her desperate attempt to forget her Indian roots due to the demands of American life and her assertion of independence from her overbearing and insensitive husband.

Jasmine, Mukherjee's third novel is about Jyoti, a simple peasant girl from Punjab who grows up in a semi-feudal, patriarchal and rural society until she marries Prakash Vijh, a progressive and bright young engineer. Prakash believes in "trashing traditions" and breaking off from the past. Their happiness is however short lived as Prakash is killed by a terrorist bomb. Jyoti is told of how on being widowed her friend Vimla had committed suicide by burning herself with fire from a kitchen stove. Even her mother had tried to kill herself when Jyoti's father had died. Having failed in the attempt, she shaved off her head and now sits in a corner all day, and has to be forcibly spoon-fed. Jyoti also undergoes gender discrimination from childhood. Her mother had tried to strangle her as soon as she was born, saying: "Daughters were curses...Gods with infinite memories insisted girl children on women who needed to be punished for sins committed in other incarnations."[1]

She had to struggle for an education because her father believed that girls were meant only for housework. But Jasmine was a rebel even as a child. Against all opposition from her father and uncles, with the support of her "masterji" and mother, she determines to study. Early in her childhood she realises that the lot of women is different from that of men:

"Nothing is fair. All over our district bad luck dogged dowry less wives, rebellious wives, barren wives. They fell into wells, they got run over by trains, they burnt to death heating milk on kerosene stoves."[2]

The novel is about Jyoti's metamorphosis from Jyoti to Jasmine to Jase and finally to Jane. As she moves from one territory to another, Jyoti undergoes a transformation. At a deeper level, the novel is about a woman's quest for her own happiness and sense of self. Jyoti's entry to America as an illegal immigrant is a violent one. She is raped by Half-Face, the captain of the boat which smuggles her in. However instead of suffering in silence or resorting to suicide, Jyoti finds in herself the strength and will to take revenge. Slicing her tongue, in the form of "Kali" she kills Half-Face with a knife.

From this point onwards Jyoti takes her destiny in her own hands. A brief spell with "Professorji", the teacher known to her husband and to whom Prakash had initially planned to come to in America, makes Jyoti realise that Indians tend to make their "little Indias" in America. They are physically in America but they blank out any outside influence of the new land. Jyoti notices the relationship which "Professorji" has with his wife. He was following an ancient prescription for marital accord; silence, order and authority. So was she: "submission, beauty, innocence. Nirmala had no idea where her husband worked — he never told her…She had no idea what he did."[3] Finally, stifled in this environment, Jyoti breaks out. She finds a job as a governess with the Taylor family and gradually adapts to American lifestyles. Her peaceful life is disrupted when one day she spots Prakash's killer near the Taylor residence. Fearful for their safety, she leaves them and finally settles into a live-in relationship with Bud Ripplemayer. Her lingering loyalty towards India and Indian values forces her to stay with Bud when he is shot at by miscreants, an accident which leaves him paralysed. But at the end of the novel when Taylor comes to take Jane away so that they could begin a new life together, she does not refuse. She is "greedy with wants and reckless from hope". Her decision to leave Bud and go with Taylor can be seen as her final rejection of the values which force woman to put duty, loyalty and responsibility before their own personal happiness. In making her leave with Taylor the novelist seems to assert that life offers endless opportunities to those who have the will and courage to take them. Jasmine achieves that which neither Tara nor Dimple could, because they lacked the courage to free themselves from their bonds. Mukherjee seems to be of the view that destinies can be altered. Jasmine repositions her stars with new hopes in accepting marriage to Taylor. Jasmine feels no guilt as she walks away from Bud.

"I am not choosing between men. I am caught between the promise of America and the old word dutifulness. A caregiver's life is a good life, a worthy life. What am I to do..? It isn't guilt

I feel, its relief. I realise I have already stopped thinking of myself as Jane. Adventure, risk, transformation...watch me reposition the stars."[4]

Jasmine, throughout most of the novel, finds herself caught between two different worlds. She recognises within herself a person who is a caregiver, showering concern and love on others and living for other people. On the other hand she discerns in her own personality a tireless adventurer engaging in risk and leaving behind the old world dutifulness. Conflicting forces thrill her. Jyoti would have saved her salary like the Vadheras. But Jase went to the movies and lived for the day. "For every Jasmine the reliable caregiver, there is a Jase, the prowling adventurer. I thrilled to the tug of opposing forces."[5]

The Holder of the World is also an attempt to portray a woman's quest. The character of the protagonist is based on one of the greatest heroines of American literature, Hester Pryne. The novel is the story of Hannah Easton, a white Puritan woman from Salem, Massachusetts Bay Colony. She makes a trip to the exotic Coromandal shores in the late seventeenth century and finally becomes the mistress of Raja Jhadev Singh, an Indian king. The inspiration behind this story was an Indian miniature painting that Mukherjee saw in an auction of Sotheby in New York. The painting was entitled "A European Woman in Aurangzeb's Court". The painting displayed a Caucasian woman in full Mughal dress. On seeing the painting, Mukherjee said: "I suddenly realised that I was looking at a woman who, three hundred years back had taken a lot of risks and transformed herself."[6]

In the novel, it is Beigh Masters, an asset hunter by profession and a modern day American woman, who comes across such a painting. Masters is looking for the most perfect diamond in the world, 'The Emperor's Tear', for her client. In the Museum of Maritime Trade in Boston she sees a painting of 'Salem Bibi' clad in a Mughal dress. During this treasure hunt Beigh discovers that the 'Salem Bibi' was Hannah Easton, a New England Puritan woman and also one of her ancestors. As the layers of Hannah's life start unravelling one by one, Beigh gets more interested in her life than the diamond. The novel therefore traces the journey of Hannah Easton, from puritan New England to England, then to exotic India and finally backs to America. The diamond called the 'Emperor's Tear' which Aurangzeb hung in his war tent and which Hannah is supposed to have stolen is said to be lost in history.

Hannah Easton, the second narrator is the figure, central to the novel. Hannah, having been adopted by Mr. And Mrs. Fitch after she is orphaned comes to live in Salem. Her father had died when she was a year old and her mother eloped with her Nipmnc lover during an attack on the Puritans by the Nipmnc tribe. People however thought that Rebecca Easton had died in the attack. Hannah alone knows the truth. The seeds of revolt, of breaking the traditional barriers are therefore already sown in Hannah from a young age. In Salem, Hannah is forced to live the repressive Puritan life of simplicity, hard work and charity.

Hannah is unable to reconcile this life with the sin her mother committed. She learns psalms, does needlework and does not indulge in the activities which occupy most girls of her age. At the age of fifteen she is married to Gabriel Legge who is a seafarer. With him she moves to England and then to India where Gabriel joins the East India Company. Arriving at the Coromandal Coast, Hannah feels a sense of belonging while Gabriel pursues his career first as an officer and then as a pirate. Hannah gradually undergoes a transformation. She absorbs the new world around her and realises how empty her life had been with Gabriel. After being separated from Gabriel, Hannah escapes with her maid, Bhagmati to Panpur under the protection of Raja Jhadev Singh of Devgad.

Hannah now finds new roots though she is torn between the diverse worlds of Hinduism and Puritanism. With Gabriel, Hannah had clung to the restrictions of the Puritan world, even though Gabriel had acquired a mistress, 'a bibi' very soon after coming to India. However, Hannah finds her real self and happiness with Jhadev Singh after she rejects the old world rules. With him she realises the emotional realities of human life. Now she finds her real passionate nature and "the first hint that a world beyond duty, patience and wifely service was possible, then desirable, then irresistible." She experiences real love and the life of emotion and passion. Hannah is portrayed as different from the other American women whose husbands' careers had brought them to India. They closed themselves to the environment around them and considered themselves superior to the Indians. Hannah "was alert to the novelty but her voyage was mental, interior." The life around Hannah thrills her and she enjoys every bit of her stay in India. She establishes a kind of "unspoken" bond with exotic India. Beigh Masters is able to identify and relate to this particular quality in Hannah. The sub-plot of Beigh Masters is linked to Hannah's story in many ways. At first Beigh Masters appears to have little in common with Hannah except her New England background and her Indian lover Venn Iyer. But as she gets more and more involved with Hannah's life, she begins to discover other points of contact. She begins to feel that she is a kindred spirit. Both Hannah and Beigh are impelled by curiosity and romance, a thirst for the unknown and a passion that transforms their lives. In trying to understand and piece together Hannah's relationship with Raja Jhadev Singh, Beigh consolidates her own relationship with Venn. She goes back to his roots and tries to reach parts of him that he had hidden away and at the same time exposes to him parts of her that he has been afraid to ask about. As she unravels the mystery of Hannah's life, Beigh tries to make sense of her own life. Her research on Hannah teaches her to go beyond her "well trained feminist self" and to be aware of the multiple contingencies of life. After Jhadev Singh's death Hannah returns to Salem with her daughter, "Black Pearl". Like Hester Prynne in Hawthorne's *The Scarlet Letter*, she is a rebel living on the fringes of society. Sandhya Rao Mehta comments:

> It is a novel of expatriation, of a quest and a journey, not only to geographically diverse lands but to culturally variant societies which help to question and abandon conventional moral and social values. Hannah succeeds in questioning and discovering new ways of defining reality in a world, which was essentially Orthodox.[7]

Through cross-cultural interaction and East-West encounter which is a major dimension in the novels of Bharati Mukherjee, the novelist furthers the feminist question. In most of the novels the protagonist is an Asian immigrant confronted with a different set of conditions in the West. Psychological anomalies result but ultimately the protagonist must rise above these with a conscious ability to survive, change and succeed, as Jasmine does and Dimple fails to do. Mukherjee's novels explore the East-West encounter from an Indian woman's point of view. *The Holder of the World* is the only exception where the protagonist is a woman from the West, journeying to India.

Usually the protagonist experiences the pull of Indian traditions, which are in constant conflict with Western attitudes. The point of interest in the novel usually lies at those critical junctures where the protagonist must make decisions, where old habits and beliefs must be discarded in favour of new ones. Mukherjee creates women characters that attempt to realise themselves and thus attain an identity and individuality of their own. After gender-related titles of 'daughter' and 'wife' in *The Tiger's Daughter* and *Wife* respectively, *Jasmine*, the title of the third novel suggests the progression in the views of the writer. The protagonist rises above the role of a daughter and wife. "The Daughter-Tara and, the wife-Dimple evolve into Jasmine—an individual with a personality unbounded by traditional limitations."[8]

In the journey towards discovering oneself there is a progression from novel to novel. Tara and Dimple seek refuge in escape and Jasmine and Hannah through sheer will to survive, overcome the situation of crisis. Mukherjee says, her protagonists have no role models. They must invent their own roles, revise old ones and survive as best as they can. The new world, in which they negotiate, holds promise of a new self-hood and self-assertion is the power that her protagonists soon begin to enjoy. The enthusiastic affirmation of the immigrant condition becomes a metaphor of hope and survival.

Anjana Appachana's *Listening Now* is a complex and gripping novel set in the middle class community of Delhi. With deep insight the writer has probed the problem of women's subjugation and suffering. The main thread in the novel is the strange relationship of Padma and Karan. Karan undergoes a deep association with a young Padma, but deserts her when she is pregnant. In a moment of weakness he yields to his mother's demands and marries a woman of her choice, thus betraying Padma and the child within her. One wrong decision leaves many lives destroyed. Padma is left destitute and alone. It is only the love of her elder sister Shantacca, her brother-in-law and her mother that sees her through the pregnancy and the birth of her child. Determined not to be defeated, Padma brings up Mallika alone. She gets a job as a teacher and struggles to give Mallika a normal, loving home. Her own shortcomings are overcome by Shantacca who gives Mallika more love than her own mother can. However Padma must suffer the rejection of her father and brother who never forgive her. Interwoven with the main plot are many threads which portray the strains on women in modern India. Confined to their homes, betrayed by their men, they live monotonous lives day after day – their dreams shattered, ambitions left unfulfilled. Through Madhu's story we get a glimpse of what happens to hundreds of girls. Madhu's father wanted her settled before he died, as he was suffering from cancer. So even though she was a promising student, she never finished her B. A. and got married in the third year. Madhu lives in a fool's paradise convincing herself and her friends that she is happy. She says: "Padma, satisfaction I have. Too much satisfaction. He gives me everything. My children give me everything. I don't need degrees to get satisfaction".

She considers herself far more fortunate than Anu or Padma. But nothing can fill the void within her, neither houses and cars, nor sarees. Even the sexual side of her marriage leaves her feeling empty and used. Anu too shows the world a "smiling tip". The picture that remains hidden is a grim one. Abused by her mother-in-law, she lives like a stranger in her own house. Yet Anu has learnt to laugh, to believe that "this is your life now..As much happiness as you can get out of it, get, there is no other place to get it from." But Anu's real worry is her daughter, Prabha. Intelligent and observant, Prabha never hesitates to point out the differences in her mother's treatment of herself and her brother Anirudha. She also observes how her mother is treated by her grandmother. "Dadima, you were saying Mumma's food is very bad..but everything you have eaten three times." But this does not make Anu feel happy. She is troubled and worried by her daughter's precociousness. Her own life has taught her that women cannot question things. In a woman's world, words like justice and fairness rang hollow. It is Anu who reveals the truth and her deepest fears for Prabha:

> Acceptance that was the truth. Justice, there was none. Truth meant violence, assault. On the surface it was what had happened to her and Madhu and Padma that day at the mela,

> but that was just its outward manifestation. The everyday violations did as much damage. Prabha would have to learn to accept both.[10]

"What a kind man your husband is," Madhu says to Anu again and again. But Anu's husband with all his kindness, integrity, high principles of justice and honesty is unable to understand or even realise what his wife undergoes everyday. They live together, one happy family, but there is a gulf as wide as the sea between them. Anu cannot complain because everything she says is misunderstood. The sexual side of their marriage is as empty as Madhu's.

> Now the nearest he came to her was when he wanted sex, and she never felt so distant from him as she did then. Two minutes it took, as quick as her single early morning cup of tea, and the tea was infinitely more satisfying.[11]

Rukmini, the mother of Shanta and Padma, says that thinking is a luxury only men can afford. She tries to teach Shanta to give everything and expect nothing in return. But Shanta had always been rebellious, even as a child. She asked questions, demanded that she be treated equally as her brother, Madhav, and after marriage expected her husband to be vocal about his feelings for her. Rukmini tries to make Shanta understand that books, thinking, and intellectualising got women nowhere. She hardly knew a man who asked for brains in the woman he wanted to marry. Common sense, beauty, accomplishment in the kitchen—these were acceptable. A woman commanded respect if she was resilient, tolerant, strong and submissive. Rukmini's husband had great dreams for his two daughters. But ultimately, those dreams came to nothing. Shantacca, a gold medallist, once a lover of literature and poetry, will cook and clean for the rest of her life. All she reads now are trashy novels. Ironically, when Karan returns to Padma after a gap of thirteen years, she refuses to go with him or marry him. By now Padma has found meaning in life through her child, her job, her friends Anu and Madhu, and the love her sister has for her. Marrying Karan would mean forsaking all this. Anu learnt classical music for fourteen years. She gave it up after marriage. Padma vehemently tells Karan, "So what if you were celibate for thirteen years? So was I."

Through the lives of five women, Appachana illuminates human relationships and how women must beat the odds to survive. Ruthlessly she tears away the garb to reveal the hollowness that lies within domestic bliss that most marriages wear. Violence against women in buses, trains and market places is only the outward manifestation of what women have to undergo. What is worse is its more subtle form. It may not even be physical but is a gradual breaking of the spirit and it must be endured. Like Anu, women seek whatever happiness they can and convince them that security means happiness. Padma refuses to marry Karan because having once found her identity and sense of self, she is not ready to give it up. She also tells Karan that at the time of crisis and need, only the women in her life stood by her—Shantacca, her mother, and her friends Madhu and Anu.

However, the novel does not end on a note of despair. Ultimately, through education, inner strength, resilience and courage Padma survives. After her nervous breakdown she exorcises the past and is ready to begin anew. She survives by depending on that same intelligence that Shantacca had berated as being useless in a man's world. While the novels of Bharati Mukherjee and Anjana Appachana show common themes and concerns with regard to the woman question, *Listening Now* is set in the middle class culture of urban India. It is about the troubles and turmoil in the lives of Indian women and their relationships. The novel offers a scathing critique of man woman relationships and the woman caught in a cage called marriage. Appachana draws a vivid picture of the middle class Delhi community. Bharati Mukherjee's protagonists on the other hand are expatriates. The problem of gender and man-woman relationships is inextricably woven into the cross-cultural crisis. Her protagonists are caught between the conflicting cultures of East and West. Their quest for identity and self is linked with their ability to assimilate Western ideals of self-reliance, assertion and love for life.

The novels of Bharati Mukherjee and Anjana Appachana introduce an authentic and objective perspective of the woman question. Their protagonists also show a definite development and change. Through pain and grievance they emerge whole and complete with a better understanding of themselves and what they want out of their lives. The vision of hope is therefore never missing. As Karan realises in *Listening Now*, "There is always a choice." For the woman specially, the struggle is a long and difficult one. But it can and must be endured and only with this intense struggle can she evolve an identity of her own.

Acknowledgements

This work has been supported by the UGC minor research project grant for which the author is very grateful.

References

1. Bharati Mukherjee, *Jasmine*, New York: Fawcett Books, 1989, p. 39.
2. Ibid, p. 36.
3. Ibid, p. 133-134.
4. Ibid, p. 274.
5. Ibid p 157.
6. Shakuntala Bharvani, "The Holder of the World", *The Fictions of Bharati Mukherjee: A Critical Symposium*, ed. R. K. Dhawan, New Delhi: Prestige Books, 1996, p. 188.
7. Sandhya Rao Mehta, "The Utmost Coast Abroad: Hannah Easton's Quest in The Holder of the World", *The Fictions of Bharati Mukherjee: A Critical Symposium*, op.cit., p. 195.
8. Indira Nityanandam, "Bharati Mukherjee: Striking Roots", *Three Great Women Novelists: Anita Desai, Shashi Deshpande and Bharati Mukherjee*, New Delhi: Creative Books, 2000, p. 79.
9. Anjana Appachana, *Listening Now*, New Delhi: India Ink, 1998, p. 61.
10. Ibid., p.129.
11. Ibid.

7

Dom Moraes: The Wandering Minstrel

— *N. Sharada Iyer*

When David Archer of the famous Parton Press published Dom Moraes's *A Beginning* in 1958, it was as if a contemporary younger successor to the romantic poets had been declared, a declaration seemingly confirmed by the announcement that the book had been awarded Hawthornden Prize. Moraes was not only the youngest but the only Non-Britisher to receive it. He was a student then, hardly nineteen, and remains the youngest to be honoured so.

The prize more or less settled the direction of his future. But the sudden publication had a disconcerting effect too. "I knew in my bones that this was a dangerous thing to have happened. The atmosphere of youthful genius that was building up around me was not an atmosphere in which I could get back to my work." Get back he did, for it was followed not only by several volumes of poetry but prose in the form of autobiography, journalism, criticism, TV films, etc.

The son of the well-known journalist, Frank Moraes, he was born in Bombay in 1938. He had a troubled and insecure childhood and adolescence during which his mother's attack of insanity was a persistent nightmare. She was eventually institutionalised. This led to his subsequent withdrawal from her and was forced to live with different families, and later travelled with his father to Ceylon, Pacific and Southeast Asia before returning to Bombay and finally leaving for England at the age of seventeen. The varied repercussions of these traumatic experience and his attempts to come to terms with them in adult life was the driving force behind his writing *A Beginning* (1958), Poems (1960), John Nobody (1965).

Dom Moraes's experience of being a citizen of the world, of travel, of solitude, of needing the security of love, of not knowing exactly where "home" is, of alienation and the subsequent delight in language and poetry thus began early in his life. His father's enormous library was a source and influencing factor which drew him to literature, especially poetry. He started writing very early in life at the age of twelve, and when hardly thirteen he published *Green is the Grass* (1951), a book about cricket. His poems appeared in the *Illustrated Weekly of India* and he was soon recognised as one of the new Indian English poets. From the first he was immersed in the theme, language, convention and attitude of poetry especially of the English poetics specifically the romantic.

In the post-war lower middle class a Little England of red brick universities and angry young men, Moraes continued a romantic tradition which had been sustained during the nineteen thirties and forties, by George Barker Dylan Thomas and David Gascoyne and W.S. Graham. These poets were Moraes's English friends too.

Even as a child he was passionately interested in poetry and as a poet for a time he played the sedulous ape to Eliot, Auden and Spender. At Oxford, as related in *My Son's Father* "to use the university and not let the university use him" as he wished his time at Oxford "to polish and my tools and extend my power...", what he had seen and felt during the passage of childhood and adolescence as he felt they asked for transmutation to poetry.

Deeply influenced by Dylan Thomas, the romantics and the surrealist school, Moraes wrote highly personal poetry with a persistent confessional tone, with recurring themes of loneliness, insecurity from which escape was sought either in the erotic fantasies of the febrile imagination or the self-probing of a tortured soul.

A Beginning (1958) published when he was hardly nineteen projects his family problem, loneliness and personal anxieties of imagined situation. The poems have grown out of the intense moments of encounter with reality – what George Whalley describes as paradigmatic events – but they have been translated though symbolic extrication into finished poems purged of the taint of the merely subjective and cast on the mould of universality— he does the alchemic act of turning the personal into the universal, 'In A Letter To My Mother':

> Your eyes are like mine
> When I last looked on them
> I saw my whole country
> A defeated dream
> Hiding itself in prayers
> A population of corpses
> Sorrow has stopped your eyes
> Your dream is desolate
> It calls me every day
> But I will not enter it
> Forgive me my trespasses

In a way it is any son to any mother. Moraes's lyrics have a vibrant suggestiveness, the familiar is touched with the allusive light of romance and unusual is rendered intimate through understanding.

The romantic tradition remained an influence on his idiom, diction and theme. Influenced by the romantic poetry, he wrote of the pipers, enchanting children, and wizards playing flutes, fairyland hermits and caves and of such themes as fear, loss of innocence, coyness, imagined love and sexuality. His poetry often creates a world haunted in which classical, Christian, medieval and fairytales, myths are mixed, dragon and dwarfs, Cain and the unicorn, that tomb of Mycenae and Christ come together. As a poet, he's a dreamer — a romantic dreamer conscious of hurt, failure, disappointment. As he matures he gains knowledge — knowledge of the ways of the world and develops a tougher outer skin to survive. The dreamer becomes a sinner, an exile, a wounded poet, a man without a home. Later there will be other defences, other postures but behind all the masks and at the heart of the varied personae will be found as he wrote "lonely on all lands unloved and forlorn" and his fate is to seem "unreal even to himself".

Unlike Ezekiel who was a poet of the city Moraes even when he was politically committed to Israel or Indian "invasion" of Goa he never was a poet of the city, modern condition, cultural crisis.

He was concerned with himself as a poet, his insecurities and hurt. His poems are of are of exile and isolation. He never went beyond older literary convention or places, his emotion within a larger cultural context. Their limitations come from the intensity of concern with self and its immediate world including friends and lovers. His first three books of verse move from an imagined dream world through romantic love to disillusioned romanticism. There had always been a strong destructive streak, a romantic element of death wish in his poetry and worldview.

> Dying is just the same as going to sleep.
> The piper whispered close your eyes
>
> ('Figure in the Landscape')

He had paid his dues to the tradition of late English romantics and surrealists of nineteen thirties and forties to which he was an inheritor. Bernard Kops who first met Dom Moraes in 1950 said "The Indian poet had brought a different aura to the post-war atmosphere of uncertainty and cynicism in the London literary circle we all fell in love with Dom immediately. Whenever he entered the cafe the whole place burst into light."

When *My Son's Father* was published in 1968 he was criticised by the London press for his presumption in writing an autobiography when he was only 30. But for the young poet who had a traumatic childhood and adolescence, writings served as a therapy – a cathartic effect. In the autobiography – *Gone Away* (1960), *My Son's Father* (1968), *A Matter of People* (1974) and *Never At Home* (1994) — a genre in which he excelled, he has recorded the events of his life. But it was poetry that articulates his themes most powerfully – absences departure, dislocation, loss. In his poetry we meet the isolated child, hurt and confused, the young outsider in England, making up for his insecurity by his dazzling presence, the solitary exile steering among the illusion and uncertainties of belonging. In England, he was an inexplicable Indian brilliant at his craft, and magical in his themes, irreducible to the standard clichés about postcolonial subject who mimics his master.

By 1990 Dom the stranger had found a belonging which diminished his bitterness and allowed him to burst forth in a candid and sometimes shockingly beautiful poetry, brought together in his *Collected Poems*. The last poem in the collection dwells on the future, often incarnated in the figure of a child, the magical survivor of experience who lives on to sing.

The Island with four parts—'The Burning', 'The Coming', 'The Conquest' and 'Afterward' is the most sustained of Dom's poetic flight, and it impresses by its urgency of motivation, and adequacy of articulation, as Prof. Iyenger noted, "it is a parable of the ultimate failure of even a successful war."

> It was not war, but mutual defeat
> The conquerors shriveled in the island sun.

'In the Prophet', Dom says, "a prophet and a poet both work with intractable material, the prophet with people in relation to his vision, the poet with words in relation to his readers. A moment comes, when he neither turns back not travel along."

> I followed desert sun
> Alone these thirty years
> My shelter under rocks
> My vision in my eyes ....
> Once these kept me happy
> Once - but now I have aged
> And the differences, to me.

Dom was a figure of paradoxes; belonging to him was a matter of being at home in a period rather than a place, the London and Oxford of his youth, and yet he could make himself on the road, travelling from one crisis to another, adjusting his focal length to the human condition as he confronted them. He confronted it from rural England through war-struck Ireland to the riverine darkness of Vietnam. His prose treatment of these experiences is self-deprecating while the alchemy of poetry allowed him to weave them into a tapestry of love, quest, sex and death. In *A Letter* he wrote:

> And poems grew like maggots in my head.
> In fighting Southeast Asians, with each gun
> Talking to me, then home word to the green
> And dung smeared plains ruled over by the sun
> When I had done with that I was fifteen
>
> ('Variety of Absences')

In *A Beginning* his idiom is rooted only in his imagination. The very first poem about the piper losing his children is prophetic.

> Even their voices went away
> And left an absence, glitter of loss

For Moraes, absence is metaphor of life. In a poem which gives the little to his collection of three overlapping memories over a period of three decades, he says that the world is held together by its variety of absences. He himself has lived in a state of homelessness, always ignorant of what the next step would be.

> No sound would be heard if
> So much silence was not heard
> Clouds scoff like this sheep on the cliff
> The echoes of stones are restored
> No longer any foreshore
> Or any abyss this world held together
> By its variety of absence.

Behind the façade of his tight and taut lines there is the pain of an insecure and vulnerable self which was never totally at home in this world. He found the right metaphor for the imaginative world of a man who was homeless in a fundamental sense:

> I have grown up I think to live alone
> To keep my old illusions, sometimes dream
> Glumly, that I am unloved and forlorn
>
> (*Autobiography*)

"I was never conscious of being alone, I found myself very interesting, a vice that persisted" over the years while supporting him through writing. He had stopped being a poet, a writer than an intellectual more concerned with words than ideas. He had drifted from being one of the most promising poets in England during the late nineteen fifties and early sixties to a superior writer of the superior coffee table books. It also showed that he was by no means an ivory tower poet as some thought him to be. Like his father who covered the Burma and China of World War II, Dom's sympathy lay with the impoverished, oppressed and the disempowered. He wrote an article about a prison island in

Vietnam in the early 1970s which moved the Amnesty International into action and secured the liberation of thousands of prisoners. He never spoke of his personal danger and endurance.

During the long poetic silence in which he felt the energies of mystery and lyric had deserted him. He could not shape thought and images into verse although he remained haunted by the memorable character he had created – the sinister gardener, the innocent prince, the wizard trapped in a glass, the innocent sinner and the self-mortifying prince. In these years from exile, from poetry he had led as Spender called the privileged existence as the director of topical film for TV, a highly paid roving correspondent with a private plane at his disposal, a guest of grandeur of the third world countries but had always been haunted by sense of having failed at his true calling. This prolonged dry spell was later recognised as a germination period. Coming back from England to the city of his birth, he quietly prepared for the return of the Muse, and gradually accomplished poems – *Absences* (1983) and *Collected Poems* (1987) – which were all sharper for the prolonged dormancy.

Throughout his life Dom was alternately attracted and repelled by India, its people its culture. This tension afforded him one of the most vital impulses of his art, the other being a sense of abiding loss, search for redemptive love, a feeling of being a permanent exile, no matter where he went.

Born to a Goan father and an East Indian mother, raised in a highly Anglicised ethos he saw himself and was regarded by others as an English poet living in exile in India. In England he spent a lot of his time fashioning himself into an English poet but nevertheless with a distinctive otherness about him. His expressions anticipated the context in which he and his poetry would be evaluated. He steadily disowned his Indian heritage.

> I'm Indian by birth but I have lived in England since I was a boy and I hold a British passport. The historical accident of British rule in India worked on my family, so that I lived an English life there and spoke no other Indian language...."[1] So English was my outlook. I found I could not fit in India, when eventually I came to England I fitted at once.[2]

He produced the certificate of Verrier Elwin who reportedly told him "you are very English person your reactions aren't Indian."[3] In this respect he was like Manmohan Ghose (1816-1924) who, reluctant to return to India after graduation, wrote to Binyan once:

> I shall try to persuade my father to let me stay in England for good. I am sure that with the tastes I have I shall be of no use in India. There is nothing I dream as much as going back to India; I feel quite at home with my surroundings here .There I should be out of sympathy with everything. I know neither the people nor the language all is strange and alien. And I'm four fifth an Englishman, if not entirely one, and it is in England I should do the most good to my country and myself.

But not getting a post in the British museum or the Civil Service he had to return to India. And ironically Dom Moraes was described by *The Penguin Companion to Literature* as an "Indian English poet", whether he wanted it or not.

He lived for many years in England, but after his public protestation of the annexation or liberation of Goa, he gave up his Indian citizenship for British; he was universally denounced. It was seen as a quixotic gesture. Lonely in its heroism, and its insistence of on truth, he freely conceded this in *John Nobody* (1965) alternately wistful and ironic.

> And I grew sick of an Indian day
> And there at last a moral issue rose
> I grabbed my pen and galloped to attack
> My Rosinate trod on someone's toes
> A government frowned and now I can't go back

During the nineteen sixties and seventies he was viewed by Indian readers through a frame of dogmatic nationalist sentiment as a maverick whose refusal to subscribe to the dogma of Indianness exposed to the charge of unpatriotic behaviour. People had many hard names for him, often hard ones: nostalgic, dreamer, alien. He was not a colonial hater of India that he was often made out to be; rather what he hated was the unreasonable brutality woven into the texture of contemporary Indian social structure, its capacity for self-deception and the lack of generosity, but his anger and bitterness are balanced by sorrow and compassion.

However towards the end, as he regarded the rise of majoritarian intolerance with horror and the country's future bleak, he achieved a certain compassionate equanimity towards its people, a positive sense of identification with their struggle and aspiration. In a reciprocal gesture, the literary culture that had long rejected him to the extent of excluding him from anthologies of Indian English writing recognised him with awards and more importantly with a revival of serious attention to his writings.

He was one of the small bands of good poets who wrote in English in the nineteen fifties and sixties, one of the best and well known. Stephen Spender considered him a perfect poet, William Darylmple describes him "as the finest prose stylist in the subcontinent," and Jerry Pinto wrote "he covered wars, won prizes, loved women and wrote some bloody good poems."

Prof. Naik holds, that "his imagery has strong sensuous qualities which despite the protestations so obviously stamp him an Indian poet. Of all his contemporaries he has the finest ear for the rhythm of modern English." Prof. Iyengar feels that the poem like 'Voices' has a subtle design on the listener's ear and mind:

> In my ladies chambers
> Once I found a skull
> It helps one to remember
> That she was so beautiful
> If I find the moral
> That is all my wish
> Men have fetched up coral
> When they have trawled for fish.

Dom turns "what he touches into finished art." Ezekiel felt that while Moraes's Collected Poems (1987) is an impressive collection from which much may be learned about the art yet he writes like an English poet and does not reflect any significant aspect of Indian life."

Some feel that his poetry lacks the power of plain speech and the wisdom born of self-questioning yet, no matter what the poet Moraes planned to say at the moment of speech he always inherited the subject. The music of poems brings the poetic content into a linguistically inevitable and memorable one. *In 'Type with Fingers'* he wrote:

Every word that I wrote was true
This way or that meant to praise
Whatever was worth it on earth

"Critics have said nice things about me, about the flow of my poems; my ambition now is to break my lines and impart a rough texture to my poems," He muses wistfully, "to alone mind the garden and to be the same gardener daily expecting an angel."

As he had declared himself a British poet, he had stopped publishing in India, and hence not included in the anthologies of Indian English poetry of the seventies and eighties, and treated merely as a historical figure. But he had come in the eighties to privately print hundred copies of the smaller book of poems written between 1982 and 85 called *Absences* (1983) and manuscripts of poems for publication. After the successful publication of Penguin's *Collected Poems* (1957-87), Moraes began to write some of his best, and published it in India and gradually came to be regarded as an Indian English poet.

Moraes was a loner and defied fashionable labels like post-colonial or postmodern. Had he begun to write in the nineteen eighties and nineties, his poetry would have been regarded as evidence of postcolonial play of identities, and viewed more open mindedly.

Dom Moraes, who passed away on June 2, 2004, was no ivory tower dreamer. He was not only a major poet, but a journalist and critic, secretly wrestling his scintillating verse from the combat zone of life. A victim of cancer he refused to submit to the harsh radiation. It was a consolation that he slipped away quietly in sleep, avoiding fuss, incarceration in a hospital ward. Nissim's death in January, the same year, was a long goodbye, his intellect, senses and memory drained away; it was only a shell to which one bade farewell. But Dom left mid-passage with conversion to be completed, appointments to be made, of books in progress, journey yet to be undertaken. He was a poet who nurtured his gift despite the work day demands of prose, and fought for his inner demon, giving a candid account of their encounters and distilling these struggles into haunting phrases and compelling images. The lyrical beauty and technical virtuosity that are the hallmark of his poetry have enthralled readers for decades. Drawing them into a mesmerising world of passion, romance, fear, guilt and the renewal, characterised by an elegant and hypnotic imagery the surreal texture of his poems weave together a variety of themes of love and war, friendship and alienation, myth and religion. His candour much as his brilliance will ensure that he will be remembered for generations.

References

1. Dom Moraes, "Shall I Paint Myself White' in *Impact Asian View of the West* ed. Jo Ann White. New York: 1971, p. 183-84.
2. Dom Moraes, *My Son's Father*, Delhi: Penguin, 1971, p. 162.
3. Ibid., p. 164.

Cited Works

Iyengar, K.R.S., *Indian Writing in English*, Delhi: Sterling, 1982.

King, Bruce, *Three Indian Poets*, Delhi: OUP, 1991.

Naik, M.K., *A History of Indian English Literature*, Delhi: Sahitya Akademi, 2005.

8

Generation in Exile: A Reading of Naipaul's *Magic Seeds*

— *Shweta Kushal* & *Evangeline Manickam*

Exile is one of the oldest words of human language, and it is similar in different spaces as well as in different times. It covers a complexity of significances, and it has a variety of explanations. It seems that for understanding this entire complex situation one must place the possible answer not between all these explanations, but within – in an internal exile. However, in order to understand the term certain definitions are required.

The Oxford Dictionary states that, exile "is a banishment or a prolonged separation from one's native land." The definition is easy to understand, as it is restricted within the space-time framework. However, Susan Rubin Suleiman believes that "in its narrow sense, a political banishment, exile in its broad sense designates every kind of estrangement or displacement, from physical and geographical to the spiritual" (Suleiman 1998, 3). This definition implies that a person becomes an exile through a process of estrangement, which begins within the subconscious frame, an inside exile, and ends in a very concrete reality – the labelling as an exile with all the political, mental, socio-cultural, and legal aspects involved.

An exile is an unusual, different individual in the eyes of the others, no matter where he/she may be living. Exile even as a final, factual experience is usually an individual experience, a "one" against "all" relationship.

Going to Edward Said's notion of the exile, as he stated in the Reith Lectures delivered in 1993, an exile is someone who is constantly "dyspepsic" and has "a kind of curmudgeonly disagreeableness" that makes him/her "dislike" the trappings of accommodation and national well being. At the end of Culture and Imperialism, he quotes a twelfth century monk from Saxony elaborating the journey of the exile from his "home-land" to the globe. The exile first becomes "tender", then strong, and finally perfect:

> The person who finds his homeland sweet is still a tender beginner, he to whom every soil is as his native one is already strong, but he is perfect to whom the entire world is a foreign place. (Said, 1994, 407)

Emile Cioran, a Romanian writer writing in French during his exile in Paris, fits Said's definition perfectly. He is a double exile, firstly in the Romanian community and secondly by "betraying" his native language in the adoption of French. Cioran's individuality and rejection of any group belonging is obvious in the following statement he wrote in one of the letters to his parents:

> As far as I am concerned, I live a very solitary life, I have become bored of any kind of excitement, and I began to understand that my life's misfortunes come from the belonging to a certain group. (Cioran, 1995, 27)

This is the perfect exile, one to whom the entire world is a foreign land. It is in this context that this paper places V.S. Naipaul's latest novel *Magic Seeds.* It discusses how the central trope of the journey that allows the protagonist to engage in a soul-searching exercise enables the author to create a world that is replete with individuals who experience exile in one form or another. This novel marks a subtle change from Naipaul's earlier writings as he deviates from the theme of search for belonging and steps into a universe where it is no longer important.

The novel is an account of the protagonist Willie's journey through a few years and three countries which forces him to delve deeper into himself, asking questions about his identity, his roots and his life at large. The narrative begins with Willie in Berlin who goes to India to join a revolution, is caught by the police as a revolutionary and is then sent to England as an exile. Later, the reader learns that he has been in India, England and Africa before coming to Berlin. The narrative is largely omniscient. The protagonist's personal thoughts, observations, tribulations, dilemmas and ideas are given a fair space so that the omniscient voice becomes unobtrusive. However, there are instances where the authorial or the narratorial voice is not very distinguishable from the protagonist's. In these instances, Naipaul presents his own opinions either directly or through Willie. The narrative begins with conversations between Willie and his sister Sarojini with her painting a picture that portrays Willie's attitude as she sees it. She thinks he lets life pass him by, is causeless and unmotivated, with overarching passivity – statements that are corroborated through his responses. Talking about the guerrilla war in Africa, she says, "That was a big enough cause to anyone looking for a cause" (MS 2). However, Willie is not looking for a cause and is content to lead his life in a laid back manner as he does not comprehend its usefulness. This is reminiscent of the author's position in an earlier novel *Guerrillas,* where Naipaul is unable to understand the evolution of postcolonial societies at their most essential and dynamic moment of development. Sarojini accuses Willie of being a pretender, of taking on the ways and methods of the new place he goes to too easily, thereby pretending to mingle with it and not keeping his ethnic identity intact – something even a rose-seller is capable of doing.

History is very obviously present in the pages of the book, so that it becomes a topic of discussion. In the very beginning, the concept of history as a construct created by the Imperial powers is introduced. As Sarojini argues, India's history, constructed by Roper Lethbridge and published by Macmillan, is such a colonial enterprise instilling the idea of the inferior in the Indian. She says:

> One of the most important of those ideas was that in India there were servile races, people born to be slaves, and there were martial races. The martial races were fine, the servile races were not..That idea would have been impressed on them in all kinds of ways. (MS 7)

She explains that the British army was made of largely upper class Hindus, classified as martial in this system, but the mutiny of 1857 changed that.

> So the warriors who had won the empire became servile in British propaganda, and the frontier people they had conquered just before the mutiny became the martial ones. It is how imperialisms work. It is what happens to captive people. And since in India we have no idea of history we quickly forget our past and believe what we are told. (MS 7)

This reasoning corroborates Edward Said's arguments in his book *Orientalism*, where he argues that Orientalism was not objective scholarship, but was a construct and a form of representation that aided colonial enterprise and helped in boosting "the idea of European identity as a superior one in comparison with all the non-European peoples and cultures" (Said 2001, 7). The theme of history continues when Willie and Ramachandra discuss the reading of foreign texts, imposed on them by their English or Anglo-Indian teachers, texts that they did not understand and could not relate to. This is symbolic of the way in which the coloniser's culture imposes on the colonised even when they do not understand it. They have not read the literature produced in their own country. They feel a lack of connection with their own history and are unable to associate with a foreign one. Identity creation is stunted when there is no context to place it in. This is true for both men even though one has been abroad while the other has never gone out of the country. While Willie is a physical migrant, Ramachandra is an exile in his own country and experiences internal migration.

Naipaul's narrative offers a comparison to this attitude to history in the perspectives on it in London. Presence of old editions of *The Graphic*, a reputed newspaper, being used as wallpaper in Peter's bathroom indicates the wretched status of history. Important events and history have been relegated to a place that is usually neglected and dirty. Peter, the banker who symbolises the rich and the upper classes of England, pays no attention to the history of his country chronicled in newspapers. He is not concerned about what happened in the past and has no connection with the country's history, thereby living in a vacuum. Where Willie and Ramachandra did not have a choice, Peter has willingly forsaken his past without thought. This is ironic as the colonial powers were the ones that "created" history for the colonised world and they are no longer interested in it. This hints at what is to follow regarding Willie's disillusionment with the ordered world that he thinks London is. The fact that events in the colonising country affect the colonised is highlighted when Willie reads about brick taxes in Britain, which helps him to make connections with the same practice in British India and to see the unfairness of it all – that it was exploitative, exorbitant and unreasonable. While looking at the houses in North London, he realises that the present is influenced by the past. He has tried to run away from his past for far too long, and it has always come back to him.

Willie, in his mind, divides the world into two halves. First is the ordered world where the wars have been fought and people are leading simplified lives – this is the West or the Occident as Edward Said calls it in *Orientalism*. The second half is the struggling world that is in conflict and is trying to reach this state of simplification. This could imply the East or what Said calls the Orient. However, the two co-exist.

> There were the two worlds Sarojini spoke about. One world was ordered, settled, its wars fought. In this world without war or real danger people had been simplified. They looked at television and found their community, they ate and drank approved things and they counted their money. In the other world people were more frantic. They were desperate to enter the simpler, ordered world. (MS 10)

These observations are made in a Western city, Berlin, when he believes that he is seeing order all around him, and it is evident that the protagonist firmly believes that the ordered way, or the Occidental way by extension, is the only desirable end to all the struggles of the world. Through this belief of Willie's, Naipaul announces his own allegiance to the Western world order and emphasises where his loyalties lie.

Willie's observations in the camp on the decline of feudalism in India in the wake of the guerilla war reveal that.

> The fields of the liberated areas Willie knew had fallen into ruin: the old landlords and feudals had run away years before from the guerrilla chaos, and no secure new order had been established. (MS 86)

The idea here is that the revolution may have abolished feudalism but it is not all for the good. It has not generated alternatives for the system and so there are still things that have no method to be done in the new world order created by the revolution.

> There were no cattle boys now; there were no landowners to hire them. The revolutionaries had put an end to that kind of feudal village life, though there were still people who needed to have their cattle looked after, and there were still boys who pined to be hired for the long, idle day. (MS 99)

In reflecting on Shivdas's reasons for offering his hospitality to the revolutionaries, Willie questions if this is done due to devotion to the cause or because he follows old traditions. He sums it up very well.

> We think, or they think, that Shivdas does what he does because he is a peasant revolutionary, someone created by the movement, someone new and very precious. But Shivdas does what he does because he is instinctively following old ideas, old ways and old courtesies. One day he will not give up his bed to me. He will not think he needs to. That will be the end of the old world and the end of the revolution. (MS 97-98)

It is interesting to note that Willie feels that with the end of this old world order of courtesy, the revolution would fail. Revolutions are supposed to do away with the old and bring in something new, but here if the old dies, the prospect of the new dies with it. Willie realises that a revolution does not have only positive consequences. There are problems associated with abolishing an established order. "The past was terrible; it had to be done away with. But the past also had a kind of wholeness that people like Ramachandra couldn't begin to care about and couldn't replace" (MS 118).

The changes in England are very similar to those in India. The feudal order is going out and there is nothing to replace it so that where in India the big houses are going to ruin, in London they are being changed into hotels and other things. These big houses, symbols of the feudal world, are crumbling and whatever history they have in them – as in *The Graphic* pasted in the banker's bathrooms – will die with them. While in the beginning, Willie believes in the clear division of the world into the ordered and the chaotic, he realises through his journey to India and then back to England after a gap of thirty years that these distinctions are not as black and white as he might have believed. There invariably exist certain areas of grey.

The narrative offers a comment on the expectations of outsiders, which is what Willie is when he visits the weaver's village. After all the exoticisation of the East through paintings where gorgeous women are seen to weave and look very happy and idyllic in their village, confrontation with it as a means of survival seems unreal.

> It was an unhurried scene of some beauty; it was hard to imagine that this spinning and weaving, which looked so much like some precious protected folk craft, was done only for the village, for the very poor, and was a desperate business for the people concerned, run on very narrow margins. (MS 82)

This idyllic picture of undying beauty and calm has been created through centuries by artists and painters both of Indian origins and from the West. Willie continues to believe in the pastoral vision of village life throughout his association with the movement as it is "the basis of the movement's thinking" (MS 127). He realises much later that this does not account for many realities that village people as well as visitors to villages have to contend with.

> He had persuaded himself that that was the countryside he saw; he had never questioned it. He had persuaded himself that outside the noise and rush and awfulness of cities was this quite different world where things followed an antique course, which it was the business of the revolution to destroy. This pastoral vision contained the idea that the peasant laboured and was oppressed. What this pastoral vision didn't contain was the idea that the village – like those they had liberated on the march (and then let go of) and might one day with luck liberate again – was full of criminals, as limited and vicious and brutal as the setting, whose existence had nothing to do with the idea of labour and oppression. (MS 127-128)

The pastoral vision of the village is incomplete. It does not account for thugs and looters and criminals. Any kind of vision created to serve a particular purpose is incomplete and does not account for everything that exists in reality. This is true for the exoticisation of the Orient through Orientalism as well as of the creation of an ideal for indigenous purposes. This narrative comment upholds Said's argument in *Orientalism* as it challenges the creation of these idyllic settings.

The text constantly grapples with ideas of reality – how it is not a unified whole, not a universal truth. This idea is first introduced when Willie goes to look at the police area with Raja, another revolutionary, in his scooter. Only on visiting the police area does Willie realise that his reality is connected with others. He does not exist in a vacuum or in bits and pieces, and that his actions can lead to loss of life for someone, even himself. Willie gains perspective when he sees the complete "reality". He is able to recognise, for the first time, that there is a fractured sense of truth that all individuals hold in them. It is not possible to "know" the complete reality without looking at the other side of the coin. Even then it may not be "the whole truth" but a mere gaining of perspective.

> When they were telling me about what the guerrillas were doing, I should have asked about the police. I never should have allowed myself to believe that there was only one side in this battle. I don't know how we make mistakes like that. But we do. (MS 87).

This idea is reinforced through Willie's interaction with another prisoner for whom the prison cell was bigger than anything he had ever known outside. "This man's pleasure in the jail routine helped Willie" (MS 162). The prisoner finds it an improvement over all the other places he has known as the standard rooms he has been in were cubes "ten feet in all directions, with a loft about seven feet up that provided extra space" (MS 161). The fact that the man can find pleasure in jail where Willie has to practice his "yoga" to survive and maintain his sanctity is a strong comment on people's different perspectives in the same situation. While for Willie it is a compromise, for the other prisoner it is a welcome change from his original surroundings. The theme of different realities for different people that people inhabit their own parallel universes until thrown together to discover the differences and similarities in them is built in this incident. Reality or truth, as one sees it, is fractured and no one person can "know" it completely. Naipaul uses this idea to create a world that is always unknown, where there are no absolute truths, where everything is relative – belonging, stable identity, a nation.

The central trope used by Naipaul in the text that forces the protagonist to ask questions and engage in self-exploration and self-realisation is that of the protagonist's journey from Berlin, to India and then to England. In the course of this journey, Willie is allowed space and opportunities to deal with his disappointments and to come to terms with his past. After his decision to come to India for joining Kandapalli, the camp of the revolutionaries provides him the liberty to engage in these thoughts. When he first reaches India, his perception of the country is that of a person who has been away from it for a long time and when he comes back can only see the squalour, the dirt and the heat with "the colour-destroying glare" (MS 26). The way people dress, eat, walk, carry shopping bags with large prints – everything about India, its people and even its heat begins to rankle inside him and "this India began to assault him" (MS 26). This statement reflects Naipaul's feelings about India when he had visited Bombay. Naipaul says in An Area of Darkness that India "was a journey that ought not to have been made. It broke my life in two." (Naipaul, 1964, 280). Willie's return to India also brings about a similar fracture in his self so that he has to grapple with his past and present together. Slowly and steadily, Willie moves from luxuries and comforts he enjoys to the bare necessities of "what he might subsist on" (MS 43). He is proud that he is able to reduce his needs and live on the bare minimum entailing that he is getting ready for the revolution. This also signals that he has become an "ascetic", at least in his own mind if not in habits. The chapter that starts with Willie's journey to India is titled "Peacock", which brings to notice that like the bird that shows itself off in rainy weather, Willie is trying to show himself to people like his sister and Joseph, his first contact in India in connection with the revolution. The cry of the peacock at the end of the chapter symbolises the wild, the world that he is a part of now. It is the unuttered cry of Willie in the face of all this misery that he is experiencing. This cry seems to be the anguish of the author in the face of all the unexplainable chaos that he experienced on his first visit to the country of his roots – India. However, in the novel, Willie becomes increasingly adept at handling his situation with less criticism.

Willie's journey to India does not automatically result in a change in mindset. He is still caught in the same trap of pretending—as his sister claims he does in the West – in India where he has come to devote himself to the cause. "I suppose it is a kind of training, a kind of asceticism, but for what I am not sure. I must look upon it as another chamber of experience. I must give no sign to these people that I am not absolutely with them" (MS 51). This pretending helps him to become a courier for the movement as "Willie looks at home everywhere. Even in the bagasse yard he looked at home" (MS 74). He does not wish to stand out and, consequently, he blends in. Although no place is home for him, he is able to look comfortable and mingle with the crowd everywhere. This is the result of his wanting to fit in everywhere. This becomes an asset for the movement, as he cannot be recognised as an outsider easily. He says, "It's the one thing I have worked at all my life, not being at home anywhere, but looking at home" (MS 74). He is aware that no place feels like home for him. Currently, he is not sure of his surroundings, he does not know if he is with enemies or with the leaders of the cause. This illustrates his constant state of not knowing where he belongs. He repeatedly switches allegiance to the different parts of the world – the organised and the anarchic. This switch is again a conflict that Naipaul has faced in the past for a long period of time – of deciding whether he belongs to the third world or to the West, specifically England. In Willie's state, V.S. Naipaul expresses the migrants' dilemma of belonging, of finding their space in a world or surroundings they are not sure of, of wanting to belong to a place – a cause in Willie's case – but not being able to do so. When Willie is in India, the reader learns more about his origins – that his father was upper caste, "placid, inactive with a strain of asceticism, always expecting things to work out" and his mother who belonged to the lower castes, "many stages down, wishing to seize the world" (MS 103). This hanging between the castes allows him to understand the revolutionaries. However, it also translates into a fractured identity. He understands and empathises with individuals around him but is unable to completely belong to any section of society, or the world for that matter. Confrontation with caste problems in India is like a blast from the past for him, something that he is not very comfortable with. "'I thought I had left all of this behind. But now it's all here, just as it was, leaping out at me. I have been around the world, but still its here'" (MS 103).

Willie decides to join the movement after Sarojini tells him about Kandapalli, the leader of the movement.

> After all the drama, we found him a simple man. A primary school teacher, without qualifications. A man from Warangal. Nobody in a town would have noticed him. Warangal is one of the hottest places in India, and when he started talking about the poor his eyes filled with tears and he trembled. (MS 15)

This man inspires Willie to move to India to join the revolution. Once in the camps, even when he is not sure if he is with Kandapalli's people or enemies, the movement becomes the means of self-discovery for him. Through his interactions with other people and his experiences in the camp, he is able to come to terms with his past and realities, which in turn facilitates a creation of a slightly stable identity. Initially, he allows himself to be guided by the other members of the camp like Bhoj Narayan. This is because of his enhanced desire to fit in as usual, which is seen in him even in the West. The changes in him are not substantial enough yet for him to change his basic ways of reacting to a new environment. The reminder of his past in the form of his father's illness, in Sarojini's letter, helps him bond with Bhoj Narayan and devote himself to the cause. He decides to abandon the idea of running away and wants to go back to the revolution with Bhoj. He is still running from his past and wants to stay away from his father who is described as being "damaged" (MS 71) in Sarojini's letter. This memory becomes the driver for him to stay on in the movement even when he had almost made up his mind to leave. The revolution stems out of hatred for the upper classes. Willie realises the problems of such a perspective but also tries self-assessment to see if his reasons are the same as the others – if he is continuing in this commitment because of his hatred for his past and his father, something that he constantly wants to shun. However, the other characters that are introduced to the reader are also running away from something or the other – be it boredom or the villages – and the revolution is an escape.

Willie's biggest asset in his situation is his power of observation. His first impressions of people help him in dealing with them in a specific manner, even though later he changes them making his decisions very impulsive, so that Bhoj Narayan whom he had put in the category of a killer earlier becomes a friend he has been waiting for all his life. "It is wonderful and enriching, this feeling of friendship. I have waited forty years for it. This business is working out" (MS 72). However, Willie realises that in modifying his first impressions of people and trying to understand them he is losing touch with his own instincts and his own realities as an individual. As a result, even when he is trying to fit in he does not ignore discrepancies in a situation but refrains from comment. For instance, he recognises the factual problems in the story that Einstein, another revolutionary, tells very clearly, and sees the hatred in Einstein that stems from his own incompetence realising that Einstein may not be the right kind of man for a revolution. Moreover, Willie's powers of observation are not restricted to other people alone.

> Probably without knowing it we've all become a little mad or unbalanced..It's always easy to see the other man's strangeness. We can see the madness of those villagers who wanted us to kill people for them. Those men with the badly made, twisted faces, as though they had literally had a terrible time being born. We can't see our own strangeness. Though I have begun to feel my own. (MS 133-34)

Willie turns the judgemental eye inwards and realises that strangeness is not something that exists only in other people. Self-realisation is one of his major abilities. He is objective not only in looking at other people but himself as well. At the same time, he continues living in his passive way, without getting involved in anything around him. "He settled into his new life, as he had settled into the many other lives that claimed him at various times" (MS 153). He still has no agency and is led by the events around him or the activities of others in his favour, including Einstein's negotiations with the police before his arrest. He is living without laying claim to anything, like he did with his wife where everything belonged to her. Someone else constantly decides things for him. Even in coming to the revolution, he was driven by Sarojini's words and passion. He has still not claimed his life for his own. Through Willie's passivity, Naipaul showcases the lack of agency and diminished sense of self-esteem in a migrant individual.

From this dilemma of not belonging anywhere, Willie slowly reaches a state where he gives up all claim to individuality. In the prison, he decides to keep himself separate from the throng of men in his cell as he does not want to enter the quagmire of belonging again, which involves a "prison-house of the emotions" (MS 153). He decides to move from the "political" cells that offer him some luxuries and amenities to ordinary criminal cells. This is significant as he wishes to safeguard the sanctity of his mind even if it means sacrificing space and comfort. He does not wish to be 'corrupted' by the discussions – mostly Marxist in nature – that are carried out in the cell where he has been staying with the other revolutionaries who are also political prisoners. Even though the revolutionaries are in jail, their attitudes, ways of living, concerns and discussions have not changed. It becomes more evident to Willie that he never did belong with them and was just biding his time with them. He gives up the practice of counting beds, something he engages in to create a sense of continuity in his life, thereby surrendering the only way of forming connections in an aimless existence. He is incapable of placing himself now and defining his days and existence.

> That counting of beds had become harder and harder with the undifferentiated days of marching, the villages almost the same..He felt his memory slipping, like time now, and with that slipping of memory the point of the mental exercise disappeared. It became too strenuous, too frustrating; it caused his head to hurt. He gave it up; it was like shedding a piece of himself. (MS 108-109)

Willie's life has been so scattered and fragmented that he needs to create a thread like counting the beds he has slept in to have a sense of continuity, and this is equally true of his identity. He needs that kind of an externally quantifiable object to be able to make sense of his life and even himself. Earlier, he was capable of organising his existence by counting the number of beds he had slept in. But his return to India takes that away from him because it is a false and unsteady way of defining life.

He could count all the beds of those years, and the counting would give him a strange satisfaction, would show him that for all his passivity his life was amounting to something; something had grown around him.

> But he had been undone by the India of his return. He could see no pattern, no thread. He had returned with an idea of action, of truly placing himself in the world. But he had become a drifter, and the world had become more phantasmagoric than it had ever been (MS 155-156).

This sense of fracture and fragmentation depicts Naipaul's own feelings when he visited India for the first time. Explaining this, Selwyn Cudjoe in V.S. Naipaul: A Materialist Reading says:

> this Indian experience had fractured his perception of the world and left him a prisoner of his warring dichotomous impulses: one that kept him a prisoner of the past, subjected to the Indian perception of the world; the other that willed him to break out of that past and merge with the contemporary western world to which he longed so intensely to belong (Cudjoe, 1988, 88).

In taking away Willie's exercise of counting beds, Naipaul denies him the only means of relating with the passive, unclaimed life he has lived so far. Willie needs to be able to count other things than beds to say that he has lived rather than 'slept through' life. This method of 'keeping count' emphasises the passivity and laid back attitude of his existence. The fact that this is something he is incapable of doing after joining the movement indicates at some kind of a seminal change in him, something that will hopefully be long lasting. After his return to England, he realises that something in him has changed permanently and will stay with him forever. "Some other person, not absolutely myself, began to crawl out as it were from hiding. I am not sure I can get rid of him. I feel he will always be there waiting for me" (MS 185). He recognises that there is no place he can call his own, no bed he can call his own. In all his bed counting activity, there has not been one that has belonged to him and only him. This other person, as he calls this awakening, brings him to this sense of belonging nowhere.

> I have never slept in a room of my own. Never at home in India, when I was a boy. Never in Africa. I lived in somebody

> else's house always, and slept in somebody else's bed. In the forest of course there were no rooms, and then the jail was the jail. Will I ever sleep in a room of my own? And he marvelled that he had never had a thought like that before. (MS 185)

It is possible that this soul searching and identifying himself as an individual may lead to some agency. Willie's self-search has yielded results and is likely to diminish his passivity so that he decides not to drift along with life anymore. Experiences in India with the camp and then in the jail tell him that he has a mind of his own, capable of making observations that stand him in good stead. The most impcrtant self-revelation for him is that he does not need to fight anybody else's battles or wars. "'Ten years ago in Berlin my sister Sarojini made me almost ill with stories of poverty and injustice at home. She sent me to join the guerillas. Now I don't have to join anybody. Now I can only celebrate what I am, or what I have become'" (MS 196). Now he has reached a stage where he is able to advise Sarojini on the course of life that she should follow.

Sarojini, on the other hand, has entered the stage of pretending and trying to fit in with her surroundings after her return to India. She tries to live up to the expectations of her father's visitors and 'patients' but ultimately is unable to do so. Her return to India translates into giving up her ideals and the thought of any fight that she may have fought. Ultimately, her return to Berlin restores sanity and her undying spirit to her. Unlike Willie, she is unable to confront her past and live with it, even though she is painted in stronger terms in the beginning of the narrative.

Willie's current state is no different from the past as there are constant association between the present and the events that occurred earlier. There is no real escape again from his past. However, the biggest difference in his attitude now is that he is not scared of it anymore. He does not wish away his history and the thoughts about his self because of this reconciliation with the past. He understands "with the deepest kind of ache that there is no true place in the world for him" (MS 238). In spite of this understanding, he no longer has the overarching desire to belong or to pretend to mingle. He is comfortable in this new discovery and the consequent alien identity that it creates – alien from all situations and places. After the long travel through dinghy rooms, slovenly camps, mucky roads, jail cells and three countries, Willie is able to reach a state where he has decided to "only celebrate" what he is and what he has become.

Naipaul in this narrative presents a critical and not very favourable perspective on revolution. It demonstrates the problems that accompany any kind of rebellious movement, out of which the decline of an order with nothing to replace it has already been discussed. The power enjoyed by the revolutionaries in the text, albeit of guns, allows them to behave in a certain manner that is not tolerated of any other body in an independent country, even the government. Willie, the commentator on the problems that exist within the movement for liberation of the villages, sees indifference, unconcern, irrationality, ruthlessness and even insanity in the revolutionaries. His tramping through villages with his unit shows him that the village people are really not interested in the revolution and the desire to stay out of trouble reigns supreme in them. In the light of this it does not make sense to fight for them. The arbitrary killings carried out in the name of loyalty to the movement highlight the indifference to human life and its value, especially when having witnessed Raja's killing by Bhoj Narayan, Willie is told, "'Give it six months. In my experience that's what it takes'" (MS 88). The 'sacrifices' demanded by the movement of people's lives seem senseless to Willie as he sees no real point in the revolution at all, considering that the villagers do not have too much faith in it. He questions the point behind Bhoj Narayan's and Raja's deaths. For a moment he believes that for Bhoj Narayan, it all made sense as it delivered it from his squalour to a life of glory, and almost immediately thinks, "'But that is romantic and wrong. It takes much more to be a man. Bhoj Narayan was taking a shortcut'" (MS 96). While discussing a veteran revolutionary who has been in some movement or the other for several years, the narrator's voice comments, "he liked living off the land, and this to some extent meant living off the people" (MS 101). This comment says that revolutionary living is more or less parasitic in nature. The starkest critique of the revolutionaries comes in the depiction of their treatment of what they call the liberated areas.

> This village was for the time being under the control of the movement. It was one of a number of headquarters villages

> and was subject to something like a military occupation by the guerillas. They were noticeable in their thin olive uniforms and peaked caps with a red star: trousers-people, as the tribals respectfully called them, and with guns. (MS 100)

The revolutionaries are described as laying siege to a village, highlighting that they are not all that different from the authorities they are fighting and are imposing military rule on the villagers than anything else. Moreover, the monitoring of these areas is reminiscent of the state of Nazi occupied land without even the freedom of communication with the outside world.

> Liberated areas were henceforth to be isolated and severely policed; people in these areas were to know only what the movement wanted them to know. Roads and bridges on the perimeter were to be blown up. There were to be no telephones, no newspapers from outside, no films, no electricity. (MS 142-143).

In the light of this, calling these areas as 'liberated' is a gross misnomer. The guerillas symbolise a new form of oppression after the colonial and feudal masters. The control that they wish to exercise over the villagers is similar to that of the oppressors before them. This revolution is not capable of bringing about any changes as it is following the same models of oppressing the people it claims to free. It reminds one of the "white man's burden" of liberating the Oriental from ignorance and savagery while actually spreading imperialism. However, in all this activity the villagers, just like the Oriental, remain the "stick" people without any fire to rebel against any kind of oppression, be it that of the landlords earlier or of the revolutionaries now. The fire in the movement is fading away so that it cannot be replenished further. This is beautifully brought out in the image of the pressure lamp at the end of a meeting of the guerillas.

> The pressure lamp itself gradually dimmed; and then could not be pumped higher. Afterwards – the pressure lamp fading fast to its limp brown mantle, the meeting breaking up, some people hanging around for a few last words..and then picking their way with flashlights to their huts, the flashlights making the forest bigger and the surrounding night blacker. (MS 107)

This image of the pressure lamp symbolises the movement losing its lustre and effectiveness. It also signals the lack of enthusiasm in the revolutionaries and their trying to substitute it with idle chatter. Passion needs to be pumped into the movement. The flashlight symbolises the false sense of enlightenment in the revolutionaries who think that only their way will lead to light and all else is darkness. In this enhanced state of "knowing" they have intensified the ills of the society – symbolised by the darkness in the forest – and are unable to see things objectively beyond their own circle of "light". Ultimately, Kandapalli's insanity, the man who was the brains behind the revolution, hints at the lack of order and thought in the movement. "All that was left him was this great emotion" (MS 135). This indicates that only feeling is left in the movement while the thought and mind have gone out of it. His degeneration is the degeneration of the movement. This is the end of the revolution, at least for Willie, who was motivated to join it only after hearing Kandapalli's story. Kandapalli symbolises the revolution for Willie and is now lost. This critique of the guerilla war depicts it as a senseless enterprise that engages individuals who have their own rage to cater to, and motives other than changing things for the better as their driving forces to enter a revolution – ranging from personal hatred to escape from something undesirable to plain and simple boredom. Naipaul's stance in the omniscient narrative tells the reader that he is not in favour of revolutions and believes that they entail more evils than benefits to be engaged in. He would rather uphold the old order instead of abolishing that and getting only chaos in return, with a new form of oppression. He sees these movements as illogical that want the material benefits of modernisation while rejecting the civilisation and thoughts that have made it possible.

The text is imbued with a sense of destiny, of life's decisions resting in someone else's hands. In his stay with his wife, Willie feels that everything belongs to his wife and starts to question his identity and individuality. However, from her remarks, he learns that in the sweep of colonisation, even the colonisers' fate does not rest in their own hands.

> When I told my wife I was leaving her because I was tired of living her life she said something very strange. She said

> it wasn't really her life..her life was as much a series of accidents as I thought mine was. Africa, the Portuguese colony, her grandfather, her father (MS 115).

Here, the control is not with the individual but with the system. This sense of an overarching destiny becomes substantiated in the story of Roger – Willie's friend – where all the things that have happened to him have been accidental but he is not surprised by them at all. In him, one sees complete acceptance of this destiny. The story of Roger's decline is a parable of the decline of the London he is living in. The movement from values imparted through generations in families to a stage where people are unaware of their heritage and their culture along with their history. Things are changing very rapidly so that today, to give an example, there is not even an authentic British accent. Loss of identifiable characteristics for a society and a culture could lead to loss of a sense of identity. The story of Marcus, another character, is a proof of the change in the world, which is encouraging inter-racial encounters and marriages. However, this could equally mean the end of an older era and its value system with nothing to take its place.

The only time the narrative breaks away from the omniscient mode is when Roger tells his story. Roger is like a typical upper class white man. He assumes a lot of things about Marian, a friend of Roger's father's housekeeper Joe, and sees her in a particular way so that she is denied any voice and any agency by him. He is surprised when she acts outside the expectations that he has of her – especially when she acts a little above the class he thinks she belongs to. He has stereotyped her: "I had worked out a character for her, but, as had been happening more and more in my work in recent years, I had got it wrong" (MS 256). He sees her as a sexual object, evident from the repeated descriptions of her pants slipping down and some thing more than flesh showing. His assumption that she will belong to a particular class and behave in a certain kind of way is dispelled when he actually sees her. It is significant that the first time they meet he does not see her face but only her behind and hears her voice. This creates an obvious kind of sexual image in the mind of the reader – she is objectified as the desirable thing because of that slipping down of pants. Roger's narrative is in the first person as it relates the idea of a conquest over Marian who in turn can be compared to the Orient – feminine, mysterious, unpredictable, breaking stereotypes created by the white man, unexplored, perverse and extremely attractive. It seems she is the woman who fulfils the quest for the East in Roger as she can be linked to it very obviously. Marian's movement from one European man to another of a separate nationality is like that of the Orient changing hands between colonial powers. Roger's narrative fulfils the white man's fantasy of conquering an element of this sort.

Marcus is another character that is introduced in the pages of the book, whose presence raises a lot of questions about identity, belonging and security in one's own self. He is the only one of all men in the text to have fulfilled his dream, aided by his 'magic seeds' that help him in reproducing. His clear-cut and unpretentious goal – which may have been too big for a black man to have at the time – helps him stay focused and sane in all the upheavals he has experienced. He is the only one of all the male characters that have not passed through life, have not used it for passing time. His clear goal of sleeping only with white women and having white children and grandchildren, no matter how strange and filled with inferiority complexes it sounds, indicates clearly that he is aware of what he is, of where he belongs and is not pretending in any way. However, this desire for whiteness makes it the ideal he wants to assimilate. This pattern, if followed on a larger scale, will eradicate blackness from the world. Again, the white or the Occidental becomes the ideal way to live, to look, in fact to be.

The most important concept that Naipaul puts forth in this text is that in today's world people do not have fixed identities, irrespective of their origins – be these diasporic in nature or rooted in one country. They experience internal exile which is an extraterritorial experience, implying that one can be an intellectual exile regardless of the geographical space that he or she inhabits. All principal characters in the text – Willie, Ramachandra, Bhoj Narayan, Sarojini, Roger or Marcus – are exiles in some way or the other even when they have not been physically displaced from their roots. All of them experience fractured and fragmented identities and, in the end, it is only Willie who is able to cope with this sense of not belonging anywhere, not having a place he can call home. He realises that to have an ideal view of the world –

where things exist in a picture-postcard fashion, where there is order and organisation all around, a world that is simplified – is a fallacy. While Marcus is looking for a way to assimilate himself in this 'simplified' white world, Willie understands that it does not exist. Chaos is omnipresent and all parts of the world have their own battles to fight – the decline of an old civilisation or the desire to herald a new order. In Willie, Naipaul creates a protagonist who is not afraid of uncertainty and a fragmented sense of self because he knows that the only place he can belong to is deep within himself—not to a place, a location, a country, a nation.

Works Cited

Cioran, Emil. *Letters Home*. Bucuresti: Humanitas, 1995.

Cudjoe, Selwyn R. *V.S. Naipaul: A Materialist Reading*. Amherst: University of Massachusetts Press, 1988.

Naipaul, V.S. *Magic Seeds*. London: Pan Macmillan Ltd, 2004. Referred to as 'MS' in the text.

___________ , *An Area of Darkness*. London: Andre Deutsch, 1964.

Said, Edward. *Orientalism: Western Conceptions of the Orient*. New Delhi: Penguin Books, 2001.

___________ , *Culture and Imperialism*. London: Vintage, 1995.

Suleiman, Susan Rubin, ed. *Exile and Creativity: Signposts, Travelers, Outsiders, Backward Glances*. Durham & London: Duke University Press, 1998.

9

Spell of Gandhi in Raja Rao's *Kanthapura*

— *Kalpana Purohit*

The relation between literature and ideas can be conceived in diverse ways; frequently, literature is thought of as a form of 'philosophy', as 'ideas' wrapped in form; and it is analysed to yield 'leading ideas'. Explicit statements or allusions show the allegiance of a writer to a specific philosophy or establish that he had some direct acquaintance with philosophies once wellknown or at least that he is aware of their general assumptions. This became a specific approach to comprehend literature for some. Throughout ages literature has always explored human values and their relevance in moments of crisis. This is especially evident in Indian Writing in English. They say that "a creative writer is the product of his age and is influenced by several factors –history –contemporary and personal."

From 1920 onwards, Indian thought, life and literature were affected most by the impact of the teachings of Mahatma Gandhi on Indian writings. The Indian writings reverberate with the glorification of truth, non-violence, non-cooperation, village uplift, charkha, khadi, Hindu Muslim unity, and protest against untouchability. One such writer was Raja Rao who in early years was greatly influenced by Gandhian ideology and spent a few days at Sevagram. His faith in Gandhian thought led him to idealise him as a true saint.

Raja Rao's novel *Kanthapura (1938)* is the most powerful of the Indo-Anglian novels portraying the impact of the Gandhian movement on the Indian people. The setting of the novel is

Kanthapura, a remote south Indian village near Hassan. The evolution of national movement through various stages, till it gained strength has been traced realistically. Rao's choice of this village setting is strategic in view of his Gandhian loyalties. During his times, historians attempted to demythologise the histories of the national movement and highlighted the role of the subaltern as neglected agent for the interest of nationalism. Gandhi did not ignore the aspects of subaltern. On his return from South Africa, Gandhi focused on the politics of village where the majority of population resides. Rao maintained the sanctity of the village in his novel.

Kanthapura is even more dramatic and provides an insight to the non-cooperation movement led by Gandhiji. In no other novel is the atmosphere of the whole village aflame with the intoxication of nationalism vividly portrayed, and nowhere else is the Gandhian philosophy so comprehensively and clearly analysed in all its aspects –the religious, economic and social, political as in *Kanthapura*. It captures and traces the years of Gandhi—the non-cooperation movements, non-violent periods from 1911 to 1931.

The readers witness the village Kanthapura through the eyes of a narrator, Achakka, a grandmother, exactly like Goldsmith's *Hoary Old Woman*, who had been witness to the growth and changes which took place in the village. The village is a microcosm of the Indian traditional society with its entrenched caste hierarchy. There are Brahmin quarters, Shudra quarters and Pariah quarters. Despite this stratification, the village is bound into a social harmony. The enduring quality of the Indian village is represented as ensuring an internal strength that resists external crisis.

Rao serves a mixture of facts and fancy, poetry, history and legend. The narrator describes how in the wake of the Gandhian movement, people shed their old beliefs, superstitions and took up the Gandhian path. The first Gandhian breeze for the village comes from Moorthy, the central character, an educated young man comes down from town to deliver the Gandhian message and explains the significance of it to the villagers. He uses Ganesh festival for the purpose, besides visiting the Harijans quarters and teaching them importance of education and healthy habits. He is portrayed as a spokesperson of Gandhian philosophy. In fact, he is seen as 'Avatar' of Gandhi by the villagers.

Under the determined, impeccable leadership of Moorthy the villagers join the passive resistance movement, and the entire village is charged with the spirit of revolution. Moorthy is helped in this endeavour by other characters, namely, Ratna, a young, progressive lady, Patel Ranga Gowda and Dorai. During the course of this movement, the villagers suffer a lot of atrocities at the hands of 'Red Man's Government'. This struggle proves to be unequal in front of the mighty government and at the end of the novel, the villages get destroyed, nothing is left. "There is neither man nor mosquito in Kanthapura."(p. 253)

But Rao seemed to suggest in an optimistic note the birth of a new village from the annihilation of ashes. The destruction of Kanthapura and its re-emergence symbolises the indomitable power and potency of the will and unbroken spirit. *Kanthapura* does not project the Indian spirit isolated but as a living experience moving in time and space. The three levels of action in the novel—political, social and religious—are all related to a unified concept of India both as a tradition, a living culture, and a rich past to be re-discovered. Rao knew the importance of rituals and festivals in Indian life. The ever-enriching cycle of ceremonies keep the spirit of festivity.

The novel opens up with an evocative description of the village: High on ghats is it, high up the steep mountains that face the cool Arabian sea, up the Malabar coast is it, up Mangalore and Putter and many a centre of cardamom and coffee, rice and sugarcane (p. 7). There is a neat structure of an Indian village. Interestingly, the people are referred as waterfall-Venkamma, nose-scratching Nanjanma, Temple Rangamma. This village is presented as a land of orthodoxy and therefore, when Moorthy endeavours to enlighten villagers on Gandhian philosophy, they show no concern; in the words of the narrator: "We said to ourselves, he is, one of these Gandhi-men, who say that there is neither caste nor clan, nor family....yet they pray like us and they live like us" (p. 72).

The satyagrahis have a Herculean task of fighting the superstitions of the ignorant rustics before they could comprehend their Gandhian ideas. These satyagrahis knew the impact of religion in the lives of these villagers. Hence, to win over the masses, bhajans and harikathas are organised on Kartik Purnima, Ganesh Jyanti, Dussera and the Satyanarayan puja;

Vedanta is discussed through discourses with the intention of conveying a sense of the national unity and cohesion of village society. The novel is not a political novel though politics becomes its dominant theme, its economic and social concerns and more importantly the religious undertones are subsumed into myths and legends. Indian sensibility is essentially religious and even politics gets spiritualised. The religious element and the socio-political issues are transformed into one entity. All this done precisely in the manner in which Gandhi attempted to 'spiritualise' politics. Raja Rao has elevated Gandhi as the invisible God who would end the sufferings of mankind. Even Amaury de Reincourt points out:

> with Gandhiji, it was the historyless masses of India who rose to political power and attempted to withdraw from contemporary history to hard back to an immutable past. . . .

Rao spoke to the masses of India in the language of the timeless religious myths. He abstracted in true Indian tradition, the element of eternity from time sought for religious truths, not historical significance. He mixed politics with religion: "Shiva is three-eyed; self-purification, Hindu Muslim unity and Khaddar"(p. 20).

The spinning of yarn and the reading of passages from the *Gita* helps in the initiation of a small congress formation with Range Govinda as its president. Gradually, the indifference of the villagers is replaced by patriotic fervour where everyone gets involved in riots, sabotage and picketing.

The passive resistance is brutally suppressed. The villagers launch no-tax campaign and other forms of civil disobedience. This campaign coincides with Mahatama's satyagraha at Dandi. Though, this struggle is mercilessly crushed and Kanthapura is destroyed but not 'defeated,' all is not lost for it and that is the unconquerable will. The memory of this struggle lurks in the mind of the narrator: "You will say we have lost this, you will say we have lost that, Kenchamma forgive us, but there is something that has entered our hearts, an abundance like the Himavathy on Gauri's nigh" (p. 225). The unconquerable spirit symbolises a new beginning, befitting with the Gandhi-Irwin pact and a hope: "They say, the Mahatma will go to the Redmen's country and he will get us Swaraj. He will bring us Swaraj, the Mahatma. And we shall all be happy" (p. 257).

The narrator, Achakka, initially narrates the historical struggle with an ecstatic mood which gets dislocated having gone through wounded experiences when she describes death and devastation which engulfed the village. Hence, the novel is packed with historical action and covers the span of nearly a decade of the Indian struggle, and Raja Rao's achievement lies in his total awareness of the Indian tradition. As M.K. Naik observes:

> Not only the sensibility that informs Kanthapura truly of the soil; its form and narrative technique also belong to a living tradition. Raja Rao has made an organised attempt to follow the traditional Indian narrative techniques in *Kanthapura*.

One finds Raja Rao at home not only with his own tradition but also in contemporary European tradition. His literary inspiration was derived from several sources which he inherited and provided some gleanings in an article "Books which have influenced me". Of the Indian influences, he mentions the classics like the *Ramayana* and the *Mahabharata*, which according to him, are the summations of the Indian tradition and wisdom.

Critics consider this novel as a classic of ancient India moving into modern times, a classic of the Gandhian movement raised to a national myth. Though Rao has focused on one Indian village microscopically but it becomes a symbol of all colonial countries. The village comes to life with the construction of the Kanthapureswari temple and discover 'Linga'. The beginning of Gandhian political ideas have its birth in this temple.

Like Nigerian writer Chinua Achebe, Rao was concerned with language and consciousness. In his foreword to Kanthapura (1938), he admitted the difficulties in using "a language that is not one's own the spirit that is one's own and conveying the various shades of certain thought movement in an alien language."

Rao, while tracing the human experience in its temporal aspects give to his narrations, the implications of universality. Though there is an exposition and glorification of Gandhian philosophy yet *Kanthapura* is also an account of the renaissance of Indian spiritual life. On the other hand, Rao's meditative quality unfolds itself in his deeper concerns for man's spiritual existence on earth and sets his characters on a metaphysical quest for the absolute. In short, *Kanthapura* sings about Mahatma as an 'Avatar', who preaches humanity: Hindu, Mohammedan, Christian or Harijan, for all are equal before God. Don't be attached to riches, says he, . . . passions create attachment. . . He is a saint, the Mahatma (p.209). C.D Narasimhaiah, praising Kanthapura as a Gandhian novel said:

> If ever an Indian boy or girl today or in years to come wishes to gain some insight into the story of India's struggle and sufferings for independence, it is in Nehru's autobiography that he must expect to find it and not in those tombs called histories of the freedom movement in which the suffering and the song that was—living flame. If Gandhi has been the cause of one such minor classic in the English language and has helped to exalt him (Raja Rao) who wrote it."

And this novel established him as one of the finest Indian literary icons.

Works Cited

Naik, M.K., *A History of Indian English literature,* New Delhi: Sahitya Academi, 1999, p. 167.

________________ . *Raja Rao.* New York: Twayne's World Author Series, 1973, p. 64.

Narasimhaiah, C.D. *The Writer's Gandhi.* Patiala: Punjab University, 1967, p. 79.

Nehru, Jawaharlal, *Discovery of India,* Bombay: OUP, 1961, p. 358.

Rao, Raja, *Kanthapura* Delhi: Orient Paperbacks, 1958.

________________ , "Books which have influenced me", *The illustrated Weekly of India,* Bombay, Feb.10, 1963.

Reincourt, Amaury de. *The Soul of India,* London: Jonathan Cape, 1938, p. 287.

10

Thy Hand, Great Anarch! Autobiography as History

— Basavaraj Naikar

Whereas the *Autobiography of an Unknown Indian* depicts the first fifty years of his life, *Thy Hand, Great Anarch!* may be said to be an extension and a complementary sequence to it. There is no clear-cut division between the two autobiographical works as far as the time and theme are concerned. *Thy Hand, Great Anarch!* which includes some facts of his early life, microscopically picturised in *Unknown Indian,* aims at giving a relatively vaster picture in his later life. If the *Unknown Indian* offers a close-up picture, *Thy Hand* offers a panoramic picture of Nirad Chaudhuri's life. In so far as its width and large rhythms of life are concerned, it assumes the dimension of an epic. It happens to be one the lengthiest autobiographies ever written in the world. The one autobiography that can easily be compared with *Thy Hand* is perhaps Bertrand Russell's. Normally autobiographies are likely to be arbitrary and slipshod, but writers like Nirad Chaudhuri have shown how even autobiographies could be written seriously, systematically and artistically. As Northrop Frye has pointed out, the writing of autobiographies involves artistic selection and concentration:

> Autobiography is another form, which merges with the novel by a series of insensible gradations. Most autobiographies are inspired by a creative and therefore fictional impulse to select only those events and experiences

> in the writer's life that go to build up an integrated pattern. This pattern may be something larger than himself with which he has come to identify himself, or simply the coherence of his character and attitudes.[1]

Although *Thy Hand* can be loosely called an autobiography, its detailed study shows that it is not a pure autobiography, but it contains a heavy dose of memoir as well. An autobiographer records his own experiences as a participant in the events of life, whereas a memoir writer records his experiences as an observer of other people and events happening around him. Thus the heavy element of memoir, which is just a little less than half of the whole book may be said to be complementary to the autobiographical element in it. Thus Chaudhuri, the participant supports Chaudhuri the spectator in giving a comprehensive picture of not only an extraordinarily sensitive Indian, but also of the large spans of historical events and movements.

As far as Chaudhuri's individual experiences are concerned, *Thy Hand* offers a greater number of details than the *Unknown Indian*. For example, he describes his intellectual growth by detailing the reading of important books. His reading of Falladon's *Recreation*, a collection of lectures delivered as Harvard University disturbed him deeply. But he immensely enjoyed reading Margot Asquith's *Autobiography* and was deeply influenced by Vallery-Rodot's life of Louis Pasteur, journals like *The Nation*, and *Times Literary Supplement*, etc. These details are not mentioned in *Unknown Indian*. Chaudhuri describes the poverty, personal peculiarities, love affairs, outward callousness and inward tenderness of Bibhuti Babu very realistically and graphically. The reader is easily convinced about how and why Chaudhuri was deeply influenced and inspired by Bibhuti Babu. He acknowledges the help and encouragement he received from Bibhuti Babu to write and publish his articles in the British, owned magazines like *The Statesman*.

Chaudhuri describes his mania for buying books even when he was unemployed and had his chronic poverty. His inability to pay the rent of his room (while trying to do his MA), and the dues to the booksellers and his humiliation by the landlord are narrated in a very touching manner. His poverty is closely associated with his unemployment. His temporary appointments with magazines like *Sanibarer Chitti* and *Prabhasi* did not solve his financial problems. But his appointment as a Secretary to Sarat Chandra Bose not only lessened his financial anxiety, but also enriched his experience of life in general and of political life of India in particular. Again he worked for *The Modern Review*, and *The Free Press Journal* (renamed as *Free India*) and many other journals including the Bengali ones. Because of his incurable poverty, he was compelled even to resort to ghostwriting, though it was not approved by his wife. Later, he was appointed as a literary assistant to a very wealthy Bengali Ph.D. holder, namely, Satya Churn Law for five years from 1939 to 1942. Since Dr. Law was an ornithologist and maintained many aviaries, Chaudhuri's close proximity with him helped him gain a scientific knowledge of Indian birds. But that did not solve his financial problem. A little later, Nalini Kanta Sarkar took pity on Chaudhuri and helped him to get a job in All India Radio of Delhi with a high salary, which was almost triple of what he used to get earlier. Thus Chaudhuri's long-drawn poverty fortunately came to an end. His wife never complained or quarrelled with him about his poverty – which is an evidence of greatness rarely found in modern Indian wives.

In *Thy Hand*, Chaudhuri offers a detailed picture of his professional life, which is not given in the *Unknown Indian*. He mentions the details of his strenuous life. As he worked with two masters, i.e., Sarat Chandra Bose and Dr. Law, he had to shuttle between them almost all through the day. Consequently, the strain of work told upon his health adversely. Though Chaudhuri was only forty years, he looked like a man of seventy years. But the on great advantage of working with Sarat Chandra Bose was that it helped him enrich his experience of life and he could observe the Indian political life from very close quarters. He describes Sarat Chandra Bose's discipline, liberality, generosity, efficiency and anti-British views minutely. The diverse kinds of people including the young and the old, the normal and the peculiar, who used to visit Sarat Chandra Bose, extended Chaudhuri's knowledge of human nature.

Chaudhuri's appointment in the All India Radio at Delhi at the age of forty-five brought a remarkable change in his life as far as his financial security was concerned. He records his impressions about Delhi very honestly. He, for example, suffered a lot in the summer heat of Delhi and even had a heat stroke. But he was quite successful in his career as a military commentator and earned the admiration of British officers for his intelligence, good English (both spoken and written). Thus he had some temporary professional satisfaction in the All India Radio at Delhi. But this sense of satisfaction did not last long. At the time of retirement Chaudhuri's publication of his *Autobiography of an Unknown Indian* caused a great deal of jealousy among his colleagues, who tried to harm him materially. His service papers were not properly recommended or attended to, in spite of his serious attempts and appeals. Consequently he was retired on the due date, but his gratuity was not sanctioned to him on technical grounds. Thus his professional career ended on a note of disappointment. Finally after retirement he was offered a job of an editor of an English bulletin on a meagre but fixed salary. *Thy Hand, Great Anarch!* thus, offers a panoramic picture of his professional life from his youth up to his old age with all the oscillation of his financial status. The reader cannot help pitying the financial insecurity of Chaudhuri in spite of the latter's being a brilliant scholar of international reputation. Chaudhuri has, obviously, shown how a sensitive soul is compelled to suffer in the callous bureaucratic set-up of India.

Chaudhuri's literary or scholarly growth is closely linked with his professional life. *Unknown Indian* has already described his scholarly quest microscopically, but *Thy Hand* offers some more details of his scholarly life, which are complementary to those of *Unknown Indian*. His scholarly attitude and obsession could be seen in his habit of voracious reading of encyclopedic range. Eager to find a direction for his life in the form of a vocation, he went on reading Margot Asquith's *Autobiography*, Vallery-Radot's life of Louis Pasteur and journals like *The Nation* and *The Times Literary Supplement*. He mentions how his bibliomania in spite of his chronic poverty was disapproved by his relatives. One can easily perceive how in his life, reading, reflection and journalistic publication went almost hand in hand, thereby helping him consolidate his vision of life gradually and microscopically. Though he was initially interested in Bangla literature, he could not approve of the crude treatment of sexual life in it. He, therefore, grew disillusioned with it so much that he finally gave it up. But he kept his interest in journalistic writing in English alive and was appreciated by many intelligent British officers. Because of his scholarly pursuits, he was in epistolary contact with great scholars of the world. Being a student of history, he was in touch with the great historian Arnold Toynbee and used to get replies from him for his queries.

Thy Hand assumes the meta-autobiographical dimension in its description of the genesis, composition and publication of the earlier one, i.e., *Autobiography of an Unknown Indian*, which may be compared to a box within a box. *Thy Hand, Great Anarch!* thus achieves a sort of self-reflexivity and reveals several interesting details. Chaudhuri mentions how in 1947 he thought he might die within two or three years and how he decided to write his autobiography as he could not write a history of India for lack of facilities required for it. He is characteristically frank and honest in confessing that his insomnia and distress egged him on to write his autobiography. He mentions how he took nine months to write the first draft of it. He wanted to publish it abroad, but did not know any publisher. But luckily his colleague in the AIR, Melville de Mellow took the manuscript to England and arranged for its publication by the Macmillan publishers of London in 1951. Chaudhuri was naturally very grateful to Melville de Mellow. The book was reviewed favourably in the Western press, especially in England and America, which gave him a sense of fulfilment. It also gave him some sort of material success. It widened the vista of his social life including the circle of friends. Consequently he was invited by the BBC to go to England for five weeks in 1955.

But there was a negative side to the publication of the autobiography. The Indian reviewer condemned the book totally. Krishna Menon, the Indian High Commissioner in London, was said to be very angry about it. Chaudhuri's success created great jealousy among his close Bengali friends, who tried to harm him materially. A close friend of his wrote an anonymous letter to the government department to proscribe the book. Though the green-eyed monster played havoc with Chaudhuri's life, he could not harm him totally. On the contrary, it inspired Chaudhuri to write more and more so that he could scale greater heights of literary success.

The family life depicted by Chaudhuri in *Thy Hand, Great Anarch!* is more elaborate than the one briefly mentioned in his *Autobiography of an Unknown Indian.* The emotional ups and downs experienced by him are graphically described here and touch the chords of our heart. Like any autobiography written honestly and realistically, it offers a wealth of material for psychoanalytical critics. The first major event in his emotional life happens to be the death of his mother when he was only twenty-six. As he mentions, this event had a very deep influence upon his mind and made him very sad and pessimistic in life. Under the pessimistic influence of his mother's death, he wrote a short story about funeral ceremonies.

Although Chaudhuri had the juvenile habit of dreaming about a girl of seventeen years, he was not lucky enough to go in for a love marriage. Though he postponed his marriage about ten years, he was compelled by the contingencies of his life to get married finally to an educated girl in 1932. But after marriage, he never repented over it, as his wife happened to be not only educated but also very understanding and cooperative. Chaudhuri honestly confesses that marriage gave him an emotional stability and a direction to his life. That is the reason why he says:

> Had I not married, my life would certainly have been lost like a river in a desert. Marriage made the river cut through rock and push through shoals to reach the sea.[2]

He also mentions how he was lucky in the sense that although he was physically unimpressive, he was given the daughter by his parents-in-law considering his 'education'. Chaudhuri thus settled down to the regular matrimonial life. Later he narrates the expansion of his family gradually. He got a baby boy, who was pet-named as 'snubby' and christened as Kirti-Narayana. Again joy and sorrow went on alternating in his life. Chaudhuri, for example, lost his father when he was thirty-six years old. A little later he lost his mother-in-law also, who was about fifty years old and who was worried about his financial insecurity.

Chronic poverty seemed to be a very close companion of Nirad Chaudhuri. His life was not a bed of roses but one bestrewn with thorns all along. He was so impecunious that he could not pay the bill for the daily milk required for his children. Chaudhuri is very honest in acknowledging the humanitarian help of the milkman, who went on supplying milk to his family although he was not sure of the payment of his bill. Similarly, he records with gratitude a boy-servant's loyalty to him and his family. He acknowledges the greatness of his wife, who never complained about his poverty or quarrelled with him. This is, indeed, a very rare quality in a normal Hindu wife.

Chaudhuri's honesty of expression and purity of character are at once revealed in his reference to an incident that happened in Delhi. When he was passing through a lane of Delhi, some pimp tried in vain to ask him if he wanted 'a pretty little wench from Bombay.' But the second pimp told the first that the gentleman i.e., Chaudhuri never went to prostitutes. Chaudhuri rightly mentions that "that was the most resounding and prized certificate of character I ever got in my life" (p. 713).

Chaudhuri's sense of humour may be seen in his description of himself as a 'Kuttawallah Bengali Babu,' a nickname given to him by the people of Delhi, who used to observe him going every evening with an Alsatian dog.

Chaudhuri happens to be a very keen observer of life around him and has a novelist's capacity to describe the scene in a very graphic manner. He, thus, brings the richness of fictive narration to the autobiography, which could have been a bald reportage in the hands of a lesser writer. His microscopic observation and almost photographic capture of the details of Nature and its beauty are remarkable. In *Thy Hand, Great Anarch!* he has a few passages describing the beauty of Nature of different parts of India. For example, while he deplores the Bengali insensibility to Nature, he mentions his own sudden discovery of the beauty of Bengali Nature by saying that there is a close connection between water and Bengali life. Similarly, he refers to River Meghna and compares it with the other lakes and oceans of the world. He describes the autumn season in Bengal in 1935 including the dust in the street very minutely.

Likewise, Chaudhuri's description of the narrow lanes of Benaras and the serene sculpture of Sarnath is very graphic and almost photographic. It is because of his fascination for Nature that he studied the Himalayan hydrology, and tried to learn some moral and political lessons from it. Similarly, his description of the Temple of Jagannath at Puri and the ocean is very elaborate and picturesque.

After getting a regular job at the AIR of Delhi, Chaudhuri migrated to Delhi, where the contrast between Calcutta and Delhi enabled him to observe the latter city very meticulously. He was really struck by the unimpressive look of the city of Delhi and suffered a heat stroke in summer. He honestly records the dust, dust storms and locusts of Delhi. His observations of Delhi and its life are very sharp. He refers to seven Delhis and calls New Delhi the eighth one. He observes the habit of the people of Delhi urinating at a wall or a post. He points out the dominance of commercial life in Delhi including wholesale business and import of foreign goods. He observes how the population of Delhi consists of Muslims and Hindus. He shows his scholarly admiration for the architectural beauty and grandeur of Red Fort and Qutub Minar, the melancholic grandeur of Tughlaqabad. He exhibits his perceptiveness of an art-critic and art-historian in his admiration for Islamic architecture, painting and civilisation. He rightly opines that one can study the evolution of Muslim architecture from the twelfth century to the eighteenth century of Delhi, although not all the greater monuments are there.

Chaudhuri's close association with Sarat Chandra Bose gave him a rich experience and knowledge of human nature in particular. This aspect of experience was not offered in *Unknown Indian* but it occupies a major portion in *Thy Hand*. Nirad Chaudhuri brings in the richness of fiction and its narration to his autobiography by offering a very graphic picture of his daily experience at Sarat Chandra Bose's house. His description of Bose's palatial house with all its paraphernalia like the furniture, garden, servants, maids, Eastern and Western type of cooking is very minute, elaborate and vivid. One easily gets the impression that Chaudhuri has written a chapter of a novel. Similarly, he captures the characteristic features of Sarat Chandra Bose's personality like his discipline, liberality, generosity, efficiency and anti-British views. Chaudhuri's close proximity to the great man taught him how to face the obstacles ort crises of life immediately. He also came to know all the major cross-sections of the Indian society – rich and poor; normal and abnormal; rational and irrational; educated and illiterate – which converted him from a taciturn into a relatively social man by rubbing off his rough edges.

Chaudhuri's autobiography *Thy Hand* has a big biographical chunk devoted to the life and career of Rabindranath Tagore. But he is very critical of both Tagore and Bengalis. The biographical-critical account of Tagore reveals as much about Tagore as about Chaudhuri's approach. Personally he had great respect for Tagore the poet, although he deplores the Bengalis' inability to understand or rate him in spite of their provincial vanity. He reveals some very interesting facts about Tagore's personal life and temperament. He mentions how Tagore was a product of interaction between European and Hindu life. He also points out Tagore's contempt for English novels (and even the Russian novel *Anna Karenina*) and even greater contempt for English criticism, especially that of Dowden. He shows the paradox of Tagore's life by remarking how Tagore had to depend upon Europe for literary recognition and appreciation in spite of his dislike for British people. Similarly, he points out Tagore's alienation from the Bengali society and readership and contempt for their clichés borrowed from English literature. His mention of Tagore's further alienation from Bengali society after receiving the Nobel Prize for his *Gitanjali* in 1913 and his inability to get a D.Litt. degree from Oxford University and many other facts are very interesting revelations not easily available in Tagore criticism elsewhere.

One of the striking features of *Thy Hand, Great Anarch!* is that far from being a bald impersonal account, it projects a typically Chaudhurian point of view, which is critical and idiosyncratic at the same time. Being a highly original thinker and widely read scholar, Nirad Chaudhuri never accepts any fact or interpretation blindly. He analyses everything from his own rationalistic viewpoint and shocks the people including his readers by rejecting popular, fanatic and convenient views. It is not justifiable to brand his rationalistic views as only Anglomaniac. He uses almost Bertrand Russellian type of chopping logic to deconstruct the meaning of people, things, events and movements. Among many things that Chaudhuri says about Gandhi, a few may be noted here. His opinion that Gandhi's upbringing in the Vaishnava atmosphere was responsible for his quietist views held later and that he did not have a higher Brahmanical Hinduism is sophisticated as well as acceptable. His attribution of the Western –especially Christian –admiration for Gandhi to the Christian pacifism is very insightful.

Chaudhuri offers a very subtle and contrastive picture of Nehru and Subhas Chandra Bose, and admires their convictions and qualities. They were two towering personalities, who could never meet each other ideologically. Chaudhuri's interpretation of the collaboration between Nehru and Gandhi is interesting and realistic as he calls such collaboration opportunistic and calculated. In spite of his admiration for Nehru, Chaudhuri comments on his British leanings.

Similarly, Chaudhuri is very critical of the Hindu-Muslim as well as Indian-British relationship. He points out how the Hindus and Muslims distrusted and hated each other privately although they pretended to the contrary. Likewise, he shows that the Indians and the British hated each other on political grounds, although they had cordial relationships in private emotional aspects. Chaudhuri does not spare the Indians either. He points out the paradoxical nature of Indians, who hated the British and yet tried to imitate them. He laughs at the Hindus' oscillation between xenolatry and xenophobia; between chauvinism and mindless imitation. Thus, Nirad Chaudhuri's observation of the contradictions of people living in India is an evidence of his perceptiveness and clear-cut thinking backed up by his deep knowledge of Indian history.

That Chaudhuri is an extraordinary intellectual is evident in everything that he writes. That he is one of the great modern thinkers of India is incontrovertible. But his thinking is not abstract one like that of philosophers, but concrete one that is typical of historians, sociologists, ethnologists and political thinkers. Since Chaudhuri himself is a very perceptive student of history, his thinking is naturally backed up by a sharp historical sense and contemporary observation. From his childhood itself, he had a fascination for an intellectual life. He says:

> I never lost my capacity to think even under the worst of conditions. In fact, it was during this period that I arrived at the ideas about our life, history and civilisation, which have remained the basis of my interpretation of these things (p. 392).

He had thus a great respect and capacity for 'mental creation,' but he did not like to be trapped in grooved thinking. He did not have any respect for a closed system of thought, which is normally enjoyed by a large number of traditional scholars of India. On the contrary, he has great love and respect for liberal thinking, which is based upon the past experience and revised by the fresh one. His intellectual sharpness, meticulousness, industry, precision and abundance of information are more than evident in *Thy Hand, Great Anarch!* There is ample evidence in it to show how his intellectuality is supported by his bibliomania, journalistic career and intellectual interaction with great scholars of the world. The external evidence for his intellectuality may be seen in many of his brain-teasing books like *The Continent of Circe, To Live or Not to Live, Hinduism* and so on. His comments on the Indo-British relationship, the Indian National Congress and the international situation of the two world wars are pregnant with vast historical and contemporary knowledge.

It is but natural for an extraordinary intellectual like Nirad Chaudhuri to codify the philosophy of his life, at least in the evening of his life. Whereas the *Autobiography of an Unknown Indian* was written during the meridian stage of his life, *Thy Hand, Great Anarch!* is written at the dusk of his life. There is, therefore, no attempt at the codification of his worldview in the *Unknown Indian*, but *Thy Hand* has a place for such codification as it helps him to look back at his past life – doubts, beliefs, dilemmas, frustrations and joys – and generalise the essence of his existence. Hence, his generalisation or codification tends to be philosophical and formulaic. The crystallisation of his worldview is marked by his transparent honesty and scintillating ideation. He relegates the codification to the Epilogue of his epical autobiography and names it as *Credo ut Intelligam*, a typically pedantic label. The straightforward observations made in this section are very significant in that they help the reader unlock the mystery of Chaudhuri's life, worldview and interpretation.

Some of the remarks made by him are very interesting and comparable to those of many philosophical thinkers. His frankness as well as honesty could be seen in the confession of his loss of faith in Hinduism as well as other established religions at the early age of eighteen. Yet he developed some faith as a rational man though he did not care for intuition or suprarational truths.

He was more inclined towards the matter of fact or cautious interpretations than towards the imaginative ones of history. But the paradox of his life is that he prematurely realised that there is much sorrow in much knowledge. He honestly confesses that he suffered more from his rational outlook than from his crushing poverty.

Chaudhuri, in spite of being an agnostic, has developed a kind of philosophical faith. He says:

> I have found peace in a new form of monism. I have been able to realise that the universe and I are one, and not at odds with each other. This is the very basis of my new faith (p. 945).

He has achieved some kind of unity with the world. This union happens to be more an intellectual one than an emotional one. He also knows how he has to undergo the dark night of the soul before achieving the enlightenment of faith.

> I would say that intellectual discipline is the purgatory through which a man must pass in order to reach the paradise of faith, and the passage can be, in fact, it often is, torture (ibid).

Chaudhuri has, obviously, passed through the purgatory to reach the final faith of his life, which, he says, is based upon his belief in biology and physics. One should specially note that his faith is not based upon religion and mythology. Thus he believes in a scientific or materialistic vision of life. He offers eight points of belief, which may be stated briefly: (1) The cosmos is not material in the ordinary sense; (2) phenomena or matter are subjective sensory perceptions; (3) the distinctions between matter and spirit are fictitious; (4) the universe is a flow or continuum; (5) there is no conflict in the cosmos as a process; (6) body and soul are not distinct; (7) there is neither personal God nor are there many gods; and (8) intellectual knowledge is partial knowledge and therefore it is only *credo ut intelligam.*

Many of Chaudhuri's philosophical observations are very deep and interesting and invite comparison with those of other serious thinkers of the world. According to him, man's body procreates, but his mind creates cosmos in a new dimension.

Showing the difference between man and animal he says, "The animal is an automatic creator, but man, besides being that, is also a creator by volition" (p. 952). He confesses, "I myself have arrived at a non-religious view of the universe as a creative process on the strength of the theory of evolution" (p. 955). Though his faith is based on science, he knows that it is nearest to Hindu monism. He confesses that he believes in biological evil and not in theological or ethical evil.

Thus the philosophical strands of his worldview are made explicit at the end of his autobiography. The existential abundance of experience is followed by a process of essentialisation. This kind of codification of his faith or vision of life naturally gives wholeness to the autobiography, which shows the transformation of the protagonist's experience into knowledge.

The most conspicuous aspect of *Thy Hand, Great Anarch!* is that only less than half of it may be called autobiography in the strict sense, whereas more than half of it has the quality of a memoir. In other words, Chaudhuri the spectator happens to be more dominant than Chaudhuri the participant. But what one appreciates in it is that the memoir element is organically linked to the autobiographical element. What disappoints the reader is that the memoir element grows far too unwieldy to balance the autobiographical one. In this respect *Thy Hand, Great Anarch!* invites comparison with Nehru's *Autobiography* in which Nehru the spectator appears stronger than Nehru the participant. A large part of the memoir element in *Thy Hand, Great Anarch!* is devoted to the depiction of the political pictures of India, especially the pre-Independence one. He offers an elaborate picture of the Hindu-Muslim hatred; the dynamic role played by Mahatma Gandhi, Jawaharlal Nehru and Subhas Chandra Bose; the Congress Party, governmental and civic politics in Bengal, India's struggle for freedom with exact dates, facts and documentary evidence. A large part of the book, which has the quality of a memoir about it, tries to relate Chaudhuri's individual life to the larger rhythm of national life. Yet one is compelled to say that this section is more enjoyable for political scientists and historians than for students of literature. The memoir element is so dominant that Chaudhuri's strictly autobiographical life appears to be rather insignificant comparatively. This is not to deny the evolutionary importance of the historico-political picture of India offered by Chaudhuri as a contemporary record of life. What is disconcerting to a literary critic is the disproportionate combination of the elements of autobiography and memoir.

Nirad Chaudhuri has given an artistic beauty to his autobiography by the use of his imagistic style. He exhibits his great scholarship in the employment of images borrowed from a wide range of fields of knowledge. The width of his field of references is almost Shakespearean. Geographical images are quite common not only in his autobiography, but also in his other works. For example, referring to his late marriage, Chaudhuri offers the metaphor of a river. He says, "Marriage made the river cut through rock and push through shoals to reach the sea" (p. 343). Describing his experience of poverty and insecurity, he says, "It was like being on a raft after being picked up by a ship" (p. 364). He describes the conquest of Bengal through a geographical simile.

> The recovery and conquest of Bengal by Clive in 1757 was like the breaking out of a river through the highest section of a mountain range near its source, whereas in the period in which I am dealing in this book the river of the British Empire in India split itself into narrow and sluggish channels in a flat delta to be silted up wholly or to grope its way out in mangrove swamps (p. 394).

Being an ardent student of history, Nirad Chaudhuri is naturally inclined to use many historical images to highlight his point of view. Referring to the unromantic ugliness of New Delhi, he says that it could not be depicted in a very romantic style. He employs a historical image to convey his sense of irony, "Cleopatras did not lie on the beds of New Delhi bungalows and so there could be no question of raising the ghost of a rose in any of them" (p. 730).

Chaudhuri employs many socio-political images to convey his ideas powerfully. He describes the shameless opportunism of Indian politicians, who showed their true colour after the transfer of power from the British to the Indians, through a very frank socio-political image:

> All the nationalist beggars, who filed into the enormous buildings bequeathed to them by the fleeing British, realised

> what treasures were to be looted by them, and they must have thought their sacrifices were at last rewarded (p. 383).

Chaudhuri's comparison and contrast between Mahatma Gandhi and Stalin is expressed through political images:

> In nothing else have Western writers gone more wrong about Gandhi than in overlooking his insatiable love of power and implacability in its pursuit. In this he was in no way different from Stalin. Only he did not have to kill because he could eliminate his opponents equally well by means of his non-violent Vaishnava method (p. 528).

Chaudhuri offers a very interesting animal image to describe Mahatma Gandhi, "On the animal plane Gandhi suggested the primitive terrier to me" (p. 437). Such an image speaks of Nirad Chaudhuri's uninhibitedness and liberal imagination.

Likewise he is quite fond of using medical imagery whenever it is required. Pointing out the sympathetic relation between Bengalis and the Japanese, he says, "The truth was that the Bengalis, who had become nationalist drug addicts, were bringing down the Japanese to their level" (p. 650). At some other place, Chaudhuri describes the Indian officers through a clinical image:

> They were overwhelmed by the patriotism and self-sacrifice of Subhas Chandra Bose. He was the man, who wiped some of the filth from the body of these dirty military prostitutes (p. 787).

Many matrimonial images are employed by Nirad Chaudhuri at appropriate places. Describing the relationship between Subhas Chandra Bose and Mahatma Gandhi, Chaudhuri points out the period of waiting and anxiety for the two brothers through a matrimonial image, "For Subhas Bose and his brother Sarat Bose these months were a period of fervid pre-marital honeymoon" (p. 500). When in 1939 Paderewski sent a telegram to Gandhi for sympathy towards Poland longing for freedom, Gandhi sent a very sympathetic reply. But he also knew that

> to ask the Indian people to have any sympathy for the Polish people at that time was like asking a wife to have sympathy for the cast-off mistress of her husband (p. 552).

Nirad Chaudhuri's use of the matrimonial image to describe the political situation is an evidence of his liberal thinking and imagination.

Because of his wide range of scholarship and voracious reading, Nirad Chaudhuri employs a variety of literary images in *Thy Hand, Great Anarch!* as also in his other works. The international range of his literary scholarship could easily be sensed in his imagery. When Nalini Kanta Sarkar took pity on Chaudhuri and helped him to finally get a job in All India Radio in Delhi, Chaudhuri was very grateful to him. He describes his dire need through a literary image, "I accepted the offer at once. For me it turned out to be like the camel's thrusting of its nose into the Bedouin's tent" (p. 405). Referring to the Bengali envy, Chaudhuri says that all that great Bengal produced in the nineteenth century was "a group of Dantean figures, in death sleeping far away from their ungrateful country" (p. 665). Chaudhuri describes his own rational growth in a literary-cum-eschatological image, "I would say that intellectual discipline is the purgatory through which a man must pass in order to reach the paradise of faith" (p. 945).

Nirad Chaudhuri is very fond of using Biblical imagery (which is part of literary imagery) to describe various situations of life. It shows his subtle understanding of the Biblical lore and his imaginative capacity to use it appropriately. He employs a Biblical image to describe Mahatma Gandhi's relationship with the Working Committee to the Congress:

> Mahatma Gandhi was never a member of the Working Committee. But he hovered above it like the Holy Spirit, and sometimes even descended in the form of the dove of peace (p. 444).

Referring to the corruption of the Congress members, he says:

> It was as if the Congress organisation as Adam had been coaxed by the practical leaders as a Congress Eve formed out of the ribs of Gandhi, to eat the forbidden fruit (p. 445).

Chaudhuri opines that Indian politicians like Subhas Chandra Bose would be happier in prison than being pestered by visitors.

He, therefore, says, "Forced imprisonment was for them what self-imposed retreats were for devout Christians" (p. 478). Chaudhuri makes very harsh comments on Nehru's pro-British policies:

> Joan of Arc was inspired in her patriotism by the vision of the Virgin, but Nehru was both inspired and sustained in his by the apparition of Britain as the Evil One (p. 543).

All these Biblical metaphors testify to Nirad Chaudhuri's sound knowledge of Christian theology as well as very perceptive observation of Indian things, beings and situations.

Since Chaudhuri knew the private as well as the public face of the Gandhian Congress, he describes it through a theatre image:

> or varying the metaphor, I would say that I saw something of the greenroom behind the lighted stage and the actors without the make-up as well as with its application (p. 434).

One may easily understand how the metaphor is resonant of many things connected with drama acting. Sometimes Nirad Chaudhuri uses architectural imagery to drive home his point. That is ascribable to his sound knowledge of art-history and theory. He describes the ICS officers and clerks through an architectural image:

> When Llyod George described the Indian Civil Service as the steel frame of the Government of India he forgot to mention that the Bengali clerk was its concrete foundation (p. 729).

Referring to Gandhi's encouragement of bogus membership of the Congress by rich people, Chaudhuri says, "While this was happening on the ground floor of political life, on the upper floors there was vicious competition for office and other profits" (p. 456).

Thy Hand, Great Anarch! is thus an important autobiography, which gives a very honest picture of Nirad Chaudhuri's life of continuous struggle and of the major historical events of Indian life in general. Although one may not like the disproportionate elements of autobiography and memoir in it, one feels that both the student of literature and the student of modern history may benefit from it by turns. It is easily one of the great cultural records of India with epic proportions.

References

1. Northrop Frye, *Anatomy of Criticism.* New York: Athenium Press, 1970, p. 307.
2. Nirad Chaudhuri, *Thy Hand, Great Anarch!* London: Chatto & Windus, 1987, p. 343. (All the subsequent page references are to this edition.)

11

Indian Diasporic Writing from Singapore: A Broad Outline

— *Malati Mathur*

The truly heroic saga of the Great Indian Diaspora – those who were taken as indentured labourers *(girmit)* by the British to work on far-flung colonies of imperialism – has never really been told. They were the men and women, nineteenth-century indentured labourers who left the shores of their homeland to be transported to Sri Lanka, Mauritius, Singapore, Malaysia, the Caribbean, Guyana, Africa and Fiji. Most of them had never seen an ocean before, all of them perhaps without exception, illiterate so that links with their home and kin were snapped completely once they set sail.

The practice of indentured labour has been described quite accurately as another form of slavery. Unfortunately, the term 'slavery' has always been associated with the black populations of the world and hence is a term that does not resonate with meaning in the context of the *girmitiyas.* It is probably for this reason that they have remained invisible to the eyes of the advocates of human rights, sociologists and historians alike. Arising from this neglect/lack of knowledge is the ugly fact of the oppression and the discriminatory and blatantly racist mechanisms deployed to keep the Indians on the margins of civil society in the countries they had been sent to.

We frequently hear of countries where the minority population is discriminated against or persecuted. But it must be a first of sorts where the majority (Indians in Fiji) community has been victimised in spite of constituting over half the population! The fact that a democratically elected government was overthrown in Fiji for the only reason that it was headed by an Indian serves to accentuate the fragile position held by people of Indian origin in erstwhile countries of indenture.

Who were these men and women, the *girmitiyas*? They were hundreds and thousands of them, ordinary people from all walks of life who took fate in their own hands, shouldered their little bundles and marched off to the far-flung corners of the globe in search of a better life for themselves and their children. What an extraordinary leap of faith that was! They lived life on the raw, without the comforting safety net of extended family and community and childhood friends in a remote, unknown country, triumphing over the brutalising ordeals of indenture. They had amazing resilience, fortitude and tenacity and were not embittered by their experiences. Instead, they met the challenges of life with determination and courage, laying a more secure foundation for their children and grandchildren. This is the most enduring legacy of the *girmitiyas*. They broke the shackles of caste and communalism and were able, through their sweat and blood, to lay the foundations of thriving nations in a new world.

The old diaspora, made up largely of subaltern and underprivileged classes, hardly produced any literature at all. Theirs was still mostly an oral culture. It consisted of stories, narratives, songs, and texts which, by and large, did not enter into the print medium. This rich archive of oral culture and the narrations of the self and community are yet to be explored. It is the descendants of this older diaspora who are now writing and giving us an idea of what the fractured consciousness is all about.

This large segment of the Indian diaspora has come to the notice of academics and other scholars only during the past couple of decades. The Indian government's interest – even, dare I say, recognition of its very existence – has come about even more recently than that. Amongst the jubilation and celebrations of the *Pravasi Bharatiya Diwas* gatherings is the undercurrent of realization and unease that many diasporic Indian communities have remained largely invisible. For instance, to Indians residing in countries like Trinidad, Guyana, South Africa, Fiji, Kenya,

Singapore and Malaysia, the purportedly global presence of India and the smug celebration of it would seem meaningless in the face of the reality of the inter-racial divide in those countries which, if not always visible, is certainly acute.

Indian diasporic writers from the Southeast have largely been ignored while there are reams and reams of research devoted to the diasporic writers of Indian origin in the UK, the USA and Canada (Salman Rushdie, Bharati Mukherjee, etc.). The older Diaspora that consisted largely of indentured labourers has been followed by educated Indians who have opted to leave India and live and work – and write – all over the globe. As the corpus of Indian diasporic writing grows larger and richer, it is important to assess the work of these varied writers and define critical parameters in the framework of which their writing may be analysed and discussed. The writing of the descendants of the girmits and the newer diaspora give off similar echoes in the awareness and statement of their diasporic condition, feeling of exile and isolation as well as an attempt to connect to the mother country in however symbolic a fashion. But they do vary greatly as far as their responses to these conditions, their narrative patterns and their manner of approaching India is concerned.

Among the Indian diaspora scattered over the world, the people of Indian origin in Singapore have scripted a great success story. Hindus and Muslims together, they are truly part of the composite ethos and multicultural mosaic of Singapore society today. The perspective from which we can view Indians in Singapore is three-dimensional. On the one hand is the detached view from outside that sees the Indians as a colourful presence on the Singapore landscape with their unique customs, attire and religious practices. On the other hand is the 'inside' picture that emerges as one ponders over the dilemma of the Indian as he strives to blend into the pluralistic society that came into being, having evolved from the insulated one into which his ancestors were plunged as a result of colonisation. And then, there is no ignoring the new, progressive society that is slowly emerging as a result of modernity and globalisation and which appears as threatening to uproot all the older concepts of tradition, culture, identity, and ethnic heritage.

Singaporean literature in English started with the Straits-born Chinese community in the colonial era and while it is not possible to pinpoint the very first work in English to be published from Singapore, we can find evidence of poetry written in English as early as the 1830s. Poetry was the foremost vehicle of expression and was later followed by fiction – firstly, short stories and then novels. After Singapore gained independence in 1965, there was the emergence of a new wave of writing in English, led by among others, two writers of Indian origin, Edwin Thumboo and Chandran Nair.

Edwin Thumboo may quite accurately be described as the father figure of English poetry from Singapore. Born of mixed Tamil-Chinese parentage and raised in Singapore, he is hailed as one of the foremost poets in English in Southeast Asia and has won several awards. He has published several volumes of poetry, which critics, local and international, have acknowledged as significant milestones in the literary history of Singapore.

Thumboo has, as do many of his contemporaries, the advantage of a multicultural environment in the social fabric of Singapore society as well as the inheritance of a pluralistic culture by virtue of his multi-racial ancestors. His writing thus comes across as uniquely Singaporean in flavour and sentiment.

Besides metaphor and rhythm, there are also concepts that have a broad application, e.g., the Malay notion of *rasa* (feeling), the Tamil dualism of *aham* (inner) and *puram* (outer) worlds among countless others that Thumboo can draw from.[1]

Having begun writing poetry as an undergraduate student in the 1950s, his attempts at creative expression were made during a time when, to be a 'modern' writer meant to write in free verse. Like Pound and Yeats who famously declared that he had no speech but symbol, Thumboo endeavoured to delve into and articulate his experiences through metaphor. His poetry is imbued with the realisation that there is a pressing need for writers to write about Singapore as Singaporeans, evoked not only in terms of the present but the past and the future as well. This is expressed through his use of symbol, metaphor and image.

It may perhaps not be wrong to state that Thumboo, of all the other Singapore writers, is the one most concerned with the role that poets must play and the responsibilities they must assume in the forging of a uniquely Singaporean identity. Going further, he is aware that, in order to present and establish a distinctively Singaporean character, it falls upon the writers to hold up a mirror to the Singaporeans through which they may learn to see themselves and recognise their own image. Both his poetry and critical writings are evidence of this marked concern of his creative sensibility.

While love is the central theme of Thumboo's poetry, it is explored not just in its romantic or idealised form but is seen as an all-pervading emotion that is expressed in conjunction with defeat, deferrals, departure and death. The common thread that runs through most of his work is his awareness and perception of the inherent transience of life.

Critical opinion on this deep and complex poet is varied and controversial. The truest test of his poetic powers lies however, in the fact that his poems continue to fascinate newer and younger critics and continue to influence a whole new generation of poets from Southeast Asia.[2]

Chandran Nair is a writer-translator who started writing at an early age. His first two collections of poetry were very well received. He won the New Nation Singapore Short Story Writing contest in 1973 and his stories have also been published in translation.

> ..of all the Indians writing in English in Singapore, it is Chandran Nair, I believe, who may be said to be the most "Indian" in terms of literary expression. His two collections of poetry...reveal fairly explicit references to Indian myths, legends, landscape and spirituality. In an early poem..written for his grandfather, Nair clearly registers the Indian nostalgia felt deeply in contemplation. The poem is suggestive also of the position Nair himself seems to have adopted in relation to living in an environment which does not always appreciate the commitment of becoming a sensitive soul.[3]

Edwin Thumboo says of him:

> Much of Chandran Nair's poetry is exploration. *Once the Horsemen* (1972) communicates the variety of Nair's poetic world and the note of urgency with which he attempts his

> themes. Image and metaphor abound and are part and parcel of "the wrestle with experience". For the raid into the articulate to achieve what Shelley called "new materials of knowledge" amounts to an essential self-understanding to harmonise the ways to thought and feeling. By taking many themes as grist for his maw, Nair's poetry ranges over the feelings of a Hindu bride to the Roman Emperor, Caligula. The simultaneous forays into life and language and the myths and legends of East and West, have strengthened and extended the coordinating power of Nair's idiom.[4]

Gopal Baratham, a neurosurgeon by profession, began his literary creative expression as a short story writer. He has maintained a steady and sustained interest in both his chosen fields and continued to write while actively pursuing a medical career. The successful balancing act that Baratham performs is evident from the fact that he won the SEA Write Award and was also elected the president of the ASEAN Association of Neurosurgeons. Some of his writings like *A Candle or the Sun* and *Sayang* that came out in 1991 were controversial due to their political undertones. These were followed in 1994 by *The Caning of Michael Fay*, an account of the Michael Fay incident in which an American, Michael Fay was sentenced to a caning in Singapore for vandalising property.

Kirpal Singh has written three books of poetry and edited over fifteen publications, including the prestigious literary journal, *World Literature Written in English*. He is a scholar of great repute whose research articles and critical writing have been published widely in major international journals. He has had the distinction of being the first Asian director of the prestigious Commonwealth Writers' Prize in 1993 and 1994. In 2004, Singh became the first Asian and non-American to be made a director on the American Creativity Association's (ACA) board.

Another writer who has successfully balanced two disparate careers is Philip Jeyaretnam. While devoting himself to a full career as a lawyer at the Singaporean Bar, Jeyaretnam has published two novels that have received very favourable reviews, a linked collection of short stories, individual stories and essays rising out of contemplative thought. He was declared Young Artist of the Year for 1993 by the Singapore National Arts Council. Jeyaretnam is passionate in his espousal of the cause of a liberal, democratic process that reflects what ordinary Singaporeans think and feel as opposed to the pervasive, prescriptive mode of governance in Singapore. His discomfort with the term of 'political writer' notwithstanding, he is aware that, in order to give voice to Singaporeans' wishes and ideas, he cannot skirt sensitive, politically charged issues. His writing expresses his concern over the ways in which economic and social 'development' impinge upon individual lives and how the monopoly of the government forces a curtailment of freedom of various kinds ranging from the physical to the intellectual.

Other Indian diasporic writers in Singapore include Basanti Karmarkar, who was born in India but later migrated and has been living in Singapore since 1920; KR Menon, Nirmal Ghosh, Ravi Veloo and A. Rajendran.

Diasporic writing deals with the diasporic experience in its various contexts as well as the problems of socio-political and cultural transformation, adaptation, accommodation and integration. The question of self and identity and the importance/relevance of one's ethnic, cultural identity *vis-à-vis* the national identity of the host nation is another issue that the Diasporic Indian confronts and resolves. Where writers are concerned, the manner in which the cross-fertilisation of cultures impacts their creative sensibility and the linguistic challenges they face is of great academic interest. Apart from this, the question of how far they have been accepted and recognised in the literary tradition of the host countries as well as a study of those features that distinguishes them from other minority/diasporic writers in those countries, is another fruitful area of research.

References

1. Ee Tiang Hong. *Responsibility and Commitment: The Poetry of Edwin Thumboo*, ed. Leong Liew Geok, Centre for Advanced Studies/ Singapore University Press: Singapore, 1997.
2. Ibid.
3. Kirpal Singh. "Staying Close but Breaking Free: Indian Writers in Singapore", *Reworlding: The Literature of the Indian Diaspora*, ed. Emmanuel S Nelson, Greenwood Press: NY 1992.
4. Edwin Thumboo ed. *The Second Tongue*, Heinemann Education Books, 1976.

12

The Primacy of Connectedness in Amitav Ghosh's *The Hungry Tide*

— *Subbulakshmi Sundaram*

Amitav Ghosh belongs to the group of migrant intellectuals who have been preoccupied with issues of hybridity, in-betweenness, mobility and crossovers of ideas and identities. While Ghosh's novels are set against the backdrop of these general issues, his primary concern is with the individual. All his novels tell human stories combining elements of biography, history and reportage. Free from the fetters of a linear plot, sequenced time and space, his characters, most of them anonymous individuals unrecorded in history—an obscure slave (*In An Antique Land*), a mysterious urchin in (*The Calcutta Chromosomes*) and an overlooked fisherman (*The Hungry Tide*)—are born out of situations at different points of time. The situations alternate between nostalgia and relief, terror and hope and violence and peace. Ghosh connects them by verbal and psychological coherence and achieves totality of vision or structure. The several narratives of *The Hungry Tide* grow out of the need to relate, and this paper examines how Ghosh integrates a whole spectrum of perspectives underscoring the unbroken thread that allows the past to possess the future as well as the present.

The concept of connectedness works at personal, emotional, spiritual and relational levels in *The Hungry Tide*. The locale of the novel, the islands of the Sundarbans, is a new territory, another world as it were, which has its own ebbs and flows of the natural tides that tend to obliterate the sense of permanent division between land and sea. The settlers in the land firmly believe that anyone without a pure heart who enters into the watery labyrinth will never return. It is a difficult life that the islanders live in the hostile environment—most women are widowed at a young age since men who go out fishing are devoured by crocodiles or mauled by tigers or drowned in the tides and the land is barely farmable even if the salt water from the hungry tide can be kept from flooding their fields. Still they try to scratch out a living there. They are attached to their tide country and cannot think of living elsewhere, even if there are better prospects. This attachment to the land is seen in the dream of Sir Daniel Hamilton, a white man who buys 10,000 acres in 1920's and actually names the islands after his wife and relatives: Lusibari, Emilybari, Annpur, Jamespur, etc. His dream is to build a new Utopian society, a new kind of country run by cooperatives where "people wouldn't exploit each other and every one would have a share in the land; and where men and women could be farmers in the morning, poets in the afternoon and carpenters in the evening."

Nilima and Nirmal who make an exploratory visit to Lusibari three decades later feel the peculiar irony of the fact that a place dominated by the British colonies should be chosen by another white man to form a colony based on the principles of equality and fraternity. They are amazed at the marks of reverence with the ceremonial trappings of a puja offered to the founder on his birthday

> ..it shamed them to think that this man- a foreigner, a Burra, a rich capitalist – had taken it upon himself to address the issue of rural poverty when they themselves, despite all their radial talk, had scarcely any knowledge of life outside the city (78).

Nirmal and Nilima settle down at Lusibari and rebuild the place, where hunger and catastrophe have become a way of life and the inhabitants who are oppressed by the estate managers and owners are rescued from the atmosphere of a penal colony/ a prison camp. In another thirty years Nilima's doggedness and tenacity build the Badoban Trust into an organisation widely cited as a model for NGOs working in rural India for the cause of the widows and the poor freeing them from a lifetime of dependence and years of abuse and exploitation. Nirmal on the other hand, ends up as an ageing bookish schoolmaster who cannot realise his leftist dreams. After his retirement, he happens to visit the Morichjhapi, a settlement of dalit refugees originally driven from Bangladesh and who had fled from a concentration camp like place at Dhanbad set for them by the Indian Government.

Nirmal sees the vital difference between Hamilton's experiment and the efforts of the refugees. The former was by a person with learning and power but the latter by those without them. The thirty thousand settlers, divided into five zones organise themselves into "What might become if not a Dalit nation, then at least a safe haven, a place of true freedom for the country's most oppressed." When Nilima refuses to support the refugee settlers against the eviction procedures of the government, Nirmal realises that he and his wife have lived side by side for years but are unknown to each other, divided by different dreams for their lives, and by a lack of respect for the other's way of embracing life. He becomes aware, as never before, of all his unacknowledged regrets and leaves Nilima only to return after a few days and die. Nilima cannot understand or appreciate Nirmal since according to her "to build something is not the same thing as dreaming of it: building is always a matter of well chosen compromises."

Nirmal writes about his specific predicament in a letter, puts it in a sealed envelope and leaves it to his nephew Kanai. Nilima feels the gulf that separates Nirmal and herself. However her mainstay is her Badoban Trust for which she lives as the one and only 'Mashima'. Nirmal feels connected to Kanai with whom he has shared his dreams and aspirations, his doubts and fears. It is important for him to bequeath all his thought to Kanai. Strangely enough Kusum is the girl to whom Nirmal and Kanai had been drawn.

Piya, a cetologist who comes to study the movements of a species of dolphins called Orcaella, arrives at the same time when Kanai comes to his aunt's place. One may be led to think of a possible relationship between them both but then Amitav Ghosh shows that there cannot be any illusion of a relationship between them because their priorities are different. Kanai, a sophisticated Delhi businessman, looks at Piya only as a Bengali woman from the U.S.; he cannot like her fierce independence or understand her commitment to her work in the midst of hazards in her expeditions in different parts of the tide country. On the other hand, Piya finds empathy in Fokir, a local fisherman, from whom she is separated by language and class and more importantly by the social institution of marriage. The harmony of their communion does not require verbal communication. Though outwardly utterly incompatible, two different people pursuing their own ends simultaneously, he, at his fishing rod and she, at her observation and recording of the dolphins' movements, she feels "the seamless intertwining of their pleasures and their purposes."

In Kanai's view, Fokir is 'a peculiar sulky fellow.' But he regards Moyna his wife as an unusual and remarkable woman who knows what she wants. He knows Fokir means everything to Moyna and that she is terrified he is going to leave her. Keeping in mind Moyna's instinctive fears and also being attracted towards Piya, Kanai offers to accompany Piya and Fokir. During their perilous journey, he reasons with her

> He's a fisherman and you're a scientist; what you see as fauna he sees as food
> ...
> Piya, there's nothing in common between you at all. You're from different worlds, different planets (268).

Kanai fails to see in Fokir and Piya their harmony with Nature. Fokir, the son of the soil, communes with every mood of the tide country. Piya appears to be a foreigner in the eyes of others, especially the forest guards, but she is more interested in the tidal ecology than those people. In fact her 'foreignness' makes her react violently against the killing of a captive tiger by villagers in a village on their way. Fokir forcibly removes Piya for fear of any possible attack on her by the villagers. When it comes to forest officials only Kanai can protect her.

The situation is reminiscent of the Morichjhapi incident in which Horen and Nirmal try to protect Kusum from the attack by the 'dadas' engaged by the Indian state to evict the refugee settlers from the island. A study of comparison and contrast can be made between contemporaries Horen/Nirmal, Kusum/Nilima,

Moyna/Piya and Fokir/Kanai and across generations between Nirmal/Kanai, Kusum/Moyna and Nilima/Piya. All these characters are united in their reverence for the Bon Bibi myth that stands for the preservation of the good in the face of evil forces and also for the conservation of the ecological balance against threats posed by human beings.

Gajrontola, the place where Kusum's father had built a shrine for Bon Bibi, assumes great significance connecting the generations. Kusum had the habit of taking Fokir to the shrine every year since she believed it was Bon Bibi who had saved her father from the tiger. After Kusum, Fokir too makes the annual visit with Tutul his son.

Kusum saw Bon Bibi's messengers in the dolphins whereas Nirmal saw the gaze of the poet when they raised their calm eyes and saw through him. For Nirmal, "everything, which existed, was interconnected: the trees, the sky, the weather, people, poetry, science, nature." He was a 'historical materialist' but Piya following Nature closely in the midst of many practical difficulties, is a pragmatist. As a committed scientist, she realises that there is a big difference between preserving a species in captivity and keeping it in its habitat. She is excited at the prospect that after nearly a hundred years, she will be the first to carry back a report of the current situation of the cetaceans and she does not want to turn back from the responsibility.

> If I thought giving up my life might make the rivers safe again for the Irrawaddy dolphin, the answer is, yes, I would (301).

Kanai calls the dolphin *'ridiculous porcine little thing'* and asks Piya *'Couldn't you have picked something with a lot more sex appeal.'* He is not aware of the magnitude of the scientific pursuit. Hence Piya tells him "Orcaella have a lot of appeal Kanai. You just have to have the patience to discover it."

Fokir's immense personal courage matches with Piya's fortitude and dedication. In an environment where life is fragile the essence of their personality is broken to its core. The storm that breaks at Garjontola gives them what life could not; it fuses them and makes them one.

Fokir's dead body is the barricade that protects Piya during the storm. That is why when she is rescued, she becomes a kind of human wraith, inward, uncommunicative and leaden faced. But Fokir's wife Moyna's grief is all-too-plainly visible in the redness of her eyes. Piya's face is stonily expressionless, as if to suggest that she had retreated deep within herself. Kanai, too, is quietened after the fearful incident.

The narrative comes a full circle when Piya comes to Nilima with a request to sponsor her project. She wants to involve the local fishermen too in the project. And Kanai has the plan to return to Lucibari and write Nirmal's story even though Nirmal's notebook got lost in the storm. The Badabon Trust holds all the characters under its care—Nilima, Moyna, Piya, Kanai and Tutul. Amitav Ghosh lets the tide country break down the barriers of both society and his characters. Actually Ghosh is more interested in characters than issues. He himself refers to it while talking about researching his novel *The Hungry* Tide, "The characters absolutely,' he said, 'That's why I write novels, because novels are about people."

Amitav Ghosh blends both verbal and non-verbal communication of his characters with interpersonal, historical and mythological elements. He demonstrates the complexities of historical as well as contemporary relations between different classes of people who use English as a language of power, Bangla as a local language and a mix of Bangla, Arabic and Persian to sing the praise of Bon Bibi and other local legends. Piya's Kolkata cousins wield English as the insignia of their upper middle class upbringing and deploy English as 'armament' or 'laser guided weaponry' against the locals. Kanai can have his way with the forest officials because of his 'superior' deportment and also because of his connections with Mashima.

Piya is caught between the forces of Bangla and English. Though she feels 'protected by her unmistakable foreignness' at the beginning of the novel, she is unnerved by the Bangla sounds she hears around her in the Tide country. Fokir's movements remind her of her mother's; his 'gamchha' (towel) takes her down memory lane to her childhood. She struggles to retrieve the word from her memory.

How do you lose a word? Does it vanish into your memory, like an old toy in a cupboard, and lie hidden in the cobwebs and dust, waiting to be cleaned out and rediscovered? (93)

Piya's father who had migrated to the US did not want to use Bangla since it meant ties with his past in India. As far as Piya could remember Bangla was the language of sadness, since that was the language her parents used in their quarrels. She wanted to have herself anchored in English.

> She wanted words with the heft of stainless steel, sounds that had been bred clean, like a surgeon's instruments,tools with nothing attached except meanings that could be looked up in a dictionary- empty of pain and memory and inwardness (94).

Here Amitav Ghosh deals with the part played by language in located ness, dislocation and relocation, which are very important in the global context. Piya travels from the warm security of the US, to the terrifying and exhilarating promise of imminent dislocation. Her growing consciousness of locatedness is strengthened by Fokir's communication that transcends language, Nirmal's experience of the dolphins and her own observations of those mute but communicative animals and her ability to relate to the Bon Bibi myth.

If Bangla and English converge in Piya's personality, the two languages serve the integrative and instrumental purposes in Nilima's life. Nilima's English is flawless:

> Nilima's English had survived like a fern suspended in amber,untouched by time and unspoiled by the rigours of regular usage, a perfect specimen of a tongue learnt in the schools of the Raj (141).

Bangla is the language spoken by the people of the Tidal islands. Kusum, who is stranded in Bihar, joins the Bangladeshi refugees fleeing Dhanbad a 'city of rust' to Morichjhapi.

> We shared the same tongue, we were joined in our bones; the dreams they had dreamt were no different from my own (165).

Bangla-speaking refugees have a catastrophic struggle for a new lease of life at Morichjhapi. But the whole land is bulldozed by the politics of power. Ghosh narrates India in its postcolonial context here: the native (and not colonial) 'masters' crush the poor displaced. The memory of de-territorialisation in Morichjhapi in the past animates the desire for re-territorialisation in future in the Tidal islands by the concerted efforts of Nilima, Piya and the local community.

The message of *The Hungry Tide* is quite clear: myth, religion, language and other belief systems can promote the unity of human beings only when the individual truly connects with his fellow men in tune with his environment. Narrating the stories of the tide of emotion, of the suffering and recuperation of individuals across generations Amitav Ghosh underscores the need for a symbiosis between human beings and the flora and fauna of the fascinating Tide country.

Works Cited

Bhabha, Homi, ed., *Nation and Narration*, London, New York: Routledge, 1990.

Bose, Brinda. *Amitav Ghosh: Critical Perspectives*, Delhi: Pencraft International, 2005.

Chrisman, Laura and Parry, Benita. *Post Colonial Theory and Criticism*. Cambridge: D.S.Brewer, 2000.

Dorairaj, A. Joseph. *Interventions: Essays in Philosophy and Literary Theory*, Palayamkottai: FRRC, 2006.

Ghosh, Amitav. *The Hungry Tide*, Delhi: Ravi Dayal Publishers, 2004.

Hawley C. John. *Amitàv Ghosh*, Delhi: Foundation Books, 2005.

Tiwari, Shubha. *Amitav Ghosh: A Critical Study*, NewDelhi: Atlantic, 2003.

'The Tide of Emotion: The Hungry Tide by Amitav Ghosh, in http:// www. ReviewsOfBooks.com

Interviews, Amitav Ghosh, November 2004; http://www. Readers Voice. com

Singh, Amardeep. "Short Review of Amitav Ghosh's The Hungry Tide" August 25, 2004; http://www.amardeepsingh.com

13

A Search for Dreams in Chitra Banerjee Divakaruni's *The Queen of Dreams*

— Shubha Mukherjee

Chitra Banerjee Divakaruni blends together her Indian heritage and her immigrant encounters of seclusion and acceptance. Caught between cultures and combating loyalties she has come up with different resolutions and commitments in most of her writings. An admirer of magic realism she finds resemblance between Indian folktale traditions and Indians settled in America.

Born and brought up in Calcutta, Chitra Divakaruni went to US to attain higher studies at the age of nineteen. She completed her Master's degree from Wright State University in Dayton and then her PhD from the University of California at Berkley. For quite a number of years she was very much interested in pursuits concerning women and continuously worked with Afghani women refugees, women from shattered families and in shelters provided for destitute women. She has been the President of MAITRI, a South Asian Women's service since 1991.

Having authored several books that include poetry, short stories and fictions, she has brought out the pains and the passions of immigrants settled in countries unknown and also the traditional chain that pulls individuals to their native land of superstitions and charms. Diaspora is the dominant theme in most of her novels and she handles it with great care and concern. She has endured and adjusted, felt alienated and consoled herself, and it is her heroines who portray her longings and sufferings with a very delicate touch. For Chitra Divakaruni the move from her home country to a foreign land was a difficult one and she herself, in one of her interviews, has recalled this shift with pain:

> It was a difficult transition. I lived with a traditional family in India and was very sheltered. I really had to learn how to live on my own and learn to survive in an environment where I didn't have a family.

Writings are the reflections of a writer's mind at work and Chitra Divakaruni does her best to justify herself through her characters. In *The Vine of Desire* she portrays the lives of two young women, Anju and Sudha, who after years of spending separate lives renew their friendship in an alien country far off from the city of their childhood, Calcutta. The novel is a continuation of another novel, *Sister of My Heart*, where the novelist projects the early lives of the two dominating characters. The deep-seated love that the two women have for each other, may be because of their similar origin, binds them together and supports them throughout even during hours of crisis. The feeling of oneness imparts Anju the strength to fight all odds after an unhappy miscarriage and instills the confidence in Sudha to make a life for herself and for her baby daughter even without her husband.

The Unknown Errors of Our Lives is a collection of tales set in the context of India and America where Divakaruni tries to enlighten the transformations that take place in personal arenas caused by the choices that men and women prefer at different stages of their lives. *Love of a Good Man* is the tale of a happily married Indian woman who is compelled to confront her past when her long estranged father pleads to meet his only grandson. Another story, *Mrs. Dutta Writes a Letter* which was selected for the Best American Short Stories in 1999, describes a widow living in her son's home in California discovers to her astonishment that her old worldly ways embarrass her daughter-in-law. In *The Blooming Season for Cacti* the two women who are uprooted from their native land because of cruelty and dishonesty, find unexpected solace and comfort in each other. And in the title story it is the artist who is faced with her fiancé's past just a few days before her wedding and is overpowered to make an important decision immediately. So in every story it is the past that haunts over the present and the present that submerges into the profundity of the past.

The Mistress of Spices revolves around a magical figure, Tilo, who runs a grocery store and uses spices to assist her customers' triumph over obscurities. Her spices are meant not only for cooking but also the sensation that the Indian immigrants experience during moments of nostalgia and alienation. And then her dilemma arises when she falls in love with a non-Indian. This leads to great divergences in her mind as she has to make a choice between serving her people and nurturing her own happiness. Tilo has to decide which fractions of her heritage she has to preserve and which dimensions of it she has to discard. It is a conflict beyond comparison, an impasse without resolution.

Arranged Marriage, Divakaruni's award-winning poetry, blends with prose and creates eleven overwhelming portraits of women who are on the edge of a memorable conversion. The women who are brought to life in these stories are challenged with the possibility of starting anew in a far-off land — a land completely different from their protective homes in India. From the story of a young bride whose fairy-tale image of California is traumatised when her husband is murdered and she faces the challenge of encountering the future on her own, to a proud middle-aged divorced woman determined to be successful in San Francisco, it is the story of pain and dilemma, alienation and isolation.

Chitra Divakaruni follows the same trend of diaspora in *Queen of Dreams* and focuses on the immigrant experiences — fluttering between the old and the new, the ache and the adjustment — from the perspective of a woman. In Divakaruni's writings women play a very prominent role and the writer herself justifies her choice.

"What has impelled my writing so far," says Chitra Divakaruni, "is the desire to put women in the centre of stories, to have their voices be the voices of interpretation, their eyes the ones that we see through. There just hasn't been enough of that in the world, if you look back at literary history."

Rakhi, the protagonist of the novel, is a young Indian brought up in America and has adopted the American standard of living but deep beneath; she craves for the country of her origin — India.

It is her talent for painting that gives her solace in hours of trouble and makes her calm at times of chaos. But her paintings are also not abandoned from her imagination about India and she tries her best to give shape and colour to her ideas in the best possible manner:Until now, most of her paintings had been about India — an imagined India, an India researched from photographs, because she'd never traveled there" (p.10).

From a very young age Rakhi has longed to be exactly like her detached and enigmatic mother, who is the 'queen' of Divakaruni's dream novel. Mrs. Gupta has the power to dream other people's dreams and she warns them about the approaching doom. She possessed this gift from a very young age and her aunt, who followed the same tradition of dream interpretation, recognised the talent in her and took her away to the caves where they lead a completely different life of seclusion and detachment. For them the outer world is a world beyond reach and beyond acceptance. Thus Rakhi's mother grew up in the caves — isolated and distant, surrounded not by realism but by dreams. It is only when she breaks the rule and commits the sin of marrying the person she falls in love, she is disowned by the family of dream interpreters. She leaves behind everything to start a life afresh in America with her husband but fails to achieve pleasure and peace. Desperately she attempts to dream but fails and then suddenly discovers that she gets the power back only when she keeps the sand that her aunt had given her as a symbol of their parting. This revelation brings her self back to life and she starts dreaming the dreams of others in an alien land. To Rakhi it is as if her mother has carried India to America and she desperately wants to be like her mother with an aroma of Indianness around her:

> To be an interpreter of the inner realm seemed so Indian. (In thinking this, of course, I deluded myself. Weren't the American papers filled with advertisements about psychics?) I hungered for all things Indian because my mother never spoke of the country she'd grown up in — just as she never spoke of her past (p. 35).

Rakhi grows up fascinating and admiring her mother and then a strange space grows between them when it is ascertained after experimenting that Rakhi does not possess the gift of following her mother's path. The more she tries to hold on to her mother the more she slips away from her clutches. She even becomes irritated when she realises that an unbreakable bond of love has taken form between her estranged husband, Sonny, and her mother. She is very possessive about her mother but cannot cling on to her. She feels that her mother blames her for this break up in relationships but she ignores the guilt showered on her. She is confident of having taken the correct decision and she spares her parents thinking that they had not confronted the truth. But at the same time she becomes annoyed with her mother's attitude as she feels that her mother avoids her purposefully. She wants to be closer and familiar to her native country but apprehends that her mother tries to restrict her from approaching the world of mysteries and illusions. Her mother, on the contrary, is not ready to take the charge on herself and has sufficient reasons to defend her approach:

> You're right. It is my fault. I see now that I brought you up wrong. I thought it would protect you if I didn't talk about the past. That way you wouldn't be constantly looking back, hankering, like so many immigrants do. I didn't want to be like those mothers, splitting you between here and there, between your life right now and that which can never be. But by not telling you about India as it really was, I made it into something far bigger. It crowded other things out of your mind. It pressed upon your brain like a tumor (p. 89).

But this doesn't satisfy Rakhi's thirst for knowledge about the country of dreams and charms, superstitions and beliefs. She tries to convince herself by justifying her talent in her paintings in the best possible dimension — an India created not on the basis of reality but by imagination. Art sustains her throughout and consoles her at critical situations. After having divorced her husband she has to maintain herself and her six-year old daughter, Jona, and so she partners her friend Belle to run a tea shop, 'The Chai House'. Rakhi hardly leads a smooth life and she is caught unawares into trouble and misfortune. Breaking up with her husband she settles down, along with her daughter, in a flat, taking turns in managing her painting as well as her tea shop, when suddenly the man in white shirt haunts her memory. This makes her restless and apprehensive. Trouble also surrounds her when in the form of a rival the coffee shop comes up on the opposite end and attracts customers. Even their regular customers prove themselves disloyal by transmitting to the low-priced competitor. Amidst all these confusions and contradictions she receives the welcome news of the acceptance of her work for display at a prestigious art gallery and she is even surprised to learn that one of her paintings has been bought by a man in white. Her parents proudly attend the show but on their way home they are met with an accident that injures her father and kills her mother. Rakhi's instant reaction is against her father as she believes that he must be responsible for bringing in some heated discussion while her mother was driving which led to the cause of misfortune. She misses her mother and at this tragic hour she fails to shrink away from Sonny, her ex-husband, who does his best to support the family in trauma.

Rakhi's father breaks the ice between their relationships by telling her that he was in no way responsible for the mishap. Her mother was actually trying to follow a car and despite his cautious pleadings she had not reduced the speed. With a smile on her lips she had chased the car as if she was pursuing death and Rakhi knew that her father was speaking the truth for she knew whom her mother must have chased — the man in white shirt. But is it completely an illusion? Rakhi is uncertain and this makes her nervous.

Mrs. Gupta's death is a turning point in the novel. Until her presence Rakhi's father played an insignificant role. His wife's death allowed him to come to the limelight and he emerged as a hero in his own way. He starts translating the dream journals written in Bengali to English so that Rakhi could understand them. He even narrates stories of his past and quenches Rakhi's thirst for India. Rakhi had pestered her mother throughout to reveal her past but she had never yielded. She had never approached her father as she did not have a very high opinion about him. But now things start changing and her views about her father takes a different turn, and gradually a strong and unbreakable bond ties them together.

Mr. Gupta even proves his talent in cooking and then in singing old Indian songs and these help them to rebuild their faith and determination. 'The Chai House' is given a new look, a novel Indian perspective and this changes the scenario. It is as if under a magic spell everything keeps moving to the satisfaction of all.

> "But I suspect that the listeners keep coming back because they are drawn, like me, to the old men. There's an enigma about them: where they have come from, why they left those distant places. What they've to give up in order to survive in America. Watching them pulls us out of the cramped familiarity of our own lives into a larger possibility, once upon a time, in a land far, far away. It's what I'd wrestled my mother for, even as she'd insisted that the only magic lay in now." (p. 196).

After a progressive run for quite a few days a fire accident in the kitchen shatters all hopes. But Mr. Gupta does not readily submit himself and is resolute to keep the restaurant running though Rakhi feels it to be a crazy decision on his behalf. Then another misfortune strikes, not personal but unanimous, when the Trade Centre is targeted by terrorists killing hundreds. America is suddenly under threat and a sense of fear and shock fills the atmosphere. Some mourn, some panic, some flare-up. The situation becomes atrocious and grave as everyone is apprehensive of the unknown future and the role they play. Suddenly at this crucial moment the definite vision of keeping the restaurant open grips Rakhi and no one is able to dissuade her from such an outrageous decision. It is only her father who supports her and the others, including Sonny, Belle and Jespal just accompany them with cynicism. Viewing fire, smoke and horror doesn't distract Rakhi's daughter, Jona. Throughout she had only painted fire and Rakhi had wondered why and now her explanation that she had always dreamt about it clarifies everything. It becomes clear to Rakhi now that the family legacy, instead of coming to her, has been inherited by her daughter. They go to the shop with a feeling of patriotism which is shattered in a blow when some civilians attack them with the emblem of immigrants. Rakhi is totally shattered. She never belonged to India. Now she does not even belong to America: "But if I wasn't American, then what was I?" (p. 271).

Caught between two cultures, her identity is suddenly in crisis. Throughout she has tried to justify herself in the best possible manner and throughout she has faced criticism and cruelty : she wanted to be like her mother – a dream interpreter—but it is her daughter who inherits the quality; she wanted to belong to India at least by knowing about the past of her mother but her mother never exposed herself to her; she broke-off her relationship with her husband at one stroke and later situation forces her to reconsider; she wanted to be a part of America and America disowns her. At this juncture she realises that her life revolves around her family and close friends only. This gives her peace of mind as she tries to hold on to her individuality: the identity that she had lost comes back to her in a different way. It is family that gives one an identity naturally; one need not seek for it.

The book exposes the world of reality and the world of dream and in a shadowy way intermingles both. Rakhi's uncertainty and Mrs. Gupta's death defies all explanation. And then going through the dream journals the speculation that Rakhi and her father has: "Did she only imagine it all?" is quite vague as if Mrs. Gupta's past is merely another dream. This intentional vagueness proposes a dreamer to reality, reflecting Rakhi's gradual perceptive of herself and her mother.

Divakaruni's characters are trendy, young artists making a mark in the smart Californian gallery, successful DJs, single woman entrepreneurs. But something is missing in them – their continuous search for identity. The young Indians feel the crisis more than their parents do. Maybe because the young feel uprooted and do not know whether to cling to the past or hold on to the present whereas their parents know how to adjust in the present without leaving the past. The older generation is acquainted with their past – a past explicit in its own way – whereas the younger generation knows neither the past nor the present. The house stands sturdy if the foundation is strong; the tree stands straight if the roots are tough; and the generation stands upright if the past is identified.

It seems that *Queen of Dreams* has helped the author to be in touch with her Indian heritage and in one of her interviews she has accepted her involvement: "I interviewed a lot of people in India, and I asked my mother to send me a lot of Bengali books on the tradition of dream interpretation. It's real way for me to remember how people think about things in my culture".

Our dream world is flooded with perplexed images: at times ornamented with joy, at times dark with sorrow and often blurred without meaning. This gulf between dream and reality is narrowed down by Divakaruni's wishful desire of encroaching in the world of dream interpreters. The dreams take on a prosaic experience, filled with imagery and folklore that reveal to the readers an illustration of India; not the physical facets, but the cultural beliefs and values, the myths and the legends. It projects the contrast between the Western world of modern thinking and the Eastern world of superstitious beliefs.

Very beautifully does Divakaruni bring the two worlds together in a community whose historical identity adds to the great blend of ethnicity in a country built on assortment. The irrational brutality on eleventh September, fed by fear of the unknown, leads to shock and despair and the confused community is expected to recover from the trauma refusing to be separated from the country of their birth. The pain of alienation hurts and the agony of non-acceptance pinches.

'Home is the sailor, home from sea': home is love, home is haven, and home is identity. Man has suffered this shock of uprooting and separation throughout and authors have taken the responsibility of carrying the heart-felt emotions to the readers so that they can be acquainted with the anguish and the pain. Chitra Divakaruni has herself sensed the trauma of antagonism and she does her best to justify the situations that crop up unexpectedly in the novel. She knows how to handle pain, how to comprehend circumstances and how to merge cultures. The bridge that she tries to build is undoubtedly strong but at times when the wind is forceful it swings hard showing signs of collapse. But one should cling on with hope and passion, emotion and anticipation. Situations change, circumstances differ but the human heart doesn't yield. It keeps searching for an identity which goes missing in a crowd of strangers. It wants to belong, to own but often fails to move on with the flowing stream. For the older generation who knows the past the crisis is not that desperate because they know that the roots, though invisible, are there and somehow try to fix the tree to the soil. For the younger generation the situation becomes pathetic as they are unaware of the invisible roots and so they try to look back in search of something which they, too are, not clear about.

To accept is impossible, to adjust painful: who else can feel it best but the author herself who knows the pang of isolation. It is a frantic search throughout and the readers can feel Rakhi's desperation acutely. With a touch of honest realism Chitra Divakaruni paves a path backwards which leads to the caves of dream interpretation and magical mysticism so that the alienated world when tormented can fall back upon. The crisis of identity is crucial; the way to find it is difficult but the everlasting search goes on and on. The heart doesn't succumb, the mind doesn't accept and the senses don't respond. Far away from one's homeland the crisis becomes grave and indomitable. The past has to be revived to live a better present and welcome a prosperous future.

WORKS CITED

Chitra Divakaruni, *Queen of Dreams*. Abacus Publishing House, UK, 2004.

______________ , *Vine of Desire*. Anchor Books, USA, 2003.

______________ , *Sister of My Heart*. Random House, New York, 1999.

______________ , *The Unknown Errors of Our Lives*. Anchor Books, USA, 2002.

______________ , *The Mistress of Spices*. Anchor Books, USA, 1998.

______________ , *Arranged Marriage*. Anchor Books, USA, 1995. www.thedailycalifornia.htm

Chitra Banerjee Divakaruni – Wikipedia, the free encyclopedia.htm

www.desijournal.com

www.waterbridgereviews.org

www.nriinternet.com

www.imaginedhomelands.htm

14

Flood Tides of Language and Submerged Communication: Language and its Inadequacy in Amitav Ghosh's *The Hungry Tide*

— *Mini Chandran*

"..no one can ever give the exact measure of his needs, nor of his conceptions, nor of his sorrows; ..since human speech is like a cracked tin kettle, on which we hammer out tunes to make bears dance when we long to move the stars," wrote a Gustav Flaubert in despair at his inability to craft a language that, mirror-like, would reflect human ideas and thoughts without any distortion (*Madame Bovary*, 146). The opaqueness and sheer inadequacy of human language was a constant concern for this writer who persisted in the pursuit for the ideal language, and failed. Amitav Ghosh's concern in *The Hungry Tide* is similar; the novel is all about human language, language that fails to connect, language that severs man from nature, language that floods the islands of communication between man and man, much like the flood-tides that threaten to take over the country in the novel.

However, a clear hierarchy can be discerned in the various languages that are in use in the world described by the novel. On the one hand, there is the materialistic language of the 'powerful' that succeeds in the worldly sense (used by Kanai and Nilima); on the other, it posits the language of the marginalised who speak, but are not heard in the world outside (used by Kusum and Fokir). The dichotomy can also be thought of as written (constative and artificial)/spoken (performative and natural). Ghosh, being a greater artist, does not confine his novelistic world to these polarities. There are lots of in-between spaces and ambiguous positions that are often interchanged among the characters. It would also be simplistic to claim that it is built on the Foucauldian paradigm, where the successful language becomes only that which produces/sustains a discourse; for we see that even the 'subjugated knowledges, which according to Foucault are "..located low down on the hierarchy, beneath the required level of cognition or scientificity" (82) are also worthy of attention. The novel looks at various aspects of the spoken and written language, without necessarily privileging one over the other.

The narrative alternates between the protagonists Kanai and Piya, who inhabit two different poles as far as language, is concerned. The dissimilarity between the two is highlighted in the first chapter that introduces us to them. Piya looks Indian, but is an 'outsider' who stands out among the local crowd in Dhakuria station by virtue of her spoken language (she knows no Bengali) and an alien body language. Kanai 'belongs', as he is a Bengali and uses his body language to assert his urban superiority. If it is words – his uncle Nirmal's – that draw Kanai to Lusibari, it is nature and one of her gentlest creatures – the river dolphins of the Sunderbans – that beckon Piya. Ghosh's alternating narrative allows no space for the reader to sympathise with just anyone of the two, but seems to swing between the two poles of linguistic skill and the lack of it.

As opposed to Kanai who knows six languages, Piya knows only English and she admits to being not very good at it either. Piya does not consider this as a shortcoming as her line of work as a cetologist allows her long hours of solitude that do not demand speech, and it is not surprising that her seeming inadequacy in the world of human beings is shed once she is in her element which is open water. The 'language' that she uses first with the forest guards and then later with Fokir is the display cards that depict dolphins. However, Ghosh emphasizes the inherent treachery of even these signifiers when the forest guard looks at the display card upside down and asks Piya if the picture is that of a bird (*HT* 33). It is clear that language, even the performative one, fails miserably. Her body language too, fails as is evident from the over familiar and patronising way they treat her on the launch. She is not obviously 'foreign' nor is she like her Kolkata cousins or Kanai, "who wielded the insignia of their upper-middle-class upbringing like laser-guided weaponry" (*HT* 34).

However, Piya's failure is successful with Fokir, who himself is uncommunicative and sparse with words. Fokir speaks extensively only with his son Tutul. Fokir's first wordless gesture of covering himself with his dhoti, on seeing Piya is an acknowledgement of her as a person/woman: "..it seemed like the first normal human contact she had had since stepping on the launch" (*HT* 47). It is appropriate that this should become the prologue to a language-free relationship that achieves the perfection of human understanding.

Fokir, like the dolphins to Arion's rescue, saves Piya from the water (and necessity of language) and conveys her to the space of his narrow boat, "the small island of silence, afloat on the muteness of the river" (*HT* 84), that offers her a means of escape from the world of language to her world of the dolphins and nature. Fokir's boat becomes the stage for a mime language that is perfectly understood by them; even complicated concepts of monetary reward are negotiated by them with ease. The signified is in perfect harmony with the signifier here—there is no treacherous sliding that defies human efforts.

The 'ritual of naming' (*HT* 93) as Piya terms it, is minimal on the boat as Fokir desists from pointing to things and telling her their Bengali names. However, it is a Bengali name *gamchha*, the towel that Fokir uses, that evokes memories in Piya – of a home with estranged parents, of her desperate attempts to break free of the linguistic fetters of Bengali. The innocuously named object breaches the dam that she had wilfully built against the bitter memories that are inextricably intertwined with language:

> There was a time once when the Bengali language was an angry flood trying to break down her door. She would crawl into a wardrobe and lock herself in, stuffing her ears to shut out those sounds. But the doors were no defence against her parents' voices: it was in that language that they fought, and the sounds of their quarrels would always find ways of trickling in, under the door and through the cracks, the level rising until she thought she would drown in the flood ...The

> accumulated resentments of their life were always phrased in that language, so that for her, its sound had come to represent the music of unhappiness. As she lay curled in the cupboard, she would dream of washing her head of those sounds; she wanted words with the heft of stainless steel, sounds that had been boiled clean, like a surgeon's instruments, tools with nothing attached except meanings that could be looked up in a dictionary – empty of pain and memory and inwardness (*HT* 93–94).

It is not surprising that Piya aspires to and achieves an uncomplicated and monolingual world, very similar to that of Fokir.

Language is the barrier that Fokir and Piya surmount to attain the communion of silence. The melody of Fokir's song is to Piya unrecognisable and the lyrics incomprehensible, but she is sensitive to its palpable touch of grief. Music transcends the spatio-temporal boundaries of human language and communicates the sorrow of a land that is plagued by demons through the legend of Bon Bibi. Listening to the song, Piya understands the communion between Fokir and the wilderness of water and the tide country. The unerring accuracy with which he directs Piya to the stream where dolphins gather is indicative of his instinctual understanding of natural phenomena and creatures. As his mother Kusum points out, "he has the river in his veins" (*HT* 245). Fokir can be seen as the holder of the Foucauldian "local, discontinuous, disqualified, illegitimate knowledges" (83).

It is this language-less wisdom that the sophisticated and worldly-wise Kanai lacks. The fact that he uses the currency of language to build a business (*HT* 199) surprises Piya. It is not surprising that Kanai, who is a translator and interpreter by profession, inhabits a linguistic world. He makes sense of the world through words, be it his own or Nirmal's. Even his attempts to understand Piya are through language; her dedication to work is to him like that of a "textual scholar poring over a yet undeciphered manuscript:" and reminds him of his own efforts to understand other languages, "how other realities were conjugated." The pure desire he felt for the unknown then, is transcreated in the thrill of desire he feels for Piya, as "a language made flesh" (*HT* 269).

However, despite knowing six languages he is hopelessly out of depth when it comes to understanding Moyna or Piya. The breakdown of communication here gestures towards a difference in language use between men and women, a fact that George Steiner emphasizes in *Understanding as Translation.* He acknowledges the stereotypical assumption that women are garrulous, but points out that women have a similar view of men's language: "Men are deceivers ever. They use speech to conceal the true, sexually aggressive function of their lips and tongues ... Women's lore and secret mock record him as an eternal miles gloriosus, a self-trumpeter who uses language to cover up his sexual or professional fiascos, his infantile needs, his inability to withstand physical pain" (43). Piya and Moyna see through Kanai's linguistic façade. Ironic as it may appear, it is the uncommunicative Fokir who is liked by both the women, a fact that Moyna senses with womanly intuition. And it falls upon this village woman to instruct Kanai about the power of the silence that is hidden by words: "Because words are just air, Kanai-babu...When the wind blows on the water, you see ripples and waves, but the real river lies beneath, unseen and unheard" (*HT* 258).

Fokir does not have a space in the world of words and efficiency occupied by Kanai and Moyna. Caught in the drab surroundings of his own home, Fokir seems to have a 'fugitive sullenness' (*HT* 207) to Piya, an aspect that had not struck her while she was spending days with him on the boat. It is also significant that Piya feels the need for a translator in this context, where both she and Fokir are out of their element in their respective ways. Faced with Kanai's patronising tone, Fokir responds with his 'instinctive mode of defence' which is silence (*HT* 210). There is evidently a chasm separating Fokir's and Piya's world and the world of Moyna who wonders what Piya would want to do with an illiterate man like her husband. Moyna obviously does not appreciate the intimate bond that Fokir has with the environment around him, a bond that is unsullied by language and other acquisitions of the all too human world. Although Moyna occupies subaltern space, her language has affinities with Kanai's in its desire to perform and succeed. It is no surprise that she has the sympathies of Nilima, who is also a doer and not a dreamer.

If Fokir in the seclusion of his boat is representative of the ideal symbiotic relationship between man and nature, Kanai is the urban man cut off from his spiritual moorings. This binary is accentuated in the short span of time that Kanai and Fokir spend with each other in the loneliness of the boat. If Fokir was sullen and silent with Kanai on land, on the river he is confident and able to deal with Kanai's familiar 'tui' with him. He is able to cut short the conversation and provoke Kanai to an ill-advised encounter with the 'spirit of the wild' in Garjontola. What Kanai perceives to be Fokir's attempt to make him submit to the terror of the unknown forest is also predicated on language. Naked fear that produces goose bumps on Fokir's skin is instinctive; equally instinctive is Kanai's response to Fokir's question whether he felt the fear: "It was as though his mind had decided to revert to the functions for which it had been trained and equipped by years of practice. At that moment nothing existed for him but language, the pure structure of sound that had formed Fokir's question" (*HT* 322).

Garjontola becomes a primeval setting for Kanai's moment of reckoning, where he is made acutely conscious of the drawbacks of his language. This is Fokir's territory where there is a reversal of roles and Fokir addresses Kanai in the familiar 'tui'. The primal land provides appropriate backdrop for the human soul that looks deep into itself and recognises the ugly spectres of prejudice, fear and insecurity that it never realised it contained in its depths. Kanai's response to Fokir's taunts is visceral: "His anger came welling up with an atavistic explosiveness, rising from sources whose very existence he would have denied: the master's suspicion of the menial; the pride of caste; the townsman's mistrust of the rustic; the city's antagonism to the village" (*HT* 326). Interestingly language ceases to become a barrier between the two as Kanai is literally able to see through Fokir's eyes and understand why he would want Kanai to be judged, for "he had become a token for a vision of human beings in which a man such as Fokir counted for nothing, a man whose value was less than that of an animal" (*HT* 327). Language fails Kanai at this crucial moment when he sees/fantasizes the tiger, making him realise that human language and all the accoutrements of human civilisation are as fragile as foam on the river. He leaves Garjontola a humbler and wiser man, realising how little he knew of himself and the world.

But words remain Kanai's gift to Piya, when he later translates the content of Fokir's song which is the Bonbibi legend. Kanai's words are tentative and unsure, "inspired by a genuine perplexity" (*HT* 353) and his translation, he confesses, has imperfections. Words crumble against the implacable reality that Kanai faces, and his words remain words, incapable of transporting him out of the linguistic cage. It requires an illiterate Horen to make him aware of the deep love that Fokir has for Piya. Horen draws a parallel between him and his uncle Nirmal, who similarly was unable to recognise Kusum's love for Horen. The tensions latent in the Kusum – Horen – Nirmal triangularity prefigure those of the Piya – Fokir – Kanai bond later.

This parallel is not unsurprising as Nirmal the dreamer and revolutionary, like Kanai, inhabits a world of words, making sense of the world around him through words, especially those of his favourite poet, Rainer Maria Rilke. To him, Kusum is the muse who draws him back to letters, while to Horen she is flesh and blood. Both Nirmal and Kanai who see the world through the opaque lenses of words, are blind to the raw emotions that bind people together. The Kusum – Horen and the Piya – Fokir relationships, both of which elude the banal clutches of human language, have a halo of mysticism reminiscent of the tentative attempts made by man to attain the realisation of the divine. While language is what Kusum inspires in Nirmal, in the moment when she gives proof of her love to Horen, "there were no words to chafe upon our senses", recalls Horen (*HT* 364). Piya and Fokir's moment of realisation of the intense love they share is also marked by silence, where there is only "a hand, hidden in the water's depths, [were] writing a message to her in the cursive script of ripples, eddies and turbulence" (*HT* 352). The silent communion that is reminiscent of the mystic union that eludes speech, is, as Derrida points out, an "ascent": "This ascent corresponds to a rarefaction of signs, figures, symbols – and also of fictions, as well as of myths or poetry" (10).

Nirmal, unlike Kanai, realises that his words are pathetically inadequate to this bond that man can have with Nature, and that even the unlettered little boy Fokir is superior to him in this respect. Garjontola that becomes the testing ground for Kanai is kinder to Nirmal. Like Kanai, he is posed with the same question whether he is not afraid to go ashore on Garjontola, but Nirmal does not feel the need to feign fear. He is alive to the love as well as the terror that pulsate in the tide country, epitomised in Bon Bibi and the evil demon Dokkhin Rai. Words come to his rescue again, as he appropriates the Bon Bibi legend in his own linguistic terms: "..the mudbanks of the tide country are shaped not only by rivers of silt, but also by rivers of language: Bengali, English, Arabic, Hindi, Arakanese and who knows what else? Flowing into each other they create a proliferation of small worlds that hang suspended in the flow" (*HT* 247). However, Nirmal lives and dies a dreamer, one who aspires to revolutionise the world through his writing/teaching, but in vain. It is significant that Kanai loses his notebook in the water; for Nirmal's words, and by extension, any word, are as transient as those written on water.

However, the argument that the novel is about the breakdown of language will appear unconvincing for *The Hungry Tide* in which the Bon Bibi legend appears as a leitmotif. But here I would like to emphasize the orality of the myth as presented in the novel. It is significant that the only two people who attempt to capture it in writing are Nirmal and Kanai. Kusum, Fokir and Horen have grown up on this myth and internalised it, and can read the language of Nature spread out over the universe. Derrida, quoting Dionysus on the language that attempts to describe the divine essence, says: "We thus learn to decipher symbols, we understand how "the love of God for man envelops the intelligible in the sensible, what is beyond Being in being, gives form and fashion to the unformable and the unfashionable, and through a variety of partial symbols, multiplies and figures the unfigurable and marvelous Simplicity" (50). It is this ability to 'read' that enables Kusum to see the dolphins as Bon Bibi's messengers, while Nirmal can see them only as 'some kind of susuk' (*HT* 235). Piya, despite being corrupted by human language, can be considered semi-literate in this sense, for she can respond to the magic of the land when guided by Fokir.

However, a word of caution has to be sounded about reading this as the privileging of speech over writing. My intention is not to say that the speech-centric language is performative and natural while the other is constative and artificial. Both languages are found wanting in the tide country. The language that is spoken is also not heard, making it the language of the subaltern who cannot always speak. Paralleling the world of those enabled by language, is the world of the subalterns where the act of speech goes largely unheard.

Drawing on Ranajit Guha, Gayatri Spivak defines the subaltern space as "the space that is cut off from the lines of mobility in a colonised country" (288). She states that there is "something of a not-speakingness in the very notion of subalternity" (289). In this sense, the refugees of Morichjhapi are subalterns who cannot make themselves heard in the power centres of Kolkata. Nirmal is made acutely conscious of the inadequacy of subaltern language when he is questioned by the leader of the refugees: "We need to let people know what we're doing and why we're here. We have to tell the world about all we've done and all we've achieved. Can you help us with this? Do you have contacts with the press in Kolkata?" (*HT* 172)

As Spivak points out, 'speaking' is a "transaction between the speaker and the listener" (289). The subaltern language of Morichjhapi fails spectacularly on this front as is evident from the unsympathetic treatment they receive from the government despite their attempts to show the world what they are doing and how they are treating the environment around them. Kusum's words that question the system that would save the animal and damn the human, also fall on deaf ears:

> Who are these people, I wondered, who love animals so much that they are willing to kill us for them? Do they know what is being done in their names? Where do they live, these people, do they have children, do they have mothers, fathers? As I thought of these things it seemed to me that this whole world has become a place of animals, and our fault, our crime, was that we were just human beings, trying to live as human beings always have, from the water and the soil. No human being could think this a crime unless they have forgotten that this is how humans have always lived – by fishing, by clearing land and by planting the soil. (*HT* 262)

This 'speech' goes unheard, underscoring Spivak's point that the subaltern cannot speak, meaning that "..even when the subaltern makes an effort to the death to speak, she is not able to be heard, and speaking and hearing complete the speech act" (292). There is a continuity of subaltern voices that seek unsuccessfully to be heard, from Kusum to Fokir. The brutal killing of Morichjhapi is a concretisation of the metaphoric silencing of subaltern concerns; likewise is the death of Fokir in the onslaught of the flood tide.

All subaltern voices, however, are not seen as futile; Nilima's success with the Badabon trust being a case in point. Nilima can be seen as the traditional intellectual who becomes the voice of the subaltern, quite unlike the Gramscian 'organic intellectual', or as Spivak defines it, the subaltern who attempts to enter the world of intellectuality (292). Nilima is not the dreamer that Nirmal is, and is shrewd enough to realise the futility and folly of the 'rescue Morichjhapi' exercise. Nilima recognises the prosaic commonsense in her stance when compared to the poetic idealistic fervour of Nirmal, as well as the materialistic quality of her enterprise. She is perceptive enough to understand that her language which succeeds in one sphere is inadequate in Nirmal's realm. It is this that prompts her to ask Kanai: "..the dreamers have everyone to speak for them. But those who're patient, those who try to be strong, who try to build things – no one ever sees any poetry in that, do they?" (*HT* 387) In a different way, Nilima's desire to be heard makes her occupy subaltern space.

Piya provides the link between these differing speech acts, which is manifested concretely in the final act of finding resources for Badabon trust and the research foundation she plans to name after Fokir. It is a chain of words that are set in motion by her that results in money; Piya, like Kanai, is eventually successful in the business of words: "I sent out some letters explaining what happened during the cyclone and how Fokir died. Some of my friends and colleagues took up the cause and circulated a chain letter, to raise money for Moyna and Tutul," she explains (*HT* 396). Interestingly, the vehicle for this modern language is the Internet. Kanai, on the other hand, divests his words of their mercantile nature by deciding to relocate to Kolkata for a while, where he proposes to give life to Nirmal's lost diary.

The lost islands of communication between man and man are seen to emerge as the flood-tide of language recedes. Piya and Moyna establish a sisterhood of sorts, which is manifested in the eerie resemblance they bear to each other in the hour of bereavement. Both appear to be widowed by the death of Fokir, an absence that cements their relationship. The cyclone that kills Fokir also seems to break down the dams separating their respective streams of language, allowing for a free intermingling, which in turn enables them to communicate with and understand each other, even if imperfectly. The Piya/Kanai divide that threatens to descend into a crude nature/culture, speech/writing binary is deconstructed, and shown to bear traces of each other even while they are seemingly opposed.

However, it is the supreme irony of the writer's trade that he is unable to lament the inadequacy of his tools without recourse to the very same treacherous words that stubbornly refuse to reflect reality. And there is no denying the fact that Amitav Ghosh uses evocative prose to great effect, to highlight the inherently flawed nature of the language at his disposal.

Works Cited

Derrida, Jacques. "How to Avoid Speaking: Denials". *Languages of the Unsayable: ThePlay of Negativity in Literature and Literary Theory.* Ed. Sanford Budick and Wolfgang Iser. Stanford: Stanford UP, 1996. 3-70.

Flaubert, Gustav. *Madame Bovary*, 1857, Hertfordshire: Wordsworth, 2001.

Foucault, Michel. "Two Lectures". *Power/Knowledge: Selected Interviews & Other Writings 1972 – 1977.* Ed. Colin Gordon. Trans. Colin Gordon, Leo Marshall, John Mepham, Kate Soper. New York: Pantheon, 1980. 78–108.

Ghosh, Amitav. *The Hungry Tide.* New Delhi: Harper Collins, 2006.

Spivak, Gayatri Chakravorty. "Subaltern Talk: Interview with the Editors" (1993 – 94)". *The Spivak Reader.* Ed. Donna Landry and Gerald Maclean. New York: Routledge, 1996. 287–308.

Steiner, George. "Understanding as Translation". *After Babel: Aspects of Language and Translation.* London: Oxford UP, 1975. 1–48.

15

Synthesizing the Orient and the Occident: A Study of Kamala Markandaya's *Pleasure City*

— *Sudhir K. Arora*

Rudyard Kipling's viewpoint *vis-à-vis* the incompatibility of the Orient and the Occident is now not in vogue as the magic of globalisation has reduced the space and provided an environment quite proper to the flowering of the proximity which has made them understand each other and consequently reciprocate the best that they have. In the present time, for a purposeful and peaceful life the materialism of the Occident is to be assimilated with the spiritualism of the Orient. It is the soul, that is, spiritualism that can work better in a *sound body*, that is materialism and hence, a balance is always required. It is the West that knows that it cannot be happy without the Indian spiritualism and India also needs to make her body burly with the help of Western materialism without losing the touch of her spiritual identity.

Kamala Markandaya is a leading woman novelist who has experienced both cultures—the East and the West—and hence, as a diasporic novelist is qualified for the depiction of the state of those who survive on a foreign land while feeling alien in an alien country and bearing affliction on account of recalling the memories of the native country. To make life worthwhile the approach of compromise is always sought, and Kamala Markandaya is the best instance as she dreams of India and offers in her texts the solution—the concept of giving and taking the best. She has become a synthesis-seeker who unites both the cultures on the basis of zero loss of identity. Calling her insider outsider,

M.K.Bhatnagar writes: She is an impressive explorer of human consciousness and of the convolutions of intimate interpersonal relationships, caught in the whirlpool of disparate and divergent cultures (p. 2).

As a diasporic writer she has endeavored with her best to bring the East and the West together in her novels, and more particularly in her swan song *Pleasure City.* Her *Pleasure City* becomes the pleasure city on account of the environment that it provides to the natives and the foreigners who come together and reciprocate the best. The friendship of Rikki and Tully is the ideal one in the changed independent atmosphere. Tully, the English officer, is the representative of the transcontinental consortium with the touch of modern technology. He comes to a fishing village in South India with the intention of transforming its face by building a holiday complex 'Shalimar'. The imperialists cross the threshold in the disguise of technocrats in the name of modernity and progress. Kamala Markandaya has presented them with the promise of fresh areas of understanding and co-operation, and it is the only approach which can bring the East and the West together resulting in the development and prosperity of each other. It is Tully, the representative of the West, who acknowledges Rikki's perception of beauty and his honesty, and the sense of spiritualism that characterises Indian culture. Knowing that there is an ocean between the East and the West, Kamala Markandaya suggests the mantra that will be helpful in crossing the cultural barriers.

My rationale in this paper is to highlight the fusion of the Orient and the Occident by highlighting the flaws and excellences and the way of achieving the target through love, affection and fellow feeling.

In *Pleasure City,* Markandaya does not appear to be a grasping storyteller as she does in *Nectar in a Sieve* but now she does not talk of poignant and heart-rending tale of Indian village; rather she talks of human relationships or in broader way of universal bond between the East and the West. The novel is not compact and intact; sometimes it is digressive and dispersed but finally all the threads are woven into the single whole. All the different episodes are the integral parts of one theme—the theme of synthesis between the Orient and Occident and it is done through the protagonist Rikki. A multinational company, 'The Atlas

International Development Corporation' founded by Herbert Boyle, is launched in independent India to build a luxury pleasure complex "which at blue print stage, with rare unity, and not entirely cynically, got to be called Shalimar by everyone concerned" (20). It was the corporation that never allowed "private feelings to interfere with business" and hence it "built anywhere, everywhere, almost anything, for anyone, with a virtuosity" (21). This transcontinental consortium was constructed "with an admirably distilled purity, of purely technological mercenaries" (ibid.). Boyle, Cyrus Contractor and Tully are the on the Board of AIDCORP. Apu, the headman has no objection if there is no harm to their water and territory. "This is our territory. The waters are our, to a five fathom depth" (26).

The village observed the activity with interest. Rikki goes to the school run by Mr. And Mrs. Benjamin Bridie for fishermen's children. But one day, Rikki who is only six years old gets the shocking news of the death of his father and near relatives in a sea storm. After this tragedy his mother also dies. Amma, the wife of the headman Apu, comes to help him and feels proud to be the foster mother. She takes care of him along with her two children—Muthu and Valli. Rikki continues to go the school of Mrs. Bridie who was childless showers her love and teaches him her language. When Mr. And Mrs. Bridie are no more, he feels much dejected at the loss. He often goes to Shalimar and one day he warns Tully against the danger of rocks in the sea. Tully searches the possibilities in this young boy who is behaving well and speaking English. He becomes the tea boy but has to leave this job as it is the 'mackerel season' and everybody has to offer his mite. As soon as the mackerel season comes to an end, he builds a boat for Tully at his asking and is paid amply.

While working he wins the heart of the officials of Shalimar. Zavera, the wife of Cyrus Contractor takes the rein of Shalimar and makes the opening ceremony successful. Corrina, the wife of Tully, Mrs. Pearl, Mrs., Lockwood, Carmen, Mrs. Lovat, and Mrs. Chari, etc., come to join Shalimar and enjoy. To celebrate the birthday party of Zavera, they go for a picnic to the caves where they find an infant. Mrs. Pearl decides to be the foster mother of the infant and names it Kali in order to invoke the goddess Kali who protects. Corrina who feels bored in India is attracted towards Ranji, the young lieutenant. When the work is complete in Shalimar, Zavera thinks of celebrating 'An Open Day' which is originally her own brainchild. Competitions like 'surfing event' become the attraction for all. When the 'Open Day' celebration comes to a close, a storm bursts out. Rikki who goes to save Corrina caught in the cross current is badly hurt. The storm affects the life of the people who do not have even the basic facilities. AIDCORP comes to the front in providing the facilities. People recall the presence of Bridies who were helpful to them. Tully makes up his mind not to go till Rikki gets well. Rikki goes to the graves of the Bridies to pay homage and becomes emotional as he still realises their influence over him.

In the name of the story, there is nothing except the bundle of the episodes; however, they are interwoven in such manner as throw light on the friendship of Rikki and Tully representing the Orient and the Occident respectively. In her last novel *Pleasure City*, Kamala Markandaya fails to spell bind the readers as she did in her first novel *A Nectar in a Sieve* but she has displayed her knack in assimilating two cultures through cooperation and understanding with the reciprocal mindset. In it, she talks of mutual understanding and wiping out of the misery of the past in the manner of Shakespeare who in *The Tempest* echoes forgiveness and reconciliation.

No doubt, the East and the West dichotomy has been the theme of her earlier novels like *Possession*, *Coffer Dams* and *The Golden Honeycomb* as, in the words of Lakshmi Kumari, "the area of divergence between the East and the West, therefore, is readily identifiable." Further she writes:

> The East signifies a sort of orientation that cares eventually more for the inner and the unseen, the categorical and the absolute. The values are associated with, or may be interpreted as passivity, stagnation, rootedness and a kind of conservatism that seems antithetical to progress and material attainments. The West likewise signifies a skeptical; hardheaded, if not cynical, attitude towards the problems of the world. (M.K. Bhatnagar, p 116).

Though the East is somewhat orthodox and has the touch of traditionalism, it can now pace with the pragmatic West if it approaches wiping out the prejudiced feelings and the West also can learn spiritualism from the East. In the novel *Pleasure City*, she has shown the possibility of fusion of the East and the West if both reciprocate genuinely and remain unprejudiced in taking the best. The friendship of Rikki-Tully is the foundation on which she makes the castle of 'Assimilation' in new surrounding where there is the fresh breeze of independence and identity.

> The friendship of Tully and Rikki is actually a friendship of moderns and traditionals in the changed environment. Through this friendship Markandaya points to fresh areas of understanding and co-operation between the West and the East in the post-colonial period. She suggests that this is how the two parts of the world can contribute their might of the development and prosperity of each other" (A.K.Bhatnagar, p. 49).

Maya offers a fresh interpretation of the friendship of Tully with Rikki as she feels that Tully is the

> decolonised Prospero returning to expiate the crimes of the past, searching for a spiritual home and place. The spiritual journey undertaken by Tully in the company of Rikki, is a regressive journey from civilisation, but a journey of progression towards complete decolonisation (M.K Bhatnagar, p. 111).

Now Tully has entered the Indian subcontinent to make amends to the wrong done previously and when Boyle reminds him that "the sun never set on the British Empire" he offers some flip trans-atlantic gibe replying, "God so ordained it because he didn't trust the British in the dark" (170). Actually, his grandfather's remark "My dear boy, India was never an occupied country. Mistake to imagine. They never felt that" (30) echo and re-echo in his mind and hence, he has not come to dominate the country but to reciprocate what is best. He learns what he can about the sea and the fishing colony from Rikki in whom he searches all the possibilities and confides in his instinctive knowledge. He asks to make a boat that will symbolise the friendship and in this way he is healing the past wounds. The following dialogue reflects the unflinching faith of Tully in Rikki who equally responds.

> 'I'm looking for a boat. An old love,' said Tully; and it was.
> 'Will you build me one?' he said.

> 'Will you trust me to?' asked Rikki
> 'There'll be reasons not to,' said Tully, 'when you supply them' (61).

Rikki is not selfish in his relations, as he believes in the bond of humanity. He presents a flower to Tully as a token of love. He tells his sister Valli that Tully is as "human as you or me" (73). Tully returns the boat to Rikki as he realises that it belongs to him. Rikki deserves the boat as he is the true owner and here Tully sees the whole scenario with the lens of equality. "The boat belonged to him" and he "would bequeath it to its proper owner, a proper resolution of at least one equation" (328). He feels sad when Tully decides to go and very emotionally he asks: "Will you come back, Mr. Tully?" Hearing this, Tully also becomes emotional and expresses his desire saying: "'I wish I could" (340). Now their friendship is on equal footing and it is too firm to be broken and he realises that "they shared a language that went beyond English, and was outside the scope of mere words. As, of course, did Tully" (ibid.).

The crucial role in making the personality of Rikki is of the mentor, Mrs. Bridie who showers her motherly affection on Rikki. For him, she becomes such a woman as possesses "the key to locked, mysterious boxes that he barely knew existed except for the barest outlines that were showing up hazily in the distance"(6). She always advises him: "If a thing is worth, it is worth doing well. You must always aim to be immaculate" (16). She takes care of him well and sees the image of her son in him. Even after her death she is present on the screen of his mind. At the end of the novel, he repeats the words of Mrs. Bridie: "There was a time and a season, for everything. A time to sow and a time to reap" (341). In spite of her infertility, she is fertile as she considers others' children as her own. She presents the image of mother—Universal Mother. Human relationship can be seen in Amma who becomes the foster mother of Rikki after the death of his parents and relatives. "Call me Amma, if you like, she said, busy with the bellows and charcoal so as not it embarrass the child. I am your mother now and lucky to be" (9). Mrs. Pearl, though a Western, loves Indian spiritualism and she takes the responsibility of the infant found at the cave. Valli is helpful to her parents and brothers Muthu and Rikki. She is more cooperative to her foster brother Rikki than her real one Muthu. Rikki saves Corinna from the currents of water but while saving her, Rikki is hurt. In the end, Corinna realises her mistake and repents for it. "I am sorry, Toby. About Rikki, I mean. It was unforgivable. I must have been mad" (317). She fails to go into the depth and to peep into the hearts of Indians. "She would never know Rikki, or perhaps the country he was bound up with, were equally outside her reach" (318). She fails to find out the key to the heart that leads to human relationship. She presents a weak image of the relationship. She is self-satisfied and wishes to live in her own world without caring for others. Mrs. Contractor is very practical lady who advises her guests what to do, where to go and what to eat. She is very polite in her treatment when the guests thank her for her precious advice and care, she tells them: "Would you not do the same for me if I were a stranger in your country? No, no, it is nothing it is simply do unto others" (151). Mrs. Lovat wishes to write a book about India. She says: "It is just that your country fascinates me. I'd like to find out as much as I can, that's al"(154). She feels more comfortable in Rikki's company. She is indebted to him for his active cooperation. When she goes away, she does not forget to wish good health for Rikki. "I want to finish my book. And don't be surprised; she said archly. If you find yourself in it" (333). Hence, human relationship is breathed almost by every character in the novel Pleasure City.

But this human relationship has the Janus face—one that is optimistic and cooperative while the other face is darkened—darkened with deep desire that has a glimpse of the possession. Now the ghost of the Occident once again has appeared in the pleasing shape of a gentleman with the new brand that can be named 'Neo-colonialism' as M. K. Bhatnagar writes: "Pleasure City seems a more sustained and simple study of the historical process of neo-colonialism through the coming together of a sensitive Britisher and an ingenious Indian villager" (Kamala Markandaya, p 4). These imperialists once possessed the land, now they have come with the intention of colonising the mind so that the Orient may become slave mentally. "The same old imperialists at it again only this time disguised as technocrats. And they saw their case proved by the balance sheets" (22). The multinational companies like AIDCORP are exploiting on the name of 'white man's burden'. In adjusting himself to the local custom, Tully reflects the mentality of the Occident of exploiting the Orient emotionally. The disguise of gentleman is for the benefit of the Occident, not for the natives. "Empires, on the whole, are not won or run for the benefit of the original inhabitants" but these empires, "like any commercial enterprise, operate for the benefit of the shareholders" and aborigines are "shunted off into second place"(ibid.).

The Occident is aware of the magical power of English language, which is the only way to colonise the mind. If the natives are taught in English language, they will be uprooted from their own indigenous culture. The English language will make them realise their inferiority and with this concealed intention, Benjamin and Martha Bridie guide the fisher boy Rikki through the Western education that makes him see with the world with the Occident lenses. Cultural hegemony through the English language becomes the objective of the Occident and herein lies their conspiracy of alienating the Orient from its culture in order to acknowledge the supremacy of the Occident.

In the post-Independence era, the permission of the Indian Government to AIDCORP to build a pleasure resort 'Shalimar' proves to be a curse as it becomes responsible for the displacement and the poverty of the natives of the village close to the coastline of the sea. Rikki, the protagonist is "a fisherman's son" who "lived by the sea with a fisherman's family" (41). The natives here live on fishing; they feel happy and eat well when there is good season but they remain hungry when the fishing is bad. At the advent of the AIDCORP, they are lured to pledge their services and the free fishermen line up to turn into coolies in order to save themselves from hunger. The novelist presents the poignant picture of the fishermen saying:

> Day after day the catch burned out poor. They ate so meagerly; the cramps were beginning. These were not unknown, but good seasons made them forget. The suicidal mackerel had spoilt them all (56).

When Rikki expresses his desire: "Wish there was more to eat,' Muthu very tartly replies to him, "Who doesn't?"(ibid.). After hot talks, they quarrel. Their sister Valli knew the reason: "when the boats came back empty it could happen that men flew at each other like fighting cocks" (57). When there is skimpy catches as "The sea is in no mood to give anything" (61), the poor state of the natives forces them to join the Shalimar as labourers. Very pathetically and realistically, the novelist presents the scenario:

> Rikki hummed. He did not wish to reveal the extent of their dilapidations, which were going from bad to worse, and were now spectacular. With prices shooting up every day it was inevitable—unless one had opted into Shalimar. Those who were in could afford far above what they were used to. Those who baulked, like Apu, could not afford even the minimum they had been accustomed to buy (65).

The poor natives were leading their lives without stir sharing among themselves their joys and sorrows but Shalimar polluted not merely the environment responsible for the poor catches but also their joys and made them slaves. The infant that is found in the cave is the result of the ill effect of the so-called progress and it shows the trade of the flesh alluring the victims with the power of money.

To think of synthesis leads one to utopia, which displays impracticability of the concept. No doubt, the text focuses the friendship of the Rikki and Tully, i.e., of the Orient and the Occident but there are many instances that prove it to be a myth. Tully tells Rikki the reason of taking over the country: "Why we took over your country, to impose our order on what seemed to us your confusion" (79). Tully is not in favour of staying too much in the country as there is, he says, "That ever-present danger, or temptation. It alters people" (ibid.). Though Tully is inspired by the spiritual remarks of Rikki who makes him see the whole ocean in spite of the cactus and lets him see two sides of the same face that look "serenely on creation, preservation, and destruction" (83). Tully finally admits before Rikki that there is an ocean between them. Rikki himself feels the division;

> between them, between one man and another, their minds, their reach and sway, the reality of the distance between himself and Tully. Distance? Notes of incredulity sounded as well. Distance between them, chipping at marble in the pool room together, sharing the light, and emotions? Where was the reality, what was vapour? Presently he had to lay

> down the chisel and simply sit, wondering, looking full face at Tully (147).

But the myth is demythologised soon when in spite of admitting an ocean between them, Tully wonders: "For was there an ocean? Really? Actually? His incredulity echoes Rikki's." He becomes aware of the feelings—touching feelings in the inner conscience and these feelings were not to subject to corruption. Now his vision is quite clear and he feels something that "washed over them like water or light, and merged them into the one landscape" (147).

The text *Pleasure City* becomes the Bible of assimilation of the Orient and the Occident on the basis of cooperation and mutual understanding without losing their identity. No doubt, there is an ocean between them but it is the touch of the water that makes the two shores realise their unity. Kamala Markandaya has presented the mantra saying: "A two-way deal, getting to know one's fellow. Advancing beyond language to contemplation. Contemplating another human, most complex of beings, each engaged in a voyage of discovery no less strenuous, or ravishing, than a physical adventure" (81). Synthesizing on the basis of the concept of discovering each other's affirmative virtues and without being prejudiced, their assimilation is the only solution that will lead them to the path of progress, peace and prosperity without affecting the roots of each other's culture. The myth of cultural hegemony of the Occident over the Orient is only a myth and will never translate into reality.

Works Cited

Bhatnagar, M.K. (ed.). *Kamala Markandaya: A Critical Spectrum*. New Delhi: Atlantic, 2002.

Lakshmi Kumari, "A Pleasure City: The New Frontier" in *Kamala Markandaya: A Critical Spectrum*, ed. M. K. Bhatnagar. New Delhi: Atlantic, 2002, p. 116.

Bhatnagar, Anil Kumar "East-West Encounter" in *Kamala Markandaya A Thematic Study*. New Delhi: Sarup and Sons, 1995, p. 49.

Maya, D., "The Discourse of Resistance: A Reading of Kamala Markandaya's, *Pleasure City*" in M. K. Bhatnagar (ed.). *Kamala Markandaya: A Critical Spectrum*. New Delhi: Atlantic, 2002, p.111.

Markandaya, Kamala, *Pleasure City*. London: Chatto and Windus, 1982.

16

Interview with Stephen Gill

— *Jaydeep Sarangi*

J.S: When did you start writing, in which language and why?

S.G: I always aspired to be a writer. I was also shy. Because of the shyness, I began to dwell in the realm of imagination. We had a good library in our house. I used to read most of the time and began to write. I was fourteen years old when my first short story appeared in a daily publication. It was in Urdu. My shyness and my mother, who was very particular about our education, must have contributed towards my aspiration. She was a good storyteller. Her stories had morals. My father who was a sort of writer must have also contributed to my development as a writer.

J.S. When did you start writing in English?

S.G: I started writing in English from my twenties.

J.S. Did your education in English literature help you to become a writer in English?

S.G. I will say no. Extremely sad situations during the days of my adolescence have shaped my path to be a spokesperson for peace. My studies of political science, philosophies and human rights have shaped the path further to find a peaceful solution for a peaceful existence. I wanted to be a political scientist. When I went to fill in my admission form for a master's programme, I wrote English literature, though I went to the college to study for a master's degree in political science.

This does not mean that I dislike the English language. I loved it then as I do now. This love does not mean that I see the English language as superior to others. I write poetry also in Urdu, Punjabi and Hindi languages. When I was in Ethiopia, before coming to Canada, I learnt Italian. I had means because Italian was extensively spoken in that part of Ethiopia. I enjoyed understanding its complexities. Shortly, I began to be admired for using it grammatically correct and also from the point of its accent. I started studying Arabic in Ethiopia because of time and availability of means. I found the grammar of Arabic more complicated than the grammar of Italian. I gave up my efforts to study Arabic. When I was in India, to be more proficient in Urdu, I studied Persian. I have found out that every tongue has its own beauty. I wanted to concentrate on English because I wanted to be a writer to share my message with as many readers as possible. For a person from the South Asian region, English is the most suitable vehicle for that purpose. Education in English literature does not improve writing skills. Sometimes, I regret giving years to the study of literature. Instead, I should have made use of that time for my writing. To improve writing skills, it is imperative to read good literature, keep the company of writers, subscribe to the publications that help writers and above all write, write and write to be in print.

J.S: Why did you go to Canada?

S.G: I felt that to join the ranks of successful writers of English-speaking nations, I should improve my language skills that is possible in a country where English is used as the first language. In addition to this, I wanted degrees added to my name for prestige. I was under the impression that these degrees would present me as a writer of value. For a doctoral degree I got admission to a university in Canada with an offer of financial assistance. Above all, I wanted to breathe in a safer place that I could call home. My introduction to my collection of poems *Shrine* throws some light on it. These factors brought me to Canada from Ethiopia.

J.S: What is the most challenging fact about being a post colonial immigrant in Canada?

S.G: In Canada persons can achieve their dreams provided they are organised, industrious, and honest.

J.S. Can you mention a few established and well-read names of this generation?

S.G. It is not possible to say who is well read and who is not. There is no such survey available in Canada. I have mentioned established Indian-born Canadian writers in my paper by the same title. Readers can form their own opinion.

J.S. Is anybody doing any project on them?

S. G. I don't know.

J.S. Dr. Gill, you are an author of so many books. Could you please list a few?

S.G. *Reflections & Wounds* (poems); *The Dove of Peace* (poems); *Divergent Shades* (poems); *Songs for Harmony* (poems); *The Flowers of Thirst* (poems); *Shrine* (poems); *Life's Vagaries* (short stories); *The Loyalist City* (novel); *Immigrant* (novel); *Why* (novel); *Scientific Romances of H.G. Wells* (critical study); *Six Symbolist Plays of Yeats* (critical study); *Political Convictions of G.B. Shaw* (critical study); *Discovery of Bangladesh* (history); *Simon and the Snow King* (children's story); *The Blessings of a Bird* (children's story); *English Grammar for Beginners*; *Sketches of India* (illust. essays about India); *Aman Di Ghughi* (Punjabi poems); *Jazira* (Urdu poems).

Books edited

Poets of the Capital (anthology of poets from Ottawa region); *Seaway Valley Poets* (anthology of poets from the seaway valley region); *Tales from Canada for Children Everywhere* (anthology); *Green Snow* (anthology of Canadian poets of Asian origin) ; *Anti-War Poems* Vol. 1 & 2; Vesta's *Who's Who of North American Poets.*

J.S. Which is your best creation?

S.G. It is like asking me which eye or hand I like the most, or asking a mother to name her best child. If you would allow me to answer using the yardstick of libraries that stock my titles, I can say, *Scientific Romances of H.G. Wells* from my critical studies, *Immigrant* from my fiction, and *Shrine* from collections of my poems are worth keeping on the shelves. Personally I like *The Discovery of Bangladesh* because of its presentation and historical value.

J.S. Your novel *Immigrant* reflects the diasporic crisis of rootlessness. Is there autobiographical hint anywhere in the theme or the protagonist?

S.G. Also I would use the term a novel of cultural pluralism or a novel of fears and hopes for *Immigrant*. In the initial stâges, particularly during the Cold War, diasporic literature was political in nature and exiled victims of persecution wrote it. Reghu Nath, the protagonist in *Immigrant*, though enters Canada as a student, has no desire to go back to the country of his birth. His dream of a democratically elected one-world government is to create suitable environment to be free from the clutches of persecutions. In the country of his birth, he suffers from one kind of persecution with all doors closed for self-advancement. In the country of his adoption he confronts another kind with all the doors wide open.

Concerning biographical hints, my answer is yes and no. Every piece of my writing is my child and every child inherits some traits of his or her father. Like any writer, I need material for the construction of my house. The closest place to collect that material is from the field of my own life. I have the option of borrowing from other sources. Events in fiction do not necessarily happen as they do in real life. Even in normal life for a normal person, it is impossible to remember objective details of every event. Retelling is a mixture of what memories choose to be retained and what the imagination presents. After choosing incidents, I shape them the way I should to suit my end. To put it in another way, I do not feel comfortable when I write directly about my experiences. At the same time, I cannot get away from myself. I have to build a house. If I am not able to get the material easily that I need, I will improvise it or go out to find it from somewhere. When the house of fiction is complete, it is hard to recognise the source of the material. Attempts to trace the source would interfere with the appreciation of the beauty that I want to present. To try to isolate an autobiographical component from what is not is like dissecting a flower.

To put it in another way, inside me I have voices. Some of these voices remain always within and some appear once in a while. Some voices are the product of my resourceful imagination. These voices shape a character to be their mouthpiece. I try to express those voices through one or other means. I may choose my disguise, but I never choose to disappear. It is similar with every artist, including sculptors, and carpenters. Let us take the case of a carpenter. Before making a table, the original of the table exists in the mind of the carpenter. That work of the carpenter, table, contains biographical elements also because that is a copy of the original that was within the maker. The table has also wood, nails and varnish that may have come from different sources. This is true with any piece of art. In that sense also, creations have biographical elements that are mixed with other elements that are not biographical. To isolate one from the other is not only undesirable but also a complicated process. It is true that Reghu Nath goes to a university as his creator does, and he is from India as his creator is. It is also true that *Immigrant* has my blood— it expresses my philosophy on several aspects. One of them is the attainment of peace through a democratically elected one-world government. Another is about prejudice. I have explained in this novel that newcomers as well as Canadians have preconceived notions about one another. Prejudice is largely the result of these preconceived notions. One way to get rid of these notions is to get out of the ghettoes of the selves to socialise freely and also to read about others.

J.S. Are you planning for a new novel?

S.G. Yes, I do.

J.S. You were born in Pakistan, brought up in India and now an immigrant to Canada. In Canada, you have visited the houses of Muslim, Hindu and Christian religions. Where do you land on or would like to land on?

S.G. My fellowship with people of diverse creeds has convinced me that people are people. This conviction is based on my visits to different countries. I have discovered that people are people no matter what their beliefs and cultural values are. Underneath their skins they are the same their hearts and thinking are the same. People everywhere have the same fears, the same hopes and the same instincts for survival. I have also discovered that environment plays a decisive role in shaping the thoughts of individuals. The individuals who were fanatical in India and Pakistan have found a vital change in their lives. They see events more objectively in the light of their latest experiences. However, the thoughts developed in childhood and adolescence are hard to change dramatically even with a better environment. Education for the betterment of self and the world should be initiated from early childhood. Wherever I go, I find that religions do not act as bridges to unite hearts. On the other hand, they have become demonic to disunite hearts. If there is any drive to destroy the modern civilisation that would be from the religious robots. The madness of this drive can be controlled through education and political steps. I believe that there should be a strong United Religions Organisation, along the lines of the United Nations.

J.S. What's about your poetry?

S.G. Although I have written also a considerable amount of prose, I am known primarily as a poet. In addition to English, I write poetry in Urdu, Hindi and Punjabi languages. I am known as a poet of peace and social concerns. It is only as a poet that I have been compared with other English poets and also with a major Urdu poet. Most of the articles and reviews that have been written are about my poetry, and most of my recognitions are also for my contributions as a poet. A prominent singer from Pakistan has provided music and sung some of my Urdu/Hindi poems in an album called Aman. I do not belong to any school or era of poetry. My poetry is the psalm of my soul. To me, a poet is a discoverer of unknown continents through the voyage of the self. A poet is also a priest who through the mantra of poetry reaches the god within. For details on my poetry, please visit my website: www.stephengill.ca

J.S. You have been published enormously in Indian journals and magazines. Did you publish your poems in Pakistan?

S.G. Yes, I have been published in Pakistan mostly in Urdu and Punjabi and my articles in English. There may be two or three poets in Pakistan who write in English. They are known not even nationally. There are not many good contemporary Urdu poets, though there are several good poems. There is no literary publication in English from Pakistan.

J.S. Would you like to comment on the poetry situation in Pakistan?

S.G. Lamentable. There are not many good poets even in Urdu. Faiz Ahmed Faiz is among the good ones. He died a few years ago. He was born in the same area of Pakistan, Sialkot, where I was born. Critics have compared our works from different angles. One reason for the lamentable situation of poetry in Pakistan is the attitude of a group of Muslims towards the arts. This group condemns music, dance and poetry for spiritual reasons, adding that the Hindus have taught these arts to the Muslims of the subcontinent of India and Pakistan.

J.S. Dr. Gill, do you read your critics?

S.G. Yes I do. If the approach is different with close attention, I take them seriously, analysing their words and sentences. I read them more than once and quote them wherever there is need.

J.S. Dove appears again and again in your poems. Would you like to share your thoughts on this particular symbol?

S.G. A symbol is something that stands for something else, such as the lion is a symbol of courage and water is a symbol of life. The dove has been used as a symbol for centuries in different cultures. In Greek mythology, Aphrodite that stands for the goddess of love keeps a dove as a pet that has become a symbol of love. A great artist, Pablo Picasso, painted doves to signify peace. In one of his paintings, a small child softly hugs a dove. Its blue and green colours make a person feel peaceful. This painting is titled, "A Child with Dove."

The name dove is given to a bird in the pigeon family. Doves live throughout the world from deserts to tropical forests. Due to its soft cooing sound and affectionate disposition it is symbolised as the emblem of peace. Among Christians, it is used for God's love in any manifestation. In Christian art it often symbolises hope, peace, Holy Spirit and even martyrdom. The dove also signifies the soul as well as gentleness and purity.

In the *Biblical* account of the flood, Noah set a dove free to find the condition of the earth. The bird returned with a green branch in the beak. After that it began to be symbolic of hope. When

Christ was baptised, the Holy spirit descended upon him in the form of the dove.

In Greek mythology, the dove was a bird of Athena that symbolised the renewal of life. *Signs & Symbols* states, "Two doves together are considered a sign of marital love and fidelity." Doves are held sacred in many countries. In Greek legend the dove was linked to Aphrodite, the infant Zeus, the Fates, and the Furies (p.65, *Readers Digest*, Montreal, 1996).

According to Jack Tresidder in the *Dictionary of Symbols*, the dove was the attribute of the Semitic love goddess Ashtart (Astarte), assimilated into the classical world as Aphrodite (in Roman myth, Venus), and also of Adonis, Dionysus (Bacchus) and Eros (Cupid). The moan of the dove was linked with both sex and childbirth. Winged phalluses shown with doves were found in Pompeii. A pair of doves has long symbolised sexual bliss, which may be why the dove came to personify the attentive and gentle wife. In China the dove is one of the many symbols for longevity as in Japan where a dove with a sword is an emblem of peace (p.67, Chronicle Books, USA, 1997). Many artists have been using the symbol of the flying dove in the corner of their paintings to acknowledge that the Lord who is the source of creativity has inspired the work.

I call one of my collections *The Dove of Peace*, that is also the title of a poem in the same collection. In *Songs for Harmony*, another collection, there is a poem, titled "Seeking the Dove of Peace". In *Shrine*, my collection of poems "To a Dove", "A Flight of a Dove", and "My Dove" are directly associated with the dove. The dove appears as symbol in several other poems also in this collection. I have used the dove in *Shrine* in sentences, including 'Relaxing/ in the nest of tomorrow/ she dreams of flying/ in the air of freedom' (50); 'the dove pleads/ that the dance of the hounds/ be stopped' (56). In *The Dove of Peace*, I refer to Canada, 'A peace adoring dove', (28). On the dove, I have written trilliums in haiku spirit. Some of them are listed below:

Dove flies towards skies
green branch in beak
message of hopes.

Dove
muses on a branch
eyes half-shut.

Dove flies
human sleep
in the fold of dreams

Dove draws no boundaries
no fuss
gypsy of hopes.

I believe that one day researchers will fathom my fascination for the dove. They may enter those ditches of agonies where I saw the innocent being killed and heard babies crying while smelling the greenery of my adolescence in New Delhi during the days of the partition of India. They can feel the pulse of the darkness when we went to bed with the darkest fears of human, and the dawn appeared with baskets filled with fresh lemons of worries.

J.S. Another symbol that appears often in your poetry particularly before *Shrine* is the wind. Could you dwell on it also?

S.G. *The Plowman* from Canada published my poems "Wind" and "A Breeze That Is Free" in issue number 3 of January 1989. I was immensely pleased when its chief editor, Mr. Tony Scavetta offered to feature me as the poet of the month for his prestigious international literary publication, asking me to give him background information on my poem "Wind." I was also somewhat puzzled because I did not know what to say or how and where to start. I had no idea whatsoever how to approach his question, or even, if it was approachable. It is mainly because poets do not always remember the circumstances under which they happen to write their poems, unless there was something very special reason attached to any of them. Even if there is something special attached to some of them, it is not always possible to carry details. However, when I started to think about the wind I began to discover many hitherto unknown facts.

I discovered that my treatment of the wind had something to do with my room where I slept. It is still the same room, upstairs. There I hear the birds welcoming another dawn; the rains striking against the windowpane producing a sonata; the winds growling and singing; and far-off the mingled sounds of trains, buses and people disrupting the night's calm. Among these sounds, the most sensuous ones are those of the winds and the rains, appearing in their different moods and tones. At one time, they produce lullaby; at another, they transport me to a solitary guesthouse with a maiden in full bloom. This guest house is a type of bungalow that one would rent at a hill-station during summer in tropical countries. Jungles and hills surround it. Wild animals shout and shriek and ferocious gales beat their heads against the doors, while inside we relax by a fireside.

Several of my poems were written under the canopy of these fancies. "A Breeze that is Free" and "Wind" are the two poems that are entirely on this subject. I wrote "A Breeze that is Free" around 1980. I wrote "Wind", another poem on the same subject, eight years after that. When I wrote "Wind", it was completely out of my mind that I had already done a poem on the same topic. However, my treatment of the wind in these two poems is noticeably divergent. I prefer my second poem, "Wind", to the first one, "A Breeze That is Free".

Both of these poems are in the form of personification, and both are on the same subject. Also, both are preoccupied with man's predicament on this earth and again in both these poems wind sees life as a whole, a complete unit, as compared with man's view of life that is fragmented and isolated. In the latter poem, the poet envies the wind because it has unlimited freedom to catch a global view. On the other hand, humans are restricted in their movements and therefore their views are fragmented.

In the first poem, the wind caresses, consoles, heals, brings sleep that is calm, enlivens lonely eyes and puts smiles where tears reign. These are some social functions. On the other hand, in "Wind" it is the philosophical aspect that has been explored. A reader can notice here evolution in the poet's idea from a social vocation to metaphysical and mystical aspect. This makes the second poem more profound than the first one.

I discovered that the wind has appeared in my poetry in various modes in the former years. In some cases, the wind is cruel and in others, benign. In "Why I Sing", "maddening winds

/ flap their wings / against the windows / of my frailties"; "In Your Presence", "intoxicating wind" is "a maid / crossing the threshold of youth"; In Stranger, "You (unnamed visitor) blew as a wind / leaving behind / a burning wood"; "In That Flower", "That fragrant whispering wind / which kisses its (flower for beloved) refreshing lips, / Embodies the flame in me" In "How Madly I Wish", "The wandering wind enlivens in me/that taste of your trembling lips"; "In Absence", "Night, /a nameless rumpled road, / watches the ghost-like winds / breaking my soul-crushing monotony"; In "Because You Are Close to Me", when "winds growl/...life becomes a light / because you are close to me"; "In Charms of Your Eyes", "Drunk with pride / the vagabond fragrant winds"; In "O Love", "Amid the frigid winds / blowing so hard, / a wave of hope you emerge,"; and in "Her Dreams", "A pleasant wind".

The wind appears also in my forthcoming collection *Flame* that is divided in cantos. There is reference to 'An intoxicating wind' and 'the wind that whispers'. The wind appears in its other forms, including breeze, air, storm, etc.

I may be asked why I am so much enamoured by the wind. My answer would be that it is perhaps my room, where I did most of my thinking and writing in longhand, when the world slept. The wind turns into a living being for me — it cries, it laughs, it moans, it recalls my past. Obviously, wind is not just another object for me at that time; it becomes a companion, a co-sharer of my secrets. Once a pastor, pointing to my room from outside, said it was like the upper room where the disciples of Jesus assembled and prayed and were filled with the Holy Ghost. Here in this room, I used to be swayed with the spirit of my muse.

Surprisingly, the wind was not prominent in my poetry before 1980. Why so, is another question that I may have to struggle to answer. This may be partly or entirely because before that I was living elsewhere, where I hardly observed the wind in its various moods. Since this question from an editor made me aware, the wind began to disappear gradually from my poetry. In my collection *Shrine*, the wind appears rarely. 'No one can buy/ nor sell/ the freedom of the winds ("Who Shall Buy"); someone should inform the winds ("The Voice of Democracy"); the wind that blows in sunny fields ("Lotus of Freedom"); A self-governing winds ("Seed of Democracy"); A running with the wind ("Somali Victim") and so on.

J.S. Why did you leave teaching for book publishing business?

S.G. Though I entered Canada as a doctoral student, my aim was also to chisel the skills of my writing and gain a deeper understanding of the English language. I was already a published book author, but I wanted to add degrees as well, to my name to convince my readers that I am a serious and knowledgeable writer.

To study the cultural life of the country, I joined groups of writers. I also devoured literary publications. It was a time and money-consuming struggle. I discovered that for a first-time author it was not easy to get a publisher. In other words, publishers invest their money on winning authors. I also discovered that it takes a year or two to find a publisher, and the publisher would take another two years to bring out the book, and it takes another two years to bring the book to the attention of readers. It was frustrating to know that some authors are publicised more than others.

For a serious writer who wants to produce books one after the other, it was a path of impatience. Moreover, there was an army of would-be writers who did not have patience to travel the long path to find a publisher and then to wait for two to three years for the book to be released. The inner world of book publishing was a mystery to new authors. To help serious writers and also to give a chance to budding writers, who had been roses in the desert, and also to help myself, I ventured into book publishing.

Publishing sector needs money and a good knowledge of the printing process, public relations, writing, editing skills, business aptitude, and above all an understanding of good literature. I was convinced that publishing would help me in my chosen field and at the same time I was going to be in a fairly good situation to help the helpless writers. These were the factors that prompted me to be a book publisher.

J.S. What were your challenges as a book publisher?

S.G. Lack of capital and manpower. A person can hire employees if there is capital. If there is manpower, the capital can be ignored for a while. But I had nothing. Moreover, I was in a new environment. All that I had was a will, knowledge of literature and skills to write. A couple of writers came forward to ask me to publish their books. They offered to buy a considerable number of books for themselves. I figured out that much money was enough to pay for the printing cost. At this stage, a printer offered to print my books and wait for a while to collect the printing cost till the book was sold. He helped me also to learn the printing process. In the first year, I released four titles; two of those were my own. I was in business as a book publisher.

Our local Member of the Parliament was also helpful. He was the minister of labour for the last fourteen years. Mr. Guindon was great as far as his heart and help were concerned. With his help, I was able to receive a publishing grant every year from the government after two years in business. I came to know that a company would become more prestigious if it was incorporated. I needed money to hire a lawyer to do it. I went to our local library and read books on how to incorporate a business. I also discussed the matter with the government people who are associated with incorporation. Several people told me that it was impossible to do the work myself. I needed a lawyer. After reading material in the library and discussions with knowledgeable persons I was able to incorporate the business myself. People still do not believe it, but I was able to do it that saved money.

Shortly, Vesta Publications Ltd. emerged as a medium-sized company in Canada. I learnt also the basics of printing. To reduce cost and to produce work on time by eliminating dependence on printers, I bought my cwn equipment. My work increased, but I became independent. I used to work for around sixty hours a week every day of the year without any day off.

J.S. Why did you bid farewell to such a meaningful profession of book publishing?

S.G. Publishing was meaningful no doubt, but also demanding. Book publishing began to interfere with my writing. Most of the time, I promoted other writers. I hardly had time for my own writing. I also discovered that book publishing was a thankless job. If a book is successful, all the credit goes to the author, and if unsuccessful, the publisher is to blame. Believe me, I made most of my friends as a writer and lost them as a book publisher. There is no doubt that publishing brought prestige, but I wanted to win friends. I am happy that I am out of it. I don't think a writer should be a book publisher. Both clash with one another.

J.S. Does your African background as a teacher have any bearing upon your writing?

S.G. Two books are the direct outcome of my experiences in Ethiopia. One is my book of English grammar, and another is my novel, why?

I discovered that British and American publishers had donated most of those books of grammar to Ethiopia. Those books were written for the students of their own countries who learn English grammar as their first language. Therefore those books were not useful for Ethiopian students. I made notes for Ethiopian students to make the grammar easy and more useful for them. Later when I came to Canada, a British publisher released that book under the title *English Grammar for Beginners*. The book gained popularity among newcomers in Britain, Europe and Canada. My novel, *Why*, is the story of the protagonist who gets in and out of love affairs with married women. Why he does so sets the tone of the book. The story is also about boredom and the cultures of North America, Ethiopia and India.

The story of *Why* revolves around Rubin Motard, who is born and brought up in Montreal, a city in the province of Quebec. When he is eleven years old, his mother elopes with a friend of his father. The only goal of his father is to make as much money as possible. A baby-sitter, who seduces him, raises Rubin. We meet Rubin later when he is an adult, in Ottawa, where he falls in love, one after another, with married women. A question arises why he always falls in love with married women.

After a while, he goes to Ethiopia on a teaching assignment. There he falls in love with the wife of his colleague. He meets there a teacher from India. They become good friends. This brings into the novel some features of traditional love in India. Ruben has affairs also with his maid, a divorcee. Ethiopia is shown as a rugged, natural country. Ruben returns to Canada after teaching in Ethiopia for three years. Towards the end, he is shown sketching a portrait of a woman. He is not satisfied with the sketch because it does not represent that woman. He destroys the sketch to start it again, without any success. While making a few trials, it dawns upon him suddenly that the sketch bears a few traits of his mother. It dawns upon him further that all the women he had loved resembled his mother. There the story ends, abruptly.

On the one hand, *Why*, is a story of Ruben's running in and out of love affairs with married women. On the other, it is a story of three cultures and their views towards love. I have attempted to show that love in North America is intellectualised. I have tried to prove through incidents, discussions and dialogue that man and woman cannot understand each other intellectually; a real understanding comes from the heart. I have tried to illustrate that North American women intellectualise love whereas for Ethiopian women it is spontaneous as the stream flowing in the jungle is. In India it is more or less traditional. I have compared the North American view of love with the Ethiopian view. The citizens of this African nation live close to nature and therefore their response to love is also natural— it is spontaneous. I have compared these two views — North American and Ethiopian — further with the traditional romantic love that exists in India. I had tried the technique of ending the story abruptly before in most of my short stories. I have used this technique also in my subsequent novels. It is because I don't want my readers to feel relieved or satisfied after the story is over— I want them to feel a thirst— I want to upset them— I want my reader to think even after the narrative is over. After all that is life. Concerning the question why the protagonist falls in love with married women I can say that there is some clue in the novel.

Protagonists of both these novels have a weakness for whiskey and both novels end abruptly. Besides, mother plays key roles in both novels, though this role is clearer in *Why* because the elopement of Ruben's mother is vital for the development of the story. It also ends with a note on his mother when Ruben discovers by chance that all the married women he had loved resembled his mother in one way or the other. My next novel, *Immigrant*, also opens and ends with a note on mother, but her presence is not vital for the progress of the plot.

Time plays important parts in both the novels. Both novels move forward and backward in time. This happens when the protagonists think of their past and future. Though I have tried to make the transition slow and smooth, yet it is difficult for an average reader to move along with the time easily. I have decided not to employ this technique any more in my next novel. In other words, the story of my fourth novel will be moving only forward, making it easier to read.

I have discovered that my novel Why is liked mostly by males whereas women, no matter which culture they are from, dislike the main character. I have also discovered that mostly newcomers and those who wish to come to Canada like *Immigrant*. White citizens do not feel comfortable reading this novel.

When I was writing *Why*, I was reading Dylan Thomas and James Joyce. Being under their influence, I wrote *Why* to be enjoyed at more than one level. The part of the story that is set in Ethiopia becomes fascinating when I bring out the moral, and culture values of that nation. Apart from this novel, I have written a couple of short stories that are set in Ethiopia.

J.S. Did any make an attempt to research for a Ph.D. on you?

S.G. There are some attempts.

J.S You have been appointed several times as examiner of Ph.D. dissertations of Indian scholars. Are you satisfied with the research works of Indian scholars?

S.G. Indian scholars have demonstrated a good knowledge of the English language and a proper use of primary and secondary sources. Because of lack of enough critical material, it is not easy to undertake a dissertation on a living foreign author. It is difficult even for scholars of the same country. Yet, Indian scholars do their jobs admirably.

J.S. You talk of world citizenship in your writing. Don't you think it as more abstract and theoretical than anything else?

S.G. The idea of world citizenship is not abstract. I have developed this idea in my poetry, have written about it in my fiction and have given talks and discussed it on radio and TV. A selection of these appearances has been put together in a two-hour DVD, titled "Interviews of Stephen Gill." I have reflected on this subject also in the introductions to Anti-War Poems, parts one and two, released by Vesta in 1984 and 1986.

Thinkers and social reformers have been talking of world citizenship for centuries. In the initial stages every idea is abstract. When people saw the denizens of the air, they began to think of flying. Man has reached the moon and is striving now to go beyond. In the same way, people saw creatures in the sea. Man has now means to touch and sail at the bottom of these oceans. Take the cases of some nations. This idea appeared abstract when the leaders wanted to form the United States of America (USA). Now it is reality. When people talked about uniting the entire Europe, the idea seemed to be abstract. Now Europe has its own currency, and its own parliament.

The idea of world citizenship is no more abstract, because the world has already been shrunk to a city. In nearly every home there are goods from different corners of the world, including computers, clothes, shoes, cameras, medical supplies, cars and other electronic and non-electronic goods. In the matter of taste and foods the world is one. Electronic devices spread the news in every corner of the world within minutes. Emails and telephone systems have united the world.

Humans are breathing in a world that has been reduced to a city, but this city is without its own council or parliament and its mayor. That is why there is chaos everywhere. We need a democratically elected world government to take care of this city. One major step that would lead to world peace is control of the international anarchy through international government.

The United Nations Organisation is a sort of world government but it has some defects. It is not effective because its representatives are not directly elected by their governments; it has veto power that is undemocratic; it has no way to raise its own finances through taxes; it has no judiciary with power; and above all, it does not have its own military force.

J.S. Can you list a few important world personalities who support the idea of one-world government?

S.G. A few utopian or crazy individuals have not launched the movement for a world government. Rather the concerned citizens of the world, including Winston Churchill, Charles de Gaulle,

Clement Attlee, Indira Gandhi, Lester Pearson, Leopold Stenghor, Jawaharlal Nehru, Pierre Trudeau, Carlos Romulo, and Bertrand Russell, have supported this movement.

Jawaharlal Nehru once said, "I have long believed the only way peace can be achieved is through world government." Winston Churchill said, "Unless some effective supranational government can be set up and brought quickly into action, the prospects of peace and human progress are dark and doubtful." Pope John XXIII in April 1963, speaking to the world, said that "the UN might eventually become a strong world authority". He argued that a super national authority must be considered.

English author and actor Peter Ustinov once said, "A World Government is not only possible, it is inevitable; and when it comes, it will appeal to patriotism in its truest, in its only sense, the patriotism of men who love their national heritage so deeply that they wish to preserve them in safety for the common good." Above all, there is the Nobel Prize-winning scientist Harold C. Urey. He was instrumental in producing the first atomic and hydrogen bombs. He died in California at the age of 87. He dropped most of his nuclear research expressing concern that this power would destroy the world. He admitted, "We may not be able to secure a world government, but we will not solve the problems of peace vs. war by any other means whatsoever."

The idea of forming one-world government has been advocated also by scientific romance writer H.G. Wells and Alfred Tennyson, a poet of the Victorian Age. I have discussed H.G. Wells in detail in my book, *Scientific Romances of H.G. Wells*. Both writers envisage a global parliament in their works. In H.G. Wells's, *The War in the Air* (1908),"scientific progress leads to a cataclysmic war, which is followed by all sorts of miseries." This makes people aware of the futility of wars, and the necessity to constitute an international parliament to ameliorate the human predicament and to avert future disasters. Wells elaborates the same view in The World Set Free that was released in 1914 (p. 135).

J.S. How can the world government make the world a better place to live?

S.G. Nearly every country has been preparing itself for wars against real and imaginary enemies. Even the poorest nations are spending their hard-earned foreign currencies on explosive to boost their national pride. This waste ought to be eliminated. Moreover, these preparations for war lead to unnecessary tensions with their neighbours.

National governments have been formed to render certain services to their citizens. One of them is to protect life and property of their people. In other words, they give security. But when all national governments become sovereign with no authority to control them and when they start arming themselves to give security to their citizens from external aggression, the natural outcome is war. The sovereignty of several states leads to clashes. The United Nations has failed to prevent several wars because it recognises the sovereign rights of national governments and resists interference in their domestic matters.

Not only is there waste in the presence of unethical national governments, there is also the real danger of the annihilation of modern civilisation through the use of nuclear weapons. It took centuries to build this civilisation, and now it may take minutes to destroy it. History tells us that every weapon that was invented has been used. Therefore, the nuclear weapons are likely to be used on a large scale. I have written several poems on world annihilation through the weapons of mass destruction.

National governments have failed to solve serious life-threatening problems, including international terrorism. Other problems include hunger, pollution, and weakening of the layer of the ozone that filters out most of the harmful radiation of the sun. The damage to ozone layer will not affect only one country. It is a concern of all humankind. Ozone is like a roof over the airship, inhabited by the entire human race. Ocean pollution also threatens the existence of human life. Pesticide, lead, arsenic, oil spills, radioactive and several forms of wastes present danger to the world's ocean system. Just in case of pollution only, no single nation can cope with this problem. Sweden with the hardest anti-pollution laws has discovered that it cannot solve their problem on a national basis. The Baltic Sea is being poisoned by pollution from other countries, and it gets acid rain that can be traced back to British factories. These are international problems and the world needs an international authority to solve them.

If there were a democratically elected world government, national governments would l not be allowed to have their military power. They would l have a police force to maintain law and order situations like the cities are allowed in any country. The military force would be under the world government only. The citizens of the world will feel safer this way.

These steps will make the world a better place to live and also save money by eliminating waste on national military budgets. This saved money will be used to open more schools, colleges and universities, more hospitals and grow more food. Scorching deserts will be changed into the smiling fields to produce crops. The money that would be saved would be used to eliminate diseases and poverty.

The world government does not mean to get rid of national languages and cultures. Countries like India and Canada are already multicultural and multilingual. World citizenship is an extension of these realities. If languages and cultures can survive in these and in other nations, they can survive also under the one-world government. World citizenship does not mean to stop loving one's country; world citizenship is to include everyone in the fold of its care for the sake of human survival and the betterment of life.

I would like to admit that it is almost impossible to form any democratically elected world government under the prevailing situation. At the same time the world cannot attain meaningful peace and prosperity without an international authority to take control of the present anarchy. To reach this goal, the citizens of the world should be educated right from the early days of their lives. I have written several articles on this subject. For my views in dętail, please visit my website: http://www.writesight.com/writers/stephen_gill/

J.S. What's your immediate wish as a creative writer?

S.G. To be a Nobel Laureate. It is not that I am hungry for such recognition. I have a serious message to share with the people of the world and that message is about peace. I am convinced that people will read my writings, taking me seriously after I receive that recognition.

J.S. Dr. Gill, finally, one old question to you. Do you feel uprooted in Canada? I would like to hear your observation on: "Home is where our feet are." Do you read it as a justified statement in the present context?

S.G. I can speak the same languages that I used to speak in Pakistan and then in India and I enjoy the same food as much as my children do. In Canada and the United States I have good friends who were born in India and Pakistan. A part of me is in the country where the bones of my ancestors have been buried; where I first opened my eyes; where I learnt to read and write; where my dear ones are still living; and where I still have my closest friends. To offer the flowers of my homage at the altar of the temple of that part, I take my poetic voyages also in the boat of the languages that I used during the early years of my life. That part spurs me to visit India more often and to keep close contacts particularly with its writers.

At the same time I believe that home is where our feet are. I also believe that our feet are in a home that encompasses safety and happiness. A home is also the evening fireside that provides warmth and cosiness. Wherever these components habitat, there habitats the heart. I see these components habitating in the rainbow beauty of Canada. Here I walk under a roof of assurances for my safety and freedoms. Wherever I go, I wear a hat that is textured with the ethnic touches of the mosaic nature of Canada. This hat is neither entirely South Asian nor entirely North American. It gives me protection, though at times it hurts a nerve.

(Published first in *The Atlantic Literary Review,* July-Sep. and Oct.-Dec. 2004, Vol 5, No. 3-4, pp. 164-183).

17

An Unknown Intellectual Made in India: An Appraisal of Nirad C. Chaudhuri's *Autobiography*

— Ashok Kumar

Nirad C. Chaudhuri (1898-1999), a man of versatile genius, and one of the most controversial writers, enjoys a conspicuous and unassailable place in Indo-Anglian literature. As a brilliant scholar and intellectual he has presented *de novo* ideas on Hinduism and the Hindu way of life. He as one of the greatest intellectuals and writers in contemporary India has been summed up by K.R.S. Iyengar in the following way:

> When all caveats have been made however, Nirad C. Chaudhuri remains the Grand Solitary, the master of a prose style that has after a fascinating spidery quality, a writer and a thinker and a universal Momus who stands apart from the muddy mainstream. His great merit as intellectual is that he isn't ever too lazy to avoid doing his own thinking or too timid to hesitate to give out-spoken expression to his views. Above all, he has the supreme faith of the moral in an amoral (if not immoral) society to make the great categorical affirmation: Whatever clever people might say in defense of unscrupulousness in politics, and about its success there is some power in the universe which sees to it that such cynicism does not pay, and nothing but what is inherently right ever success.[1]

Nirad C. Chaudhuri's *The Autobiography of An Unknown Indian*[2] is the most celebrated and the most vituperative book. The recourse to the first personal singular, far from eschewing authorial intrusion, magnifies it to the extreme. Chaudhuri persistently depends on a self-centered point of view which amounts to an unflinching self-justification. This is one of the optimum examples of this genre to materialise in English in the previous century, and the most considerable, distinct discursive work to be generated by adoration and revulsion of Indian-British interaction. It inconsistently is to a great extent more closely controlled approach. In it, Chaudhuri reveals himself as an entity in scenery or as an inclination in a more inclusive and controlling rhythm, and the entire revelation of the self is astoundingly soothing and objective. While entitled an autobiography, the tone goes beyond the extent of the author's delicate narration and encompasses a decisive interlude of the nationalised history of Bengal.

Chaudhuri initiated writing *The Autobiography of An Unknown Indian* in 1947 and got it published in 1951. This reveals the indispensable ideas that have twisted his extremely idiosyncratic scrutiny of India and the West. It is his foremost reserve but it was so well established that he became celebrated as an extraordinary Indian made intellectual throughout the English speaking world after its publication. The editor of the *Glasgow Herald* writes:

> This is an extraordinary book. It is written by a Hindu of East Bengal who has never been in Europe,[3] yet with a command of English that is not exceeded by Mr. Nehru himself. . . . No other Indian self-portrait can compare, for interest or challenge, with this product of a tortured and assertive spirit. (1)

Nirad C. Chaudhuri was born in 1897, and it is confined to reveal Chaudhuri's life up to 1921 only, when he failed to pass the M.A. examination and entered the work-a-day world to earn a living. It is written in a masculine, self-assured English of long, balanced sentences, which combine a degree of formality with considerable case and lissomness. *The Autobiography of An Unknown Indian,* in the track of revealing the delicate verve of the author, expresses in a representative approach the typical conflict suffered by a middle-class Indian intellectual in the early years of the twentieth century, because of his European sensibility acquired in the course of English education and Western influences.

Subsequently the very close reason that strained Nirad C. Chaudhuri to engrave the autobiographical endeavor seems to radiate from some individual foundation. He revealed that he wanted an avowal of self-reliance, because after passing the age of fifty he was faced with the obligation to carve off the years he had lived so far and instigate life a different. This obligation, nevertheless, arose from a heightened consciousness of being familiar in life, a truth he mentioned but disowned in the same breath. This logic of breakdown is at the derivation of his *The Autobiography of An Unknown Indian,* which evidently affects together its tone and texture, and the autobiography seems to be a research in revenge. On this score, conversely, Chaudhuri cannot be predestined, as George Misch writes, "The urge to talk about their lives is felt even more when they are smarting under the frustration of their hopes of accomplishment."[4]

Subscribing as Nirad C. Chaudhuri does, "to a creed of intellectual Prometheans" (523), he jealously guards his freedom to think and is proud of his iconoclasm, as is clear from his forceful espousal of totally unorthodox views on many issues including Indian history, the Nationalist movement, Hindu religion and culture, etc. *Autobiography* bristles with many highly controversial statements:

> Hinduism. . . has always been an admixture of foreign goodness and indigenous debasement (208).
>
> The Indian middle-class intelligentsia is too worldly wise to be swept off its feet even by the rabid nationalism which is the stable of its recreational mood (255).
>
> Neither his (Gandhi's) station in life nor his English education succeeded in making him understand the things of the intellect and civilisation. He remained profound uneducated in the intellectual sense...Gandhism... remained the morality of servos (444).

The Autobiography of An Unknown Indian was written in the recollection of the British Empire in India which completed, twisted and quickened whatever was good within Indians in

Nirad C. Chaudhuri's view. He believed that India cannot flourish without subordinating itself to the English-speaking world which owned a more humanistic and scientific culture and civilisation than India. His autobiography, thus, intends to project his anti-Indian and pro-Western outlook on life that colours his portrayal of the determining days of his life. He writes:

> My personal development has in no way been typical of a modern Indian of the twentieth century. It is certainly exceptional, and may even be unique. But I do not believe that on this account the value of my narrative as historical testimony is impaired. Rather, the independence of environment which I have always been driven to assert by an irrepressible impulse within me has given me a preternatural sensitiveness to it. In relation to modern Indian society I am like an aeroplane in relation to the earth. It can never rise so high as to be able to sever the terrestrial connexion, but its flight helps it to obtain a better view of the lie of the land (x).

Certainly, his autobiography is more of a countrywide than private narration as it reveals superiority to the upbringing greater than the product. And it is more of an implement in evocative compilation than autobiography. It is less a revelation of his living and celebrity and scarcely touches the subject matter of self-introspection. It is, on the other hand, a erudite scrutiny of his locale. He further writes:

> This book describes the conditions in which an Indian grew to manhood in the early decades of the century. . . . The story I want to tell is the story of the struggle of a civilisation with a hostile environment, in which the destiny of British rule in India became necessarily involved. My main intention is thus historical, and since I have written the account with the utmost honesty and accuracy of which I am capable, the intention in my mind which has become mingled with the aspiration that the book may be regarded as a contribution to contemporary history (ix).

Chaudhuri's fascination for the times of yore has been since his college days, and although only twenty, he wrote an incredible article on "The Objective Method in History"— and his autobiography could indeed be regarded as a contribution to the modern history. If, conversely, we wind up with K. R. S. Iyengar—which, by the way would most probably be the conclusion of every other bookworm of this autobiography is: "It is clear then that Chaudhuri's real aim is to write history and the autobiographical exercise is merely a means to get the history started."[5]

Chaudhuri's autobiography is a history of dreams; even, however, all his dreams are not adequate or sustainable in terms of logic and history what impresses most is his uniqueness, radiance and forth rightness. Opinions surge from his psyche; they however, are not supported by chronological specifics or evidences. But he seeks a validation of these dreams in history. And it is this ideational process that makes Nirad C. Chaudhuri's ingenious venture somewhat thought-provoking.

His *Autobiography* reveals not recurrently, an insight into his probing mind, which has always been vigilant and animate. The commonly· appearance is almost unconsciously given up, and before he becomes sentient of it and turns to his affirmed 'objective method', he expresses the entirely delicate surface. Such 'lucid intervals', taken together, we feel, are capable of providing with a delight no less gratifying than the luxury he has at being enlightened by a unique and original look into India of the past, present, and future, from the historical viewpoint, which is what Chaudhuri explicitly states as his intention in writing his autobiography. And a look into it in search of the purely personal element is warranted, for he does only say that his main intention is historical but not his sole intention.

However, his loom to Indian account is not at all objective but solely slanted. In the closing of his autobiography he contends that Indian customs and evolution had been produced and continued by alien influences right through the course of Indian history which is alienated into three consecutive but divergent cycles:

1) The Indo-Aryan cycle which began in the prehistoric period and ended towards the close of the twelfth century,
2) The Indo-Turkish cycle which commenced with the defeat of Prithviraj Chauhan at the hands of Muhammad of Ghur in A.D. 1191 and came to a close at the time of the battle of Plassey in A.D. 1757, and

3) The Indo-British Cycle which gained momentum towards the middle of the eighteenth century and is still continuing despite India's achievement of freedom from British rule on 15August 1947.

Nirad C. Chaudhuri revealed that in each of the three cycles of Indian history an alien supremacy appeared on the Indian vista and forced its own language, ethnicity and government on the inhabitants of the country. In the first cycle, the Aryans came to India and established the Hindu and Sanskritic empire and communal array here, in the second cycle the Turks invaded India and renewed it into a part of the Islamic territory with Persian as its common language, and in the third cycle the British imperialists took charge of the government of India and made English the common language of the Indian community. Nirad C. Chaudhuri observes:

> The foreign influences in Indian history are exceptional in their character, and are also exceptional in their operation and results. These exceptional and significant features may be summarised under the following heads: first, three of the greatest historical movements have forced their way into India in successive ages and created three different types of civilisation, secondly, the civilisations have remained essentially foreign even at the highest point of their development within India and have ceased to be living as soon as they have been cut off from the source and been assimilated by the previously existing population, thirdly, the civilisations have always been in conflict with the greater portion of the local population, and lastly, neither political order nor civilisation has come into being in India when a powerful external force has not been in possession of the country (592-593).

Nirad C. Chaudhuri contemplates in the book that the Aryans or Hindus not only shared the linguistic, mythological, cultural and social systems of the European peoples but also were cognisant of their distant derivation. He said:

> In carrying out an inquiry into the group-consciousness of the ancient Hindus, there is nothing more striking than the persistent emphasis in all their sacred books, from the Vedas to the Dharmasutras and Dharmasastras, on the distinction

> between the Arya or Aryan and the Anarya or non-Aryan. Without giving as much as a hint in these books or other books that they had ever had any notion of not being natives of the country the Hindus always advertised their sense of being an aristocracy living among hostile and inferior aliens, being always in danger of being swamped by them, and being always under the necessity of defending their society, faith and culture against these enemies. In this matter the ancient Hindu reminds one of the modern Whites, more especially the Boer, in South Africa. The Hindu notion of a hostile internal proletariat was stronger than even the Hindu notion of foreigners as Mlechchhas." (565)

The Autobiography of An Unknown Indian is framed in such divisions that the accustomed chronological sequence has been overturned in as the version of his physical and intellectual milieu had been given at first and that of his birth and rearing afterwards. The revelation again is not chronological as many later dealings and parody have been assorted with the first impressions of the emergent boy. In the prefatory note Chaudhuri reveals that he began to be redolent of his childhood when he had long passed his youth. Aksakov, Renan, Antole France and Ravindranath Tagore also had done so, but Nirad C. Chaudhuri was not, like them, calling up its memories and recording them either as things interesting in themselves or as a foil to his later life. It is not the aspiration of autobiographer to craft that kind of idealistic curiosity or gap. He writes:

> There is no room in it, since it is more of an exercise in descriptive ethnology than autobiography, for presenting childhood against the background of age, for presenting it as a submerged City of Ys or as the times when the intimations of immortality lay about us. If there is to be any vanished or vanishing Atlantis to speak of in this book, it should and would be all our life lived till yesterday. All that we have learnt, all that we have acquired, and all that we have prized is threatened with extinction. We do not know how the end will come, whether through a cataclysmic holocaust or slow, putrid decay. But regarding the eventual extinctions there does not seem to be any uncertainty (149).

The central hypothesis of this autobiography is the edifice of a scholar's acumen, and it is the recitation of a susceptible author's edification. Nirad C. Chaudhuri revealed his verve and separated it in his autobiography into four sub-sections (books). Out of the four books into which this autobiography is divided, three are autobiographical. In the last book Chaudhuri has written essays on political, historical, and sociological topics. One of the distinctive characteristics of this autobiography is that it covers his life up to the first twenty-four years, and has not only given him enough span to present a full picture of both the growth of his mind and his early milieu but it has also endowed a large part of *The Autobicgraphy of An Unknown Indian* with an exceptional vividness and immediacy, because of all human imitations it is perhaps those of early days and teenage years that are the most deeply felt by the him, and hence he can conceivably correspond them with far superior recall than any others. Among Indian English autobiographies, it is indeed unrivalled in that none of its peers reveals as lengthily and widely as it does with the early years of his life.

His autobiography is structured encircling a notion of places, which influenced him in his early life. "The first three, his birth place, his ancestral village and his mother's village are the places where Nirad C. Chaudhuri actually lived as a boy, but the fourth one is England which he had never visited."[3] Yet England has made a major influence in his. As he has recited "Earth has not anything to show fairer", the light of down in all its purity seemed to descend on him, unfolding the celestial beauty of London.

He is significantly enthralled by the vivacity and uncomplicatedness of English characters, by the intellect for the concrete publicised in English art, by the English capacity to give form and solidity to its insight, and by the English gift evident at every point and in all its productions for the differentiated and particular. Himself a man with a relish for the specific, he loved the quality of concreteness in English civilisation. And it was the absence of this in Indian civilisation to which he gave a measured philosophic expression towards the end. He writes:

> I think there is even in the highest and most characteristic teaching of Hinduisms (apart from the layer on layer of infinitely varied primitiveness which constitutes its buried foundation), something impelling a Hindu towards the simpler in preference to the more complex, towards the

> unmerged in preference to the emergent, and towards the general in preference to the particular. According to some of the noblest teaching of Hinduism, the manifested universe is an illusion, the ultimate reality attribute less, and man's supreme happiness lies in putting an end to the cycle of births and deaths, or, in other words, in eliminating precisely those particular forms possessing sensible attributes which confer qualities and values on reality, and clothe it with attractiveness for us. With such a philosophical background it is not surprising that a Hindu should tend to ignore distinctions. To me, however, Hinduism appears to be swimming against the current. Although its penchant for the undifferentiated and attribute less is undoubtedly due to its anxiety to bite on the rock of truth and reality lying underneath the flux of changes, I would still say that in actual fact it is retrograde and out of sympathy with reality. For I believe in change and hold all reality to be a process, a process which is justifying itself, as well as making itself more significant, by becoming more particular and differentiated and by endowing itself with ever more new values (526-527).

Nirad C. Chaudhuri prefaces the revelations of his hometown Kishorganj with a citation from Shakespeare's quixotic jesting *As You Like It*. He writes:

> Who doth ambition shun,
> And loves to live i' the sun,
> Seeking the food he eats,
> And pleased with what he gets,
> Come hither, come hither, come hither:
> Here shall he see
> No enemy
> But winter and rough weather (xvi).

He makes it apparent that Kishorganj had nothing of the English country town about it, since it was only a compilation of tin-and-mat huts or sheds, comprising courts, offices, schools, shops, and residential dwellings rose up in the green and brown spaces of East Bengal by the British administration.

An intellect accordingly insightful as this could not but retort to plead of temperament, and several unforgettable experiences revealed in the autobiography are those which Nirad C.

Chaudhuri's response to the beauty of nature, especially during his boyhood. He refers to a pastoral scene observed during a boyhood journey to the village of Kalikutch. He writes:

> Across the river was a small temporary hamlet such as the peasants in our parts build on the sandbanks of the big rivers. All the huts in it were thatched with bright gold-colored straw, there was a corn rick of the same happy colors in every homestead, the river between us and the village was rippling to a light breeze and shining like cut-glass in the afternoon sun. The scene almost brought tears to my eyes from a sensation of peace. I now come to the inexplicable part of the experience. It lay utterly forgotten and dormant within me for thirty-five years without being recalled even once, But that vision of the golden village across the river was brought back into my memory suddenly, at one stroke, one day in the terrible summer of defeats of 1940 by the tune of one of Haydn's quartets. How and why this happened I am totally unable to explain, because I can trace no perceptible link between the typical East Bengal scene and the snatch of a tune which was perhaps derived from a Croat folk melody (207-208).

The guy who was talented of having this sort of an incident, was no dreamy-eyed passionate vanished in the planet of gorgeousness. His unquenchable thinking oddity is visible every where in his autobiography. As he says:

> My leaning towards encyclopedic knowledge was disclosing them in every intellectual activity I undertook. . . . What I was primarily interested in even as a boy was the meaning and purpose of existence, and since existence had many facts my intellectual interests also became many-sided. Even without my being aware of its deep springs, my appetite for information and explanation became as varied as my mental detention became versatile. I could pass from physics to Sanskrit literature or from novels to astronomy with an agility which seemed like volatility to those who did not know me well...secondly, I was always very anxious to ascertain the position of any subject I was studying in the whole field of knowledge (393).

Days in Kishorganj were made for a coherent inclination of psyche. It presented strength but it also encouraged, basically since manipulate of a venerable, level-headed father, decent intellectual independent. At this time children's indulgent fed an affluent poignant life. The rhythms of the fatherland, the sentiment for blood and ancestors, the existing Bengali customs of theatre, and folk-poetry, the cherished acquaintances of relations and skill deepened and distinguished the children's impend. *The Autobiography of An Unknown Indian* reveals, throughout the minutely meticulous surrounding of everyday life, and interpretation of a decidedly enlightened society, in which theatre, verse, creed and average life were thoroughly amalgamated. He writes:

> We always had plays at the time of religious festivals and weddings, and at times also for their own sake. The repertory, though large, was almost exclusively drawn from either of the great epics, the *Ramayana* or the *Mahabharata*, and the stories were thus familiar to the audience. From this followed that the watching of the plays was even for young people like us not a passive gulping down of a story but an appraisal, in the light of a critical code which was never crude, of points of composition and acting, and, at times, even of doctrine (70).

Together the richness of Nirad C. Chaudhuri's revelation of the days of his escalation and his attempts to bestow a nationalised facet to his delicate history point to a self-centeredness which is actually vast in its self-absorption. Whereas there can, of course, be no autobiography without selfishness, in Nirad C. Chaudhuri the intention of self pre-occupation would emerge to be peculiarly sturdy one is consequently just stunned while in the concluding segment of The Autobiography of An Unknown Indian, he quietly contrasts himself by means of "the rest of the four hundred million, and averse that "while I was being carried away by the momentum of our history, most of my country man were being dragged backwards by its inertia" (522). Complimenting his personal 'emancipation' with that of the rest of his countrymen, he reveals, "They are freed men, I am a free man... I do not know why I should have been singled out for so great a gift of grace"(523).

It definitely desires extra than normal valor for a man to introduce a contrast like this and still additional to stop it with this variety of a climax. Nor is his the just paradigm of its kind in the autobiography. Earlier, commenting on the fact that during the days of the Swadeshi movement, he as a boy was made drill master to all the boys in Kishorganj (some of whom were actually older and stronger). He compares himself with "the young and slight Napoleon cowing down the Massena and Algerians" (523). Up till now, it is unerringly this rampant selfishness that reveals *The Autobiography of An Unknown Indian* its atypical demand.

Nirad C. Chaudhuri has revealed exceptionally and flamboyantly in this autobiography concerning his parents as well. His father Upendra Narayan Chaudhuri was a lawyer by profession and a humanist by conviction. Being a man of towering and honorable disposition, he did not shadow sophisticated powers and opulence. He imparted to his brood a noninterventionist edification which enabled them to widen their proficient skills as well as their oratory skills. He contracted them sovereignty of opinions and trials. He was very curious of learning English and promoted his kids to have an excellent dominion of it. His father brought to the quandary of the edification of his kids an intellectual as well as an emotional fervor. He inculcated in Nirad C. Chaudhuri "a sense that by educating ourselves we should be acquiring, not simply the means to do something else, not simply a key to other kinds of success, but some all-round and absolute goodness which was not mere skill but something desirable in itself" (167). He had a liberal view of education and he did not want his sons to become mere technicians and specialists but also to acquire some ancillary qualifications in the field of art which would lead grace to our life (175). Whitehead sets an analogous venture of edification:

> Culture is activity of thought, and receptiveness to beauty and human feeling.... What we should aim at producing is men who possess both culture and expert knowledge in some special direction.[6]

His father was not in every respect unbiased in his children's worldly wise accomplishment. Certainty, he estimated them to be booming in the human race because he unspecified worldly wise accomplishment to chase brilliance in education. As for him, Nirad C. Chaudhuri revealed that he "fell so headlong in love with the idea of being a scholar gypsy after reading Matthew Arnolds' poems that this love marked its trail on my entire subsequent worldly career" (168).

He was nurtured in an Anglicised coherent ambience which entrenched in him a subterranean adores for English life and literature. His mother used to enlighten him with the fairy-tale of Shakespeare's *King Lear* and later he became a vigorous contestant in the Shakespearean convoy by learning the stories of *The Merchant of Venice.* His father had a huge assortment at home stocked with the works of celebrated English writers. He comprehends these works incredibly ardently. They incorporated the *Holy Bible,* Annandale's *English Dictionary;* Milton's Poetical works, Cunningham's *History of Sikhs,* two volumes of Burke's speeches on the prosecution of Warren Hastings, Shakespeare's *Julius Caesar* and *Othello,* a small number of novels of Bankim Chandra Chatterji, and verse of Michael Madhusudan Datta. Besides these works, Nirad C. Chaudhuri studied in addition a book regarding the conflict of Trafalgar and thus became proverbial with the name of Napoleon Bonaparte. Furthermore, the verses of Colly Cibber, Wordsworth's *Lucy Gray, We are Seven, Daffodils* and *Upon West-minister Bridge,* Shakespeare's *Full Fathom Five,* Webster's *Call for the Robin-red breast and the Wren,* Rupert Brook's *Soldier* and Campbell's *Ye Mariners of England!* enthralled him and gave him an inspiration of the different aspects of England and English dynamism. As a consequence, it was his who culminated a keen interest for wide readings and introduced him to the world of books through his huge library at home.

He learned English from his father. His father laid identical hassle on material guidance and brought for them an assortment of appliances for calisthenics. He consequently, tried to communicate an unbiased, all-round teaching to his offspring. Nirad C. Chaudhuri could extraordinarily categorise his father, for he moved over to Kishorganj to have a self-regulating enterprise. His revelations of his parents are not only a product of his intimacy which would not have been possible in a joint family, with them, but of his self-determining and equitable inquisition of them. About his father he writes:

> In dress he was simple to the point of being shabby. I never saw him in anything but the conventional Bengali dress,

> except that when going to the courts he put on a chapkan and trousers. But in that he was only obeying long-established custom. In the cold season he wrapped a shawl round himself, sometimes also put on an ordinary coat and something even a chesterfield. But he was always giving away the more expensive articles of his clothing to us. He was a man who stood in need of very little personal service and even disliked too much attention of this kind from others. While my mother lived she looked to his personal needs. After her death he would rather be left to himself than made much of (165).

He has revealed that his father was altruistic and utterly unmoved to money, but his mother was the reverse both in manifestation and in attitude. As soon as his father with his family shifted to Calcutta in 1910, he came in contact with an innovative milieu in an electrifying metropolitan area. He acquainted himself with the contemporary legendary and academic society, moreover enlightening a vigorous awareness in existing political opinions. He revealed the roots of these movements to nineteenth-century Bengal. He refers to the latest intellectual activities based on the prescription of a "synthesis" of the values of the East and West, which passes under the names of the Indian Renaissance represented by Raja Ram Mohan Roy and his followers. He also reveals the other important strand in the nineteenth-century Bengali psyche — the Hindu revivalist trend which he feels, was represented by Bankim Chandra Chatterji. This brings him to contemporary politics. He feels that the national movement, dominated by the Hindu middle-class, was irreconcilable with the liberal nationalism, represented to some extent, by the Western trained Brahmo intellectuals who influenced Nirad C. Chaudhuri at a certain stage in his life. He reveals also the roots of the Hindu Muslim divide in the national politics to the Hindu dominated national leadership. But he tends to undermine the role of the British rulers in exploiting the Hindu-Muslim conflict, as evident from his comment that the British rulers did not formulate exercise of it to the level they might have easily done.

Nirad C. Chaudhuri learned greatly from libraries, museums and even the shabby buildings of Calcutta, but remained wholly unaffected by the surge of its daily life. He has revealed concerning his schooling in Calcutta that it was entirety frustration. Right from the start of his academic career he was drawn irresistibly towards history and offered history as the main subject of study in his B.A. course. He did very well in the examination, topping the list of successful candidates. During his M.A. course, however, he began a much wider study of history and failed to pass the examination. Analysing the causes of his failure he revealed that it was perhaps partly due to his lack of vitality and will-power and partly to an extensive reading that was rather diffuse and haphazard. But his ambition was, not merely to take the degree and get a professorship and to become a historian. He writes:

> My insane ambition was to combine Mabillon, Muratori, and Tillenont with Gibbon. The idea of a gigantic corpus piling itself up in annual volumes throughout a life-time, a single-handed Monumental of India history rivaling the corporate Monumental Germaine Historic, and the idea of a stupendous synthesis written on a grand scale over decades and revised on an equally grand scale over succeeding decades obsessed me at the same time. If the synthesis was not to be absolutely like Edward Meyer's Geschichte des Altertums, the least that it had to be was Stern's Geschichte Europass.... (420).

Chaudhuri was a brilliant student but he met some setbacks and the academic life which would surely have been his natural habitat was shut off from him. He endeavoured to scrutinise the causes of his breakdown in order to carve out an academic career for him. Among the causes he notes for his failure to pass the M.A. examination are his absolute lack of vitality and good health, his 'insane ambition' to attempt too much too fast, his tendency to get "frightened or tired out by the too exacting programmer he was always taking the virtuous resolution to put through", and his lack of "will power" (364-65). His attempts to escape the ordeal of the examination took interesting forms : "I ran up and down a ladder quite a number of times, recklessly inviting a fall", and "seeking relief, I turned to the making of card board boxes in my room and the jotting down of my ideas about the organisation of a national army for India" (365). Characteristically sufficient, he in due course unravels the derivation and escalation of his maladjustment in terms of his most wanted chronological notion.

The thrashing was adequately rewarded when he stepped into the dynamic and spirited bookish ambience of Calcutta in the course of one of his uncles who was legitimately engrossed in English and Bengali text. The furthermost occasion of his career he accredited to be his affiliation with the *Encyclopaedia Britannica*, and surprisingly as much as necessary, the opening critique fascinated was on dogs. Chaudhuri's academic career at college was promoted by his over-ambitious routine of elucidation. Regarding his obsession for erudition he revealed that however he in no way became a scholar, he experienced the emotion of scholarship (350).

Consequently, Chaudhuri's autobiography is further elaborated, illuminating and encompasses greatly superior series of incidents. Even though it lacks the structural nimbleness, it nevertheless attracts the oddity for being the accustomed version of his derivation and upbringing however with an elaborated portrayal of the places where he lived in his early days. *The Autobiography of An Unknown Indian*, S.P. Swain comments, "is concerned with Nirad C. Chaudhuri's fascination with himself."[7] The revelation is carried on chronologically, despite the fact that the incidents are not allied chronologically in the stern prudence of the term. Being vastly exploratory and having so numerous digressions, the sequence of events does not give the impression to progress on and incredibly the series of events is out of order, hitherto the revelation is made extremely intriguing by the author's extraordinary domination of estimation and psychoanalysis. *The Autobiography of An Unknown Indian* reveals Nirad C. Chaudhuri's way of life from his genealogy to student days till 1921.

In this way Nirad C. Chaudhuri's estimation as an autobiographer comes from the greatness of his writings, his intellect, his uniqueness, his contentious, recurrently inconsistent sociological theories and records interpretations, the meticulous intellectual dealing with his subjects, the absolute massiveness of particulars he revealed, and greater than that, the self-esteem and demureness of the array of English he writes, in his attempt to be straightforward and categorical in the lexis of his surveillance and credence. *The Autobiography of An Unknown Indian* may appear to be a tribute to lack of consideration for others, it reveals the manifestation of an extraordinary man who could not appreciate precisely the cessation of the huge nationalised excitement of which he was a eyewitness. Hence, this is particularly an intellectual exploration of Nirad C. Chudhuri's outlook not in favor of the background of the Hindu philosophy. These aspects of *The Autobiography of An Unknown Indian* tag it from the common run of autobiographies written by Indians in English.

Notes and References

1. K.R. Srinivasa Iyengar. *Indian Writing in English.* New Delhi: Sterling Publishing House Pvt. Ltd., 1989, 601.
2. Nirad C. Chaudhuri. *The Autobiography of An Unknown Indian,* Bombay: Jaico Publishing House, 1976. All the subsequent quotations are cited from this edition and only page numbers will mentioned thereafter.
3. Nirad C. Chaudhuri visited England for the first time in 1955 at the age of fifty-five and wrote a provocative book entitled *A Passage to England,* London: Macmillan, 1959, on his visit.
4. George Misch. *A History of Autobiographies in Antiquity.* London Routledge and Kegan Paul, 1950, Vol. 1, 10.
5. K.R. Srinivasa Iyengar. *Indian Writing in English.* 591.
6. A.N. Whitehead. *The Aims of Education and Other Essays.* London: Ernost Benn Ltd., 1970, 1.
7. S.P. Swain. "*The Autobiography of An Unknown Indian: A Critique*" in *Nirad C. Chaudhuri: The Scholar Extraordinary,* ed., R.K. Dhawan. New Delhi: Prestige, 2000, 83.

18

Third Space of Enunciation: Reading Bharati Mukherjee's *Jasmine*

— *Beerendra Pandey*

Diasporic in-betweenness empowers the migrant, subaltern subject with a hybrid location, which allows for the construction of a new identity in the crucible of what Homi Bhabha calls the "Third Space of Enunciation" (37):

> It is significant that the productive capacities of this Third Space have a colonial or postcolonial provenance. For a willingness to descend into that alien territory . . . may open the way to conceptualising an international culture, based not on the exoticism of multiculturalism or the diversity of cultures, but on the inscription and articulation of culture's hybridity (38).

The in-between location turns out to be a room for manoueuvre—a site of an enabling agency allowing for an active interference into the perpetuation of inherited tradition rather than an automatic acquiescence in its "eternal" wisdom. The hybrid subject appropriates the received knowledge and reinterprets it so as to be able to operate from a slightly inverted power field for the contestation of his or her representation both in the traditional, native and the (post)modern, alien spaces. Bharati Mukherjee's migrant, female protagonist in *Jasmine* (1989) maintains the agency to make her aphasia "speak" in order to problematise the scene of representation both in the native, third world and the alien, first world. *Jasmine* refashions *Dharma,* the Hindu social order, seen as complicating the issues of bloody violence and female subalternity in the postcolonial Indian society. The novel shows the subaltern-protagonist as bringing to crisis her subalternity with an air of subversiveness, which is reminiscent of the Hindu goddess Kali.

Jasmine points to two major flaws in Hindu *dharma* [social order]: the subaltern position of women and the refusal to acknowledge the harsh reality of the splitting of human blood in the Hindu society. A woman, according to *dharma*, should be self-effacing, submissive and true to the husband to the extent of joining him in celestial joys by performing *sati*—a traditional practice of self-immolation on the funeral pyre of her dead husband. As R. C. Zaehner says, she is "never svatantra [free], she never 'has a thread of her own:' she is not her own mistress. In childhood, she is subject to her father, in marriage to her husband, and after his death to her eldest son" (112). The dha*rma* smacks of double standard: whereas the wife should either opt for *sati* or for a highly restrictive and self-abnegating life, the husband can remarry should she die. The second flaw arises from the thinking that bloodshed is out of place and dangerous in the context of civilised order. The splitting of blood, especially resulting out of a deliberate violent act, is an affront and a threat to the neat vision of the order of *dharma*. Blood, however, has a tendency to shed accidentally and tragically; it can never be avoided as the history of the partition for Pakistan bears out and as the threat of the second partition for Khalistan unleashes in the form of terrorism.

Seized by the need to correct the *dharma* against the bloody backdrop, Bharati Mukherjee's *Jasmine* reincarnates Kali, the goddess of blood and death in the form of Jyoti-turned-Jasmine-turned-Jase-turned-Jane. By paralleling the protagonist as Kali, Mukherjee seeks to put up the order of *dharma* in the right perspective by reminding the Hindus that certain aspects of reality are untamable, unpredictable, and always threatening to society's feeble attempts to order what is essentially disorderly and violent. The hapless victims of old, exploitative society turn out to be mostly the subaltern women who, like Vimala in *Jasmine*, succumb to fatalism. The blow of fate, however, fails to unnerve Jasmine, who overcomes the odds Kali-like: violently and unyieldingly. By thus demonstrating her *Shakti*—the archetypal power of Kali—she beckons the subaltern women to seek a wider, more redemptive vision of their destiny.

The world of the subaltern woman as depicted in *Jasmine* is rural Hasnapur, which steadfastly sticks to the traditional *dharma*. It is "feudal", as Prakash explains to Jasmine, a society where "the woman is still a vassal," where wives use "only pronouns to address their husbands" (77) and "never eat before" them (213), where the husbands "beat" their wives who have to cringe with their "mouth zipped" and "veiled head down" (47). It is a society which denies higher education to girls because their father will "have to wear out (their) sandals" in trying to dispose them off in marriage (47). Girls have no preferences of their own; they are "like cattle; whichever way you lead them that is the way they'll go" (46). Their marriage demands heavy dowries that can beggar "families for generations," thereby rendering the birth of daughters a curse rather than a blessing (39). A woman begetting more females than males is considered to be "heavy with wrongs" in past life (39). All these lead to, as Mataji's abortive attempt of sniping Jasmine at birth shows, to the cases of female infanticide. The lot of both the dowry-less wife and the barren wife is worse than a dog's: "All over our district bad luck wives, rebellious wives, barren wives . . . fell into wells, they got run over by trains, they burned to death heating milk on kerosene stoves" (41). Even those married with dowry may not turn out to be lucky because of their illiteracy and early marriage. The secret of the success of Indian marriage is, as Jasmine comments about the conjugal life of Professor Wadhera and Nirmala in Flushing, which Mukherjee presents as a replica of rural Hasnapur, "an ancient prescription for marital accord: silence, order, authority on the part of Professor Wadhera and submission, beauty, innocence on the part of Nirmala" (151).

In Hasnapur, girls are confined to domesticity when still children. Instead of books to read they are given dung to make cakes. Child marriage is the rule rather than the exception: "The Mazbi maid's daughter, who had been married of eleven . . . already had a miscarriage"(78). Whether old or young, a widow is expected to spend the rest of her life mourning her dead spouse and interceding for his soul: first Mataji and later Jasmine, respectively after the death of their husbands, have to sit in a dark corner, eschewing hot food and praying for the redemption of the souls of the departed husbands. In some cases, as it happens with Mataji, women have to tonsure "her head with a razor" and cloak her "body in coarse cloth" (61). In the dark corner the widows are reduced to the most subaltern of the subalterns: "Except for the visit of my brothers on weekends, Mataji and I were alone in the widow's dark hut, little better than Mazbis and untouchables" (96). In a few cases the widows prefer to perform the sati just as twenty-two years old Vimala "doused herself with kerosene and flung herself on a stove, shouting to the god of death, 'Yama, bring me to you' " (15). As R. C. Zaehner rightly comments:

> It is true that a widow's lot was frequently so miserable that even death may have seemed preferable to a life in which she was still all too often held up to contempt and that she might be forced by public opinion to make the extreme step, but this must be regarded as perversion of dharma which regarded voluntary sacrifice as the highest virtue (112).

In this old *dharma* a widow, like a broken pitcher, has "no insides and outsides" (15). She is a real subaltern; she does not have even female identity because she is male-defined on the outside. She possesses no identity other than that of her husband. This is the rationale behind the *sati* system.

Whereas an Indian widow has to commit *sati* or else lead a dog's life, American women do not remain widow for long, as the narrator says, "With all the old Iowans in Southern California, [Darrel's sister] does not think she will be a widow for long" (9). Mukherjee dramatises the depth of the subalternity of Indian women by foregrounding the contrast between poverty-ridden rural India and prosperous urban America on the one hand and the big difference existing between the status of the women of the two countries on other hand. Rural Hasnapur, the microcosm of third world India—with its lack of basic infrastructure like water, electricity and roads—presents a stark contrast to first world America. As women in Hasnapur scramble for "muddy bucketful" of water, in America too Jasmine who is unable to give up her old Indian habit "store[s] water in orange-juice jars, plastic milk bottles, tumblers, mixing bowls" (16). The cataloguing of the containers is an ironical comment on the drudgery of Indian women in contrast to the mechanised life of abundance and comfort of their American counterparts. Carrying water reveals a truth about female identity in Indian context: it symbolises woman's subservient role in the patriarchal, feudal set-up. American women, to a great extent liberated domestically, politically, socially and sexually, are young at seventy-six (the narrator says so of mother Ripplemeyer), whereas "in Hasnapur a young woman may be old at twenty-two" (15). Even if Jasmine is young enough to reproduce, she "feel[s] old, very old, millennia old, a bug-eyed viewer of beginnings and ends" (34-35). For American women, "experience must be forgotten, or else it kills" (33). Indian women have only bitter experiences to forget since the final nature of the Indian society makes them victims of fate.

In conventional Hasnapur which still reels in backwardness, the traditional and conservative villagers believe in astrology and subscribe to the fate-as-victim belief. The astrologer forecasts seven year old Jyoti's widowhood and exile. Her fate, as he insists on and the villagers would believe, is irreversible like the fate of "Behula's bridegroom" (4). The villagers, as Mataji's remark about the partition bears out, attribute the cracking of India at the time of Independence in 1947, to God's cruelty (41) unlike the narrator who blames Mahatma Gandhi for favoring "the partition of Punjab and the slaughter of millions" (42). Jyoti's rejection of fatalism comes not primarily because of its inexactitude but due to its dismissal of the human agency in controlling future events, insinuating that she cannot carve out her own destiny. However, as long as she is in India the astrological configurations seem to be validated. Such a worldview serves to perpetuate a fatalistic view of life—What is lotted cannot be blotted. Mukherjee ties the belief to the social pressures of feudalistic rural life: "I was the last to be born to that kind of submission, that expectation of ignorance. When the old astrologer swatted me under that banyan tree, we were both acting out a final phase of a social order that had gone untouched for thousand of years" (229). Mukherjee makes astrology a trope of the master narrative of the repressive social order. Seen from this perspective, Jasmine legitimately surmises that if she and Prakash "could just get away from India, then all fates would be cancelled. We'd start with new fates, new stars. We could say or be anything we wanted. We'd be on the other side of the earth, out of God's sight" (85). The copying of the culture of the first world tantalises Jyoti with liberation, but

Bharati Mukherjee shows her as seeing the redemptive vision not in the metropolitan manners and values but in the Hindu myth of Kali.

Unwilling to assent to fatalism, Jyoti challenges the astrologer vigorously and when the latter tries to silence her by chucking on the head, Jasmine is ironically invested with the feeling of the potency of goddess Kali:

> My teeth cut into my tongue. A twig sticking out of the bundle of firewood I'd scavenged a star-shaped wound into my forehead . . . I smelled the sweetness of winter wildflowers. Quails hopped hiding and seeking in the long grass. Squirrels as tiny as mice wished over arms, dropping nuts. The trees were stooped and gnarled, as the ghosts of old women had taken root. I always felt the she-ghosts were guarding me. I didn't feel I was nothing . . . "The bleeding star on my forehead is not a scar," I shouted, "it's my third eye." In other stories that our mother recited, the holiest of sages developed an extra eye right in the middle of their foreheads. Through that eye they peered out into the invisible worlds. "Now I'm a sage" (3-5).

Very early in the novel, Mukherjee makes clear her intention of casting the heroine in the mould of goddess Kali. As her lolling tongue and lips are smeared with blood, Jyoti's cut tongue gives her a similar bloodied and fierce look. Kali's love of the woods and the wild, wherein she is believed to have been surrounded by snakes, jackals and ghosts, finds an echo in the evocation of the wildlife imagery and the ghost-like snarling and gnarling of tornado-swept trees with reference to Jyoti. Similarly, the star-shaped scar on Jyoti's forehead parallels Kali's third eye, the gift of a curse from Lord Shiva for having mocked him for his *trinetra* [third eye] (O' Flaherty 247-48). However, Geoffrey Kain wrongly associates Jasmine's third eye with Lord Shiva's: "The reference to the third eye brings with it inevitable associations with Shiva, god of creation and destruction who, by focusing this third eye on other gods and creatures, achieves periodic destructions of the universe, making way for subsequent periods of renewed life and development" (152).

The third eye endows Jyoti with Kali-like power to see into the invisible and foresee the future. The third eye blazing in the middle of her forehead sheds "a spotlight . . . on lives to come" (21) and enables her to sense "designs in history's muddles" (60). Thus invested with Kali-like potency, Jyoti does not feel herself like typical subaltern women as her older sisters for whom the only goal in life is to be an object of male desire and be accepted as wife: "'What happened?' my sisters shrieked as they sponged the bleeding star on my forehead with the wetted ends of their veils, 'Now your face is scarred for life! How will the family ever find you a husband?'" (4-5). Fleeing from the mockery of her sisters, Jyoti swims along the river until she comes across a carcass of a small dog. As her small fingers touch his body it breaks in two and the stench stays with her: "Everytime I lift a glass of water to my lips, fleetingly I smell it. I know what I don't want to become" (5). The feeling of Kali-like strength gives Jyoti the confidence not to become a conforming subaltern woman like her sisters.

Jyoti gets the first opportunity to display her Kali-like strength to eliminate the evil when, literally speaking a mad dog but metaphorically, a rapist threatens to charge at the squatting women of Hasnapur. She kills the dog in mid-leap with a staff. The killing inaugurates the grand opening of a series of Jyoti's Kali-like individual efforts like the establishing of order in the disordered society through seemingly chaotic actions. Even though the feudalistic male-dominated society, speaking through the mouth of Dida, totally discounts the significance of her individual triumph—"All it means is that God doesn't think you're ready for salvation. Individual efforts count for nothing" (50)—the snub has no effect on her as she responds to greater crises in her life by taking on the dangerous dimension of the divine feminine in full fury. Although Kali establishes order in her role as the slayer of demons, more often than not she is so frenzied that she becomes drunk on the blood of her victims and then she unleashes death. Jyoti-turned-Jasmine, likewise, becomes a "walking death. Death incarnate" (119) when she kills the rapist Half-Face in true Kali style—"above him . . . with [her] mouth open, pouring blood, [her] red tongue out" (118). As Karin rightly remarks, when Jyoti-turned-Jane whirls a trident, she becomes "a tornado" (215). Jasmine's driving with Bud on the gravelled roads of Baden—"I hear gravel chunk against the sides of Rabbit, but it's not rural routes in Baden I'm racing through. I am deep inside a crater on the moon. Before me huge, lunar hogs leap and chew on Darrel's bloodied boots"—parallels Kali's *tandav nritya* [dance of cosmic destruction] (235). The Kali-like dance for the female protagonist is so chaotic that she devours "the cosmos whole" (240).

Kali's seemingly chaotic dance, however, points towards a form of fruitful order. Even in the most violent disorderly act of Kali-Jasmine there is a deep structure of order. Jasmine's saga of self-assertion—her epic journey from feudal Hasnapur to modern America—is marked by violence. The tale of her self-identity turns out to be a parable for the social metamorphosis of post-independence India. The metamorphosis is, however, punctuated by outbreaks of sectarian violence. As Samir Dayal puts it:

> The obverse of the euphoria of Independence was the horror of Partition. The horror has continued in the unceasing violence between Muslims and Hindus, the bloody fighting in Bangladesh, the unresolved Kashmir problem. Before Indira Gandhi's "Emergency"quelled it, the Maoist Naxalite violence in Bengal was another formidable chapter in postcolonial Indian history. The violence associated with the militant Sikh factions agitating for a new Khalistan in Punjab refuses to disappear and in fact is the matrix of Jasmine's emancipatory struggle. As India moves toward modernity, it threatens to crack, if not "Balkanise" itself . . . India's progress toward the twenty-first century is anything if violent. But for the characters in Mukherjee's novel, the West to which Jasmine goes is equally violent, in different ways (66).

Mukherjee, by designing the protagonist on the lines of goddess Kali, seeks to come to terms with violence. The old *dharmic* way of life patterned on the wishful thinking of a non-violent society and Mahatma Gandhi's weapon of non-violence to fight colonialism turns out to be grossly irrelevant in the context of postcolonial realities. Mukherjee seems to suggest that Kali's perfomativity may be the one way in which postcolonial India should seek to come to terms with the built-in shortcomings of its refined view of the world. Kali is mother to her Hindu devotees because she gives birth to a wider vision of reality than the one embodied in the *dharma*. The *dharmic* order is insufficient and restricting without a context, without a frame as it were. Kali frames that order, putting it in a compelling context. Standing outside the *dharmic* order, indeed threatening it, Kali-Jasmine beckons the subaltern Indians to seek a vision of transcending their subalternity.

That Mukherjee takes the subversive activities of Jasmine in the constructive sense of establishing order through disorder is also clear from her choice of the epigraph from James Gleick's *Chaos*. Jasmine, a tornado "is not just a huge storm but a continuum, from the swirling of litter in the street to vast cyclonic systems" (150). In her role of Kali, she demonstrates her shakti, the powerful, ferocious, feminine cosmic principle in violent contrast to *sati*, the ascetic good wife who surrenders her life to the traditional *dharmic* way. Like Kali whom even Shiva cannot control but only becalm, Jasmine never gives her lovers the upper hand. Her sexual freedom functions as a measure of her rapid Westernisation on the one hand and her increasing detachment from the traditional sexual mores on the other. By deserting Bud and opting to go away with Taylor, Jasmine "is not merely choosing men; she is symbolically asserting her right to try and reposition the stars instead of . . . [resigning to] her fate [as any American women would do in normal situations]. In America she has learned that nothing lasts for ever, so she need not condemn herself to a life she does not particularly want" (Brinda Bose, 60). As the ending of the novel shows, Jasmine, Kali-like, is never going to be dominated by whoever is her consort: "I am out of the door and in the potholed and rutted driveway, scrambling ahead of Taylor, greedy with wants and reckless from hope" (241). Jasmine not only succeeds in re-positioning her stars but she also becomes "more assertive in her fight of survival" (Sampat 148). Her survival strategy in America predicates itself on her goal of staving off the common predicament of women in capitalist patriarchy: the exploitation of their sexuality. The use of the trope of Kali in the American part of the novel makes clear how the victimisation of women in a capitalist metropolis may be successfully avoided.

It will be, however, wrong to take the text's dramatisation of the subaltern protagonist's triumphant saga through the trope of Kali alone. As Hoppe observes, Jasmine "enters new and empowering possibilities, both within the aid of her culture's narratives and in other ways that are articulated through the twinned tropes of 'America' and high technology" (143). One of the most decisive moments when the subaltern migrant demonstrates her inherent Kali-like subversiveness so unmistakably—the vendetta in the hotel room of her rape—is triggered by the modern shower glass, the foggy surface of which blurs her indistinct reflection into an image of goddess Kali. Thus Jasmine's violent substitution of self turns out to be a move constitutive of her hybrid space. The transformation from the myopia of a backward Indian village girl into the far-sightedness of a metropolitan lady who finally engages herself in self-aggrandisement comes through the cumulative insight obtaining in the coalescing of the myth of Kali with "the narratives of Americanisation associated with Western locales, mobility, and frontier-hero lifestyles" (Faymonville 53). Jasmine's knack for integrating the Indian religious tradition with mythic American way of life alters the two cultural sites into a power field for her, thereby modifying both. The integration reinforces itself through the novel's support of a possible negotiation between destiny and opportunity, between a sexed subaltern and a subversive woman, and between non-violence and violence.

Finally, Bharati Mukherjee's integration of the Indian and American myths in Jasmine is what turns out to be Bhaba's third space—the in-between site of transition—wherein binary oppositions commingle through conflict. Jasmine's hybrid identity, which is a discursive product, allows itself to be remade and remodelled in such enunciatory ways which enables her to interrogate, reconfigure, and manipulate the received ideas of both native India and metropolis America.

Works Cited

Bhaba, Homi. *The Location of Culture*. London: Routledge, 1994.

Bose, Brinda. "A Question of Identity: Where Gender, race and America meet in Bharati Mukherjee." *Bharati Mukherjee: Critical Perspectives*. Ed. Emmnuel Nelson. New York: Garland Publishing, 1993, 47-63.

Dayal, Samir. "Creating, Preserving, Destroying: Violence in Bharati Mukherjee's *Jasmine*." *Bharati Mukherjee: Critical Perspectives*. Ed. Emmnuel Nelson. New York: Garland Publishing, 1993, 65-88.

Faymonville, Carmen. "Mukherjee's *Jasmine*." *Explicator* 56.1 (Fall 1997): 53-54.

Hoppe, John K. "The Technological Hybrid as Post-American: Cross-Cultural Genetics in *Jasmine*." *Melus* 24.4 (Winter 1999): 137-156.

Kain, Geoffrey. "'Suspended between Two Worlds': Bharati Mukherjee's *Jasmine* and the Fusion of Hindu and American Myth." *Journal of South Asian Literature* 28.1-2 (Spring-Fall 1993): 151-157.

Mukherjee, Bharati. *Jasmine*. New York: Grove Weidenfeld, 1989.

O' Flaherty, Wendy. *Asceticism and Eroticism in the Mythologies of Shiva*. London: Oxford UP, 1973.

Sampat, Manju. "Bharati Mukherjee: The Fiction of Alienation and Identification." *Indian English Fiction 1980-90: An Assessment*. Eds. Nilufer Bharucha & Vilas Sarang. Delhi: B. R. Publishing Corporation, 1994, 139-149.

Zaehner, R.C. *Hinduism*. Oxford: Oxford UP, 1966.

19

Land and Identity in the Poetry of Stephen Gill and Jayanta Mahapatra

— Jaydeep Sarangi

> There is no insurmountable solitude. All paths lead to the same goal: to convey to others what we are. And we must pass through solitude and difficulty, isolation and silence in order to reach forth to the enchanted place where we can dance our clumsy dance and sing our sorrowful song—but in this dance or in this song there are fulfilled the most ancient rites of our conscience in the awareness of being human and of believing in a common destiny.
>
> (Pablo Neruda, Nobel Lecture, December 13, 1971)

The Canadian nation consists of a multiplicity of cultures that is rarely found outside the Commonwealth. From time to time, a variety of people from different socio-cultural backgrounds have sought refuge in this country of the English-and French-speaking people. Multi-culturalism is an essential aspect of the Canadian scene that is reflected in the words of the writers of this land. There is a great variety in the Canadian immigrant experience as recorded in literature. During the last hundred years, many writers of Indian origin, once or twice removed from their first homeland, have gone as immigrants to Canada. The literature of these writers reflects clashes. In an interview with Bruce Meyer, Neil Bissoondath talks of his personal experiences regarding the clash of socio-cultural and socio-linguistic values in a sentimental way:

> I grew up in a culture that restricted me; a culture that imposed its values on me and that had little regard for my personal feelings and desires. From this point of view, I identify with that Japanese girl (in "The Cage") very closely? The girl can't escape her past. When I left Trinidad, I knew I was leaving for good? The girl in this story was incapable of saying that.[1]

Like Bissoondath, other immigrant writers reflect these clashes and talk of their displaced geo-national and socio-linguistic identity. While explaining the role of immigrant writer, Stella Sandahl (1985) says: "He is the one who can convey experiences from different worlds, being himself part of different worlds. Complexity does not mean schizophrenia. We can and should contribute to the common culture and still remain ourselves".[2]

One of such immigrant writers is Stephen Gill. Stephen Gill was born in Sialkot, Pakistan, grew us in India, and settled down permanently in Canada. Canada and India are separated not only by thousands of miles but also by different histories, social and linguistic traditions. In spite of this, both these countries have similarities, especially in terms of language, polity and multi-cultural ethos. Gill, a multi-talented and sensitive Indo-Canadian writer, depicts also the Canadian immigrants experience in his writings. His novel *Immigrant* waxes eloquent over the trials and tribulations of an Indian in Canada. According to P. Parameswari, "Raghunath's existence in Canada signals a shunting between a willful regression to India and a forced progression towards Canada." Canada has been described as "the land of opportunity."[3] Stephen Gill projects the identity of an immigrant:

> I came here
> some thirty years ago
> long before you
> you are not that old.?
> I would have said.
>
> I came here
> carrying the lily of my dreams.
> I have offered
> the boon of my life
> to my new mother
> where would the whites go ?
> how about the Mohawks and Inuit ?
> if you know Canadian history![4]

The poet is aware of his new geo-national identity. Gradually he comes to terms with an alien culture. He does not want to go anywhere:

> do not tell me to go anywhere
> my friend
> this is our land
> where our father lives
> we are all in exile.[4]

Canada, a nation with too much geography and no particular history, possesses a grave challenge to all immigrants, that of charting a cultural territory of one's own or to be doomed with a hyphenated identity forever. An immigrant is always troubled with the thought of going back to his motherland. The apparent similarities between two Homo-sapiens from two parts of the world are often obliterated and over powered by the differences in their attitudes:

> my children are of this earth.
> you want me to go back.
> how insensitive!
> my bones crack
> in pains of despair.[4]

The poems of Stephen Gill depict the basic loneliness / emptiness of the people in exile. Language and culture fabricate a cumulative metaphor for the identity of an individual writer or a poet:

> he views golden gates
> displaying the dances
> of the dragons of disharmony.
> Under the clouds of emptiness.[5]

The man who settles abroad as an immigrant finds himself suffering from basic emptiness and rootlessness. Then which is his home? Is it the new land of opportunity he has dreams or the one he has left behind? In this context, I think of Katherine Mansfield, originally from New Zealand but settled in England. She said that "Wherever I live I write with New Zealand in my bones." [6]

Salman Rushdie points out , "Our physical alienation from India almost inevitably means that we will not be capable of reclaiming precisely the thing that was lost; that we will, in short, create fictions, not actual cities or villages, but invisible ones, imaginary homelands, Indians of the mind."[7]

Writers in Stephens Gill's position, exiles, emigrants or expatriates, are haunted by some sense of loss, urge to reclaim, to look back, even at the risk of being "mutated into the pillars of salt".

At the same time, writers in Stephen Gill's position enrich the Canadian letters because of the uniqueness of their experiences. In his paper presented at the seminar organised by the Canadian Urdu Writers Association on the 9th of January of 1993, in Kingston, Ontario, he said:

> The material that new Canadian writers possess is unique and individual, because of their struggle as newcomers. In their writing, there is a blending of the experiences, traditions and values of the countries of their birth and adoption. This mosaic nature has and will enrich Canadian literature, giving it a universal dimension that it lacks at present.

He further added,

> Canada is in the same situation in which Alexandria and Byzantium stood which helped them grow culturally wealthy. Byzantium flourished for more than a thousand years from 330 AD to about 1400 in Eastern Roman Empire. The location of Byzantium provided the city with some excellent advantages. Byzantium emperors gave a home to refugee scholars and found time to build up lending libraries. It was a cosmopolitan society full of vitality, a half-way house between the East and West.[8]

One of the poems of Stephen Gill that concerns directly with Canada is "The Meechlake Fish" that is about the Meechlake Accord (in 1987) when Canada was badly divided over constitutional amendments. That division could lead to the territorial division of the country. He refers to "racial disharmony" that enters in his land "in the guise of Meechlake fish". It disturbs the "Crystal flow of life." History and its associated teleology have been the means by which the concepts of time have been naturalised for postcolonial societies. Gill maintains a fine balance between hope and despair. At times, his hopes borders on morbidity as he says in "The Meechlake Fish": "Why does autumn lurk on the banks?"[9]

The poetry of Jayanta Mahapatra, on the other hand, is the cross-section of an exotic culture:

> Endless crow noises
> A skull in the holy sands
> Tilts its empty country towards hunger.
> White-clad widowed Women
> Past the centers of their lives
> Are waiting to enter the Great Temple.[10]

The "holy sand" is the long sea-beach where the funeral pyres go on burning. The "Great Temple" is certainly the Temple of Lord Jagannath(a)[11] which is one of the great spiritual centres of India. India is a multi-cultural country where different religions exist side by side. Lord Jagannath(a) is one of the presiding deities, who is worshipped almost all over the state of Orissa. "White-clad widowed women" give us a picture of widows. In this part of India, widows wear dresses in white to express their sense of loss and bereavement for the death of their husband. The seascape runs parallel to the mindscape to give a composite wholeness in the subject. There lies the mastery of Jayanta Mahapatra:

> ...her last wish to be cremated here twisting
> Uncertainly like light on the shifting sands.
> Over the soughing of the sombre wind priests chant
> Louder than ever, the mouth of India opens.[12]

Jayanta Mahapatra sometimes adds notes to communicate with his readers better. About Dawn at Puri he adds: "It is the wish of every pious Hindu to be cremated at Puri. Swargadwara (Gateway to Heaven) is the name of that part of the long sea-beach where the funeral pyres go on burning."

Indian natural setting or topography is vividly expressed in Jayanta Mahapatra's poetry. When he describes the places or rivers he uses regional register, as in *Way of the River*, "The river crosses the forests of Sal and Deodar in a gleam." "Sal and Deodar" are distinctly regional trees and very familiar to Orissa.

Distinctly regional in the poetry of Stephen Gill is snow and the broad highways for which Canada is known. He refers to them when he says in "Recollections of Texas": "When I stare vacantly/ along the frozen banks/ of my land's silent highways in the winter of my visions".[13] He builds a scene of the snowflakes falling:

> White and soft
> like the wings of a dove
> they are.
>
> ...they fall silently
> on the trees
> slanted roofs
> deserted roads
> and windy paths...[14]

In "Songs of a New Canadian,"[15] he talks of seasons and other aspects of nature, including springs, summer and fall and skies and joyful birds, and also rivers and lakes/wide and long highways. In "Spring is Around", he describes the beauty of the summer when Canadians are caught in the web of spring madness. In this season, "snow frees life", "life will breathe again, as snow yields warmth."[16]

One feature of Jayanta Mahapatra's poetry is socio-cultural deterioration of the present generation. In a state of fix, he tries to go deep into the problem. He is concerned about the present state of India:

> What is wrong with my country?
> The jungles have become gentle, the women restless.
> And history reposes between the college girl's breasts:
> the exploits of warrior-queens, the pride pieced together.[17]

He moves even deeper: hiding jungles in her purse, holding on to her divorce, and a lonely Ph.D."[18] Things have changed over the years. Now new women are free to get into higher education. They can even go on for research and can mark their contribution. But what troubles him is the flexibility of the husband-wife knot in the conjugal life. Economic freedom strengthens the womenfolk to stand on their own. In his poetry, the present persistently appears grey, barren and morally corrupt. Those who live today are not alive in their own way. They are only "the grapping noise in my earth." Their courage has failed, their sexual vitality is sapped, and like the poet's one time friends, or the women in his poetry, they have betrayed the nation and the vision:

> The present opens its toothless mouth wide,
> the earth seems loose, feet are cold
> the dignity we had relied upon
> stares at us from the bottom of the sea.[19]

Stephen Gill also bemoans some losses due to the modern education. However, his bemoans are not confined to one nation. They are universal. One poem that expresses this attitude of the poet is "Contemporary Humans"; another is "A Ph.D. Says". Both are from *Songs of Harmony*.[20] *In* "We Are Proud,"[21] he says that the educated person of today has not learnt to touch the moon of human heart, though he has learnt enough about the distant planets.

Life in Indian slums is pathetic and pitiable. Jayanta Mahapatra portrays them in his poem "Slum":

> Your madness catches me:
> Scarred shacks nights begin,
> and full orange fires
> so dreadful on women's faces.
>
> Only that I must summon courage to be in,
> spits of wind chawing at the flame,
> that keep burning here, from the dark mirror
> resting on pain and plain despair.

He photographically projects "a lonely girl, beaten in battle". The girl is a representative who is like crushed flowers and feels sad. She feels limp, bruised, tired and crushed. Her sensibility is shaped by the Indian environment and climate:

> ...there stand
> only a lonely girl, beaten in battle, all mine,
> sadly licking the blood from my crazed smile.[22]

The poetry of Stephen Gill has not much to do with the local geography of Canada, except the Canadian dream of peace. With the exception of a few poems, he is largely a globally oriented poet. In the words of Dr. John Gorman, Stephen Gill's "poetry concerned with racism, violence, famine, war, ecological pollution, greeds and madnesses and every sort of exile, finds itself coming to rest every once in a while in New York at the United Nations."[23] This aspect of Stephen Gill's poetry that is based on world consciousness has been confirmed by other critics.

The recurrent theme in Gill's poetry is peace, and a recurrent theme in Jayanta Mahapatra is the sculpting of Konarak(a). "Konarak" exhibits a great tradition of Indian sculpting:

> I must carry the stone I found
> In the late afternoon light
> me not think of myself only,
> and my pain which possesses
> these last breaths of my life...[24]

The sculpting of Konark(a) casts a deep impact on the visitors. In his poem, he refers to "proud Konarka of the soul". Konarka is a true symbol of Indian heritage and culture. "the red stone walls/ of Konarak/Bhubaneswar and Puri" come again and again in his poetry.

Within the ambit of his poetry, the past holds us down. In the process, India is invoked in the generic. The timeless sculpting to Konark remains abstract, untouched by generation after generation. His language reinforces this effect:

> Konarka, black is sleep cold become of my silent land
> messenger of death.
> here the little boy in a dream waved to the Man once and
> death hund its peace;
> an indifferent time of stone marks the burnt-out funeral
> pyre and the Sunrise that journeys again and again to call
> this grief of man its own.[25]

India is a land of myths. Jayanta Mahapatra often refers to these myths to establish his point. In "Performance", he deliberately refers to Kurukshetra: *"Now is the instant when I can not recognise myself, / amazed by the silence after Kurushetra"*.[26]

Linguistic multiplicity and cultural diversity in India may apparently contribute to a poet's identity; but in reality, these forces remain committed to defining, and authenticating a distinctive identity. Jayanta Mahapatra is a Christian, living in a Hindu society— a society which pays maximum homage to Lord Jagannatha, the presiding deity of Orissa. Jayanta Mahapatra's grandfather accepted Christianity out of compelling forces of famine and poverty. There is always a sense of insecurity and alienation in his poetry. He perpetuates his quest for identity and he is keen on the assertion of his self-emanating from a veritable part of his holy land and its rich socio-religious traditions.

Contrary to this, the poetry of Stephen Gill discovers a different metaphor for identity. "As an ethnic writer and poet, Stephen Gill enriches the mosaic-tapestry of Canadian culture and values with his Indian background and Asian learning. The immigrant sensibility of the novelist Gill extends into the poet Gill, whose creative negotiation absorbs the conflict of cultures without being bitter."[27] Gill's poetry traces the nature of cross-cultural encounter and cultural-shock syndrome. Stephen Gill's poetic vision is that of a home-bound pilgrim. "His immigrant consciousness and sense of alienation are at the core of many of his poems. The Canadian in me/ works harder day after day/ to pay his bills/ hoping one day/ he would be free. He has retorted and reassured his commitment to his adopted country in the poem *Go Back.*"[28]

If at all there is any religion for the poet, that religion must be peace. Peace is the centre of his creative activities. It may be due to his experiences when he was growing in New Delhi. He witnessed people killing one another in the name of religion and he hears about such killings even now. In the preface to his collection *Shrine*, he says:

> In my early teens in those days, we used to live in Karol Bagh, New Delhi. Every time there was a stir caused by the wind, a car on the street, the bark of a dog, or the mew of a cat, we froze inside our house. Every time there was anything unusual, unseen tragedy was expected. The nights were nightmares and the days did not bring any hope. Often, the mornings dawned with more lamentable events. It was not easy to sleep when night after night the ghosts of fear looked straight into our eyes. It turned into an obsession that afflicted me every minute of every hour that whom to trust and to take in confidence. Passers-by and neighbours

> appeared to be the possible killers. Apparently to me, the dragons of religious terror for minorities roamed around freely.[29]

It was this fear that forced him to get out of that atmosphere of religious fanaticism. This fear tormented Stephen Gill and his entire life. He took poetry as a mission for peace. He writes articles and poems against religious fanaticism. In *Songs for Harmony*, he touches peace when he asks in one poem, "Angel/ if you lend me your heart/ I shall also embrace patience/ and feel the flesh of peace". In another poem, "Refreshing winds of the morning/ shape my pen into a plough/ that will prepare my land/ for sowing harmony/ wherever its blade touches".[30] In his poem "Discriminators" he calls fanatics "smiling shylocks, who rest in rusted tombs". In his collection Shrine, fanaticism "is bearer of deformed urchins/ in the ruins of assumptions. It grows/ on the babel of confusion/ in the lap of/ the blinding dust of vanity/ by the arrogant prince of ignorance".[31]

> In "Terrorists," he asks,
> Why
> do they promote
> the twisted agenda
> of insanity.
>
> Why
> do they love
> the catechism of ruin.
> Why do they commit outrages
> which are futile.[32]

The poet seeks refuge in the "Isle of Art":

> Away from the life-stifling smoke
> from the heartbreak house
> lies a lonely isle of art
> where I have carved
> an Eden...
> In this garden
> no more ice of silence
> no doors, no locks, no keys.
> The logs
> In my soul's fire-place
> burn the bigotry beasts.

No haste, no worry, no malice
no dark prejudice lurks here
eyes set on the horizon
a new Adam I breathe.[33]

Stephen Gill seeks the help of the dove to spread his message of peace. He also seeks the help of the Prince of Peace. His last poem in *Divergent Shades* is addressed to the Prince of Peace who is "Strength of the weak" and who "shall awaken/ the season of blossoming." His first poem in *Songs for Harmony* in the form of a prayer is also to Prince of Peace. Stephen Gill has written several poems about the dove and often mentions Prince of Peace in his poetry. The poem "Dove of Peace," in his collection by the same name, and "Seeking the Dove of Peace," in *Songs for Harmony*, and "To Dove," "Flight of a Dove," "My Dove," are just about this bird in his collection *Shrine*.

Because he was forced to leave the land of his birth by fanaticism, he has made Canada his home that is the symbol of peace for him. He has presented papers in international conferences on his belief that Canada provides a blueprint for world peace. He presented such a paper in 1999 at a conference of the Himachel Pradesh University that was chaired by the Assistant Ambassador of Canada in India. The gist of this blueprint is the acceptance of multi-culturalism. He adores the country of his adoption for accepting this concept of diversity. He believes that home is where our feet are and we had better place our heart where the feet are.[34] Canada is his home, that is clear from his poems, particularly from "Song of a New Canadian" in *The Dove of Peace* and "Meechlake Fish" in *Songs for Harmony*.

The realisation of a necessity to identify with a specified place along with its social, geo-historical and traditional background is obviously the epicentre of a matured creative writer's consciousness. Jayanta Mahapatra's poetry celebrates the essence of an Indian sensibility— a sensibility fostered by "The rain and the sun who seem to do nothing new to the earth" (*Summer Dusts*), a sensibility moulded by a reckless innocence, and a sensibility so exquisitely tethered to the belief that things happen as the consequence of things that happened before, and that nothing can change the entire sequence of things, amidst temples and shrines, with their festivals, feasts and fasting. His identification with Orissa is total. Orissa has been a most pleasant and painful experience for him. Orissa is the hub of Jayanta Mahapatra's iconoclastic perambulation. Jayanta Mahapatra's penetrating eyes don't leave any aspect of Orissa's culture unvisited. The temples in ruins, priests behaving like crows, lepers clotting at the gate of the Great Temple, widows standing outside the temple in a queue for "darshan" of the deity, rearing of the cows, the great car festival in Puri, the ghastly effects of the Kalinga were rituals of marriage all these images appear amply.

Jayanta Mahapatra's poetry reveals the vast range of his outlook, the multifarious themes and above all his distinct style. The use of private symbols and seemingly opaque image demand a thorough and close reading. He has consistently struggled with language to develop and use a human language in his poetry. His uniqueness as an Indian poet writing details of landscape that come out alive in his poetry suggests the voice of a true insider.

Among the Canada-based Asian poets writing today, Stephen Gill is one of the few who speak of Canadian landscapes with the assurance of an insider. He makes humble acknowledgement to Canada, his second home:

> O Canada!
> My well of love
> full for thee.
> A peace-adorning dove! (*The Dove of Peace*).

The generative power of the "dove" is used to reveal the mystery. His "dove" symbol stands for harmony in social order and in human mind. The "Dove" symbol appears again and again in his poetry. There is a hint of Christianity in the use of the "dove" symbol. Like Jayanta Mahapatra, Gill is a Christian. His dove symbol can be compared to "rain" (symbol of unity), a symbol in Mahapatra's poetry. Rain brings assurance to life. "Dove" stands for totality in life. Stephen Gill reveals this complete vision of life in a harmonised Canadian identity. His Canadian identity is comprehensive.

Jayanta Mahapatra is a greatly respected Indian poet. He was born in Orissa, India, lives in India and writes about India, observing the country closely. He is India's most celebrated poet and *"one of its best known abroad"*.[35] Stephen Gill, on the other hand, was born in Pakistan. His parents moved to New Delhi after partition. He went to Ethiopia to teach for three years. After the expiry of his contract, he went to England and eventually settled in Canada. He has been to Italy, Germany, Sweden and the United States. He has studied in India, Canada and England. His experiences and studies have made him a citizen of the world. His poetry reflects his world consciousness. He "is an impressive poet because he is compassionate, and because of the beauty of his poetry which is the voice for those who are voiceless."[36] According to Prof. Dr. John Gorman "Stephen Gill's is a visionary life that thrives among the unpredictable connections that make the characteristic experience of our odd century. From a small Canadian city on the banks of the St. Lawrence, he weaves a poetry of worldwide consciousness."[37]

Jayanta Mahapatra is also a translator of poetry from Oriya and writes in prose in this language. Stephen Gill writes poetry occasionally in Urdu, Hindi and Punjabi languages.

References

1. Qtd. In Charu C. Srishra, Discourses of Displacement: South Asian voices from Canada. *The Commonwealth Review,* Vol. XII, No.2, 2003, Page 23.
2. Stella Sandahl *South Asian Literature : A Linguistic Perspective,* A Meeting of Streams, ed.M.G. Vassanji, Toronto: TSAR, 1985.
3. Stephen Gill. *Immigrant,* Ont.: Vesta, 1982, p. 8. All textual references are from this edition of *Immigrant.*
4. *Shrine* (collection of poems) by Stephen Gill. World University Press (USA), 1999, p. 79.
5. Ibid., pp.78, *261-glimpses.*
6. M. Thope, *Modern Prose,* Oxford: OUP, 1968 rpt. In 1994, p.115.
7. Salman Rushdie, *Imaginary Homelands,* London : Granta Books, 1991, p.14.
8. A paper presented at the seminar organised by the Canadian Urdu Writers Association on the 9th of January of 1993 at Days Inn in Kingston, Ont. Canada.
9. *Songs for Harmony* (collection of poems) by Stephen Gill. Vesta Publications, 1992, p. 46.
10. *Dawn at Puri.*

11. The Oriya speakers of English tend to add "a" after Jagannath. This happens due to their mother-tongue-pull.
12. *Dawn at Puri.*
13. *Divergent Shades* (poems) by Stephen Gill. Writers' Forum, Ranchi, India, 1995, p.33.
14. Snowflakes," *Songs for Harmony*. Vesta, 1992. p.30.
15. "Song of a New Canadian," *The Dove of Peace*. M.A.F. Press, New York, 1993, p.27.
16. *Songs for Harmony*. Vesta, 1992.
17. *The Twentyfifth Anniversary of a Republic*: 1975.
18. *Ibid.*
19. *Ibid.*
20. *Songs for Harmony*, ibid.
21. "We Are Proud," *The Dove of Peace*. M.A.F. Press, New York, 1993, p.15.
22. *Slum* (poems) by Jayanta Mahapatra.
23. *Songs for Harmony*, ibid.
24. *Konaraka* (poems) by Jayanta Mahapatra.
25. *Konarka*————————————.
26. *Ibid.*
27. "A Search for Elysium" by Prof. Dr. R.K. Singh & Mitali De Sarkar. *The Mawaheb International*, Canada, June 1998.
28. "Shrine," by Dr. S. Samal. *Replica* (India). January-March 2000, pp. 64-65.
29. *Shrine* op.cit., p.8.
30. *Songs for Harmony*, op.cit., p.10.
31. *Shrine* op.cit., p.63.
32. *Ibid.*, p.154.
33. *Songs for Harmony*, op.cit., p.33.
34. Uma Parameswaram, "Home is where your Feet are, and May your Heart be there", *Writers of Indian Daspara:Theory and Practice* ed. Jasbir Jain, New Delhi : Rawat, 1998, p.30.
35. "A Conversation with Jayanta Mahapatra," by Rabindra Swain and Preston Merchant. *Contemporary Poetry Review*. April 2004.
36. "Shrine," by Bianca Elliot published in Masihi Sansar. April 15, 2001, p.7.
37. Prof. Dr. John Gorman says in his introduction to *Songs for Harmony*, op.cit., 1992.

20

Diasporic Interpolations in Indian Films

— M. Rizwan Khan

Talking about the Bollywood films and the Indian diaspora in Germany Christiane Brosius, in her essay, *The Scattered Homelands of the Migrants: Bollyworld through the Diasporic Lens*, observes:

> The South Asian shops are somewhat condensed illuminations of a parallel world: alongside trays filled with triangular henna tubes, samosas and wedding garlands, shelves offer film magazines such as *Stardust* or *Filmfare* and postcards of film stars Shah Rukh Khan and Kajol. Walls are covered with posters announcing classical and pop concerts, lectures on religious issues, as well as, the screening of the latest blockbuster. (2005:207)

The observation brings to light the relationship of Indian films with the diaspora as the other cultural entities like henna tubes, samosas or wedding garlands are related to them. Often, Indian diaspora has been talked about for its famous attachments to the popular Indian films from the time since Mehboob Khan's *Mother India* and Raj Kapoor's *Awara* were screened in the West and in the erstwhile USSR. Shooting films in foreign locations and having them screened in foreign lands is a phenomenon that goes back to the days when the films like *An Evening in Paris* or *Love in Tokyo* were made.

One can definitely say that because of the ever expanding magnitude of the Indian diaspora (or even the South Asian diaspora in general) the popularity of the Indian films has been growing too to the extent that there is huge overseas market for the Indian films today. Various studies that have been taken up to unravel the reasons behind this attachment of the diasporic communities with films range from being cultural to psychological, ethnic, etc. The aspects related to the Indian diaspora and the films in India may be discussed under the following heads:

> First of all, a few facts about the Indian diaspora and the films in India. Secondly, a mention of the reasons for which the Indian films have become a part of the cultural constructs that are fondly cherished by the Indian diasporic communities. Thirdly, a study of the ways in which the Bollywood films have been responding to the overtures of the diasporic audience. Finally, a detailed account of those films that have been made recently with interpolations that cater to the entertainment needs of the diasporic audience.

The Indian films form an intricate part of the cultural patterns carved out in the collective memory and the mass psychology of the Indian diaspora. They often look up to the films as a junction where they exchange, recall, recollect, relive, revive and remember their ethnic roots, their homeland, their culture, their forefathers, their glories, their youth , their gains, their losses, their pains their achievements and their struggles. These suppressed and not so suppressed desires are included in William Safran's definition of diaspora, saying the diaspora communities:

> Retain a collective memory, vision or myth about their homeland—its physical location, history and achievements; Believe that they are not and perhaps cannot be fully accepted by their host society and, therefore, feel partly alienated and insulated from it; Believe that they should, collectively, be committed to maintenance or restoration of their original homeland and to its safety and prosperity; Continue to relate personally or vicariously to that homeland in one way or another and their ethno cultural consciousness and solidarity are importantly defined by the existence of such a relationship (Safran, 1991: 83-84).

Most of these notions mentioned in Safran's definition of the diaspora are put forth by the Indian films to the Indian diaspora.

The process of believing, relating and retaining is fulfilled at a junction which in this case happens to be the film. In the words of Christiane Brosius this junction or the films (Bollywood) for the Indian diaspora is a 'contact zone', as she says: "In proposing a discussion of Bollywood as a 'contact zone,' I aspire to circumvent the idea of a singular cultural space from which transnational identities emerge" (2005:208).

The popularity of the Indian films among the diasporic communities across the world explicates the theoretical diasporic perspectives. Although the desire to come back to the homeland is witnessed as a common phenomena among the diasporic communities but very few actually return. Thus the 'myth of return' and 'lived experience of a locality' (Brah, 1996, 192) combine to form the notion of 'homing desire' (Brosius, 2005, 208). Smadar Lavie and Ted Swedenburg's claim to recognise the existence of 'many geographies of identity' (1996:4) also strengthens the notion of 'homing desire'. The films form a significant portion of these overlapping geographies which have 'lucid or oscillating borders' (Brosius, 2005, 208). Now when I say diasporic interpolations in the Indian films, I am to foreground these 'geographies of identity' in the diasporic communities' efforts to gratify the 'homing desire' while they enjoy the films. From Subash Ghai's *Pardes*, Aditya Chopra's *Dilwale Dulhaniya Le Jaayenge* to Karan Johar's *Kabhie Alwida Na Kehna* the Indian films are bringing forth not just the Indianness to the diaspora which traditionally reminds them of their homeland, but these films also bring forth the diasporic images and meaningful signifiers for identifications to the diasporic audience. Thus the 'diasporic interpolation' refers to the journey of the Indian films from being popular among the diaspora (for the reason that they offer Indianness) to presenting diasporic themes and plots shot in the locales that are not so unfamiliar to the diaspora but definitely etched out within the framework of Indianness that has been retained by them, i.e., by the diasporic communities.

Before going on to talk about the diaspora and the Bollywood films, certain facts about the Indian films are significant to be mentioned: According to Derek Bose, "film factotum and man about town, Amit Khanna, claims to be the first to have used the expression (Bollywood) in a news story published sometime in the seventies". *The Journal of Bengal Motion Picture Association*" had coined the word, Tollywood—way back in the thirties—to describe a certain kind of 'Progressive' ('read Westernised') cinema produced by Calcutta's Tollygunge Studios. From this somewhere along the way came Bollywood. *The Oxford English Dictionary* recognises Bollywood as a colloquial representation of 'India's popular film industry based in Mumbai—a blend of Bombay (Mumbai was earlier known as Bombay) and Hollywood" (2006:11).

Bollywood produces 200 films annually. Hindi film producers put in 3.8 billion dollars for their 200 films. The temptation to tap the overseas market spurred mainly by the multiplication factor of foreign exchange *vis-à-vis* the Indian rupee. A normal cinema ticket worth $12 in the US, for instance, works out to more than Rs.500 or 35 times what the producer gets on an average for screening the same film back home. Thus producers who were till the other day sending out only three-four prints of a film abroad, have begun releasing up to 40 prints there (Bose, 2006, 29).

It has been the dream of every Bollywood film maker to produce that one international hit in the glory of which he could bask the rest of his life. The first to get anywhere close to achieving this has been Aditya Chopra's *Dilwale Dulhaniya Le Jaayenge.* At present, there are following three key market territories where Bollywood cinema has found a degree of acceptance: Indian diaspora mainly in the US, the UK, South Africa, Canada and the Middle East. The biggest concentration of settlers of Indian extraction in the world is in Myanmar (almost twice that of US), but they remain largely untouched by Bollywood owing to political and diplomatic restrictions, and neighbouring countries where Hindi is understood if not spoken, that is Pakistan, Nepal, Bangladesh, Sri Lanka and Malaysia. The success of Bollywood cinema in these markets, is, however, driven not by content but by the popularity of lead performers. Non-traditional/ new markets like Greece and the CIS (Commonwealth of Independent States) countries where Hindi films were extremely popular till around the early seventies, Bollywood cinema is now revisiting these countries, but with the subtitled or the dubbed content (Bose, 2006, 205).

If one asks the question as to why the Bollywood films are popular among the Indian diaspora then one may often feel that the answer is too obvious to be discussed but the truth is that in the present scenario the answer to this question leads one to a whole range of interesting reasons mentioned below, which unravel new cultural trends among the diasporic audiences: Bollywood films are looked up to for the moral values and cultural identity. First-generation diasporic audiences consider the Hindi films as a 'fortress' (Brosius, 2005, 215) and agents of authority for generating and enforcing ideas of a paradisiacal homeland and notions of an authentic culture. Besides being a container of 'Indianess' – that is, idealised cultural 'Indianness'—the films lately have been projecting Westernness as not an entirely alien notion which is something that makes the diasporic audience feel at home. In a way the elders in the diaspora feel the film viewing as education and entertainment being combined together.

The idea to keep one's own cultural identity 'clean' both derives from, and results in, a constant act of imagining (South Asian) culture as homogeneous entity, by giving 'homing' a privileged place away from allegedly threatening western influences (Brosius, 2005, 220). The Bollywood film is a 'helping hand' for first generation migrants to communicate 'culture' as a given fact, something one has to keep and appreciate like family photographs. The invocation steps in when institutions, such as schools, and networks such as cultural and religious centres, in the diasporic context are seen as failing to provide adequate socialisation. Migration has become a danger zone in which essentialised values and ideals are felt to be constantly challenged, destabilised and thus weakened. The films serve as a backdrop for negotiations, dramatisations and dichotomisation.

The diasporic settlers do not actually get to see too many birthdays, weddings, and funerals. So they try to get them be seen through the films. The depiction of a wedding with the grandeur, for example, contributes to the elaboration of a vocabulary of a 'transnational realism'. With this practice 'authentic cultural practices turn into commodities' (Brosius, 2005, 223-24). In the wake of growing middle class and economic liberalisation in India in early 1990s, filmy weddings gained an inflationary popularity; many films are centred on wedding narratives.

The depiction of the protagonists in the recent films as the perpetuators of the multicultural and balanced outlook makes the films more lifelike for the diasporic audience since the cultural competence of highest value 'to be both'—to be able to comfortably navigate between two or more worlds without breaking with tradition—is a practical formula for survival. The diaspora people feel that they are foreigners there in the foreign and there in the home country also and so they wish to learn their culture in order to return to the home.

The international fame of the stars like Amitabh Bachchan (who became the first Indian to be sculpted at the Madam Toussaud's Museum) and Aishwarya Rai (who became Miss World) make the diaspora more comfortable in the foreign land as they, too, now have their own brand-names to match with the consumerism of the developed nations.

The discussion of Bollywood films as moral universes of nationhood, familial values and notions of sexuality enables to understand that a clear separation of homeland and 'exile' is neither possible nor desired by the diaspora communities. NRI patronising the Indian films abroad is not a new phenomenon. What's new is the resource pool they have come to represent. For example, following U.S. based IT baron, Kawal Rekhi's example many more silicon-valley diaspora professionals are showing the interest in investing in Bollywood.

Films in the Pre-1990s

Films made in the earlier times about the lives of the expatriate Indians dealt mostly with the problems like loneliness suffered in the alien land, struggle to strive in the hardships, earning for one's people back home, facing the discriminations of various kinds, etc. Overall, those films had an innate desire on the part of the diasporic settlers to return to their homeland, and also mostly the solution to all the problems was coming back to one's homeland. Most of the characters depicted in the films were generally first-generation expatriates.

One of the very early films of such sort is *Des Pardes* in which the protagonist is played by Dev Anand. He goes to England in order to search his elder brother (played by Pran) who had gone for a job to England and has got murdered at the hands of the agents who facilitate the illegal stay of the expatriates after charging them huge money. Such Indians are shown taking up small jobs with meagre salaries in extremely difficult conditions to survive. The film is all about how then Dev Anand gets the culprits to the book and also gets their Indian counterparts hooked. The film had a message—that the West posed only a glossy picture of smooth and luxurious life to the unemployed youths in India who would desert their homeland and would sell off all their belongings in order to fulfil their dream of earning richer currencies in the distant lands. The reality was not so glossy and there lay a grim reality which meant living a substandard life and facing all sorts of hardships for not being in one's own land.

Hare Rama Hare Krishna, another film by Dev Anand, though mainly talks of the Hippie movement of the sixties, yet is worth a mention here for being related to the lives of the Indian diaspora in the West. Dev Anand and Zeenat Aman, the two siblings' parents, while living in the US are shown to be completely callous towards their conventions and family values, which leads to a separation between them. The siblings face a forced painful separation as the son has to go with the mother and the daughter is taken away by the father. The sister is not able to fill up the emotional vacuity and undergoes traumatic depression while living a life without peace with her stepmother and father. The result is that she gets addicted to drugs and leaves her house with her Hippie boyfriend and takes to street life, running with a group of Hippies from one country to another. Finally she lands up in Nepal where her brother, who has grown up to be a good-looking, balanced mind, dutiful and patriotic young officer, identifies her. The reason for all these qualities is shown to be that he was closer to his roots and held on to his values as he grew up in his homeland after coming from the West with his mother. Though the dutiful son, loving brother and caring man is not able to bring her sister back to the family-fold as she finally dies, but definitely makes her realise that giving up one's roots and values lead one nowhere and the influence of the West in the form of Hippiism is again something to be kept off. Besides this, the homecoming, that is coming back to one's homeland is again shown as a silver-lining as the mother and father unite again and regret their past in the 'other' land as their son rekindles in them the love for one's culture, custom, religion and family.

Manoj Kumar's *Purab and Paschim* does not leave much to be guessed as the title itself declares the West as a separate and distant influence on the East. The protagonist played by Manoj Kumar is patriotic, educated, cultured, good-looking, respectful towards his upbringing, confident of his faith, modern in outlook, committed to his countrymen's welfare, honest in his love and strong enough in his will to change the heart of those expatriates who have deserted the country after having acquired a new land in their heart and behaviour as their new homeland. Saira Bano (the lady love of the protagonist and a completely Westernised girl), insists that her fiancé, Manoj Kumar, should desert his country in order to marry her. Manoj Kumar makes his fiancée agree to visit India just once before the marriage as he was confident of the change of heart that Saira Bano would undergo by just visiting India once. It happened the way he had expected and the film ends on a positive note that the homeland never goes off from the heartland; it just needs to be revisited. Thus again this film presented forth the coming back to one's homeland as the inevitable destiny of the diaspora people which brings joy and peace in the being.

Another film *Naam* depicts homecoming in a different mould. Sanjay Dutt and Kumar Gaurav play the two brothers. Sanjay Dutt goes to Dubai to try his luck in some business. His misfortune takes him to a wrong set of people and he gets charged with drug-peddling. Along with other Indians and some South Asian diasporic settlers he is also shown to be suffering in the foreign land with the pain of alienation. The brother Kumar Gaurav goes to rescue and bring back his brother. Unfortunately Sanjay Dutt is murdered in the film. In a very painful and heart-rending series of events there is one more homecoming but this time it's too late as Kumar Gaurav brings back his dead brother's ashes. Not only the mother, but also the younger brother and Sanjay's fiancée (played by Amrita Singh) all undergo an agonising pain that puts forth an advice for the distracted and unemployed youth and the expatriates—that escaping away from one's homeland under the fear of hardships takes one to further problems only because such an escape is the escape from reality. The film is based on the contemporary scenario of the South Asian region as there created a sudden popularity of settling–in-the-other-country notion in search of greener pastures which would provide wealth and welfare.

Films in the Post-1990s

The films in post-90s made with the diasporic interpolations foreground entirely different notions related to the Indian diaspora. Among the films that have been made with the diasporic interpolations in the post-90s the prominent are *Pardes, Aa Ab Laut Chalein, Dilwale Dulhaniya le Jaayenge, Yaadein, Kaante, Kabhi Khushi Kabhi Ghum, Namaste London* and *Ramji London Waaley*. I have chosen a few of these for the discussion that follows. Post-90s films depict the second or third generations of the Indian diaspora in various countries. The diaspora is not anymore the distraught, agonised, suffering, alienated, marginalised and underprivileged as was generally shown in the earlier films discussed above; instead the diaspora in most of all these films are affluent, satisfied, happy-living among big communities, educated, highly skilled, fashionable and enjoying the mainstream power positions. These films cater to entertainment needs of diaspora because there has been a major and gradual shift in the film making policy of the Indian filmmakers. The earlier films depicted the woes of the Indian diaspora to the Indians back home and with an interminable suggestion that the best solution was in the actual homecoming. The desire of homecoming has, by now, turned into the 'myth of return' which along with 'the lived experience of a locality' (Brah, 1996,192) forms 'the homing desire' (Brosius 2005, 208). By now the diasporic settlers have realised their various 'geographies of identity' (Lavie and Swedenburg, 1996, 04) in the form of hybridised cultural constructs evolved out of the canons of multicultural interactions of the diasporic settlers. The films nowadays depict these cultural constructs on a grand canvas with dexterous strokes of designer clothes, foreign locales, intercontinental plots, melodramatic lyrics and upbeat lifestyles.

Aditya Chopra's *Dilwale Dulhaniya le Jaayenge (DDLJ)* enjoys the status of being a super-hit film in India as well as in the overseas territories, and enjoys an important status in the Indian film history. *DDLJ* has an intercontinental plot that is the sequence of events run from Europe (UK) to Asia (India). The protagonists are played by Shah Rukh Khan and Kajol. Shah Rukh and Kajol are second-generation diasporic Indians settled in the UK. Amrish Puri plays Kajol's father. Kajol has been brought up along with her sister in a traditional environment close to Indianness provided by her parents even though they had been living in the UK for a long time. She is engaged to a boy in India who is the son of Amrish Puri's friend. Though she hasn't seen the boy, yet like a stereotypical Indian daughter accepts the father's wishes as her destiny. The Europe-trip on which Kajol meets her love interest, Shah Rukh, provides a scenic effect to the film with which any diasporic viewer would instantly identify.

To see one's life depicted on the big screen provides gratification to the desires of the audiences for two reasons in the case of the diasporic audiences: firstly that they have never been depicted as part of these geographical features in any kind of media portrayal as the Indians are mostly shown with the backdrop of Indian locations only and secondly the sense of belonging or the 'homing desire' that they possess with regard to the space and time shown in this part of the film provides the diasporic audience a balance between the Indianness and the Westerness.

Kajol's father would never break up his promise made to his friend in India, so he orders his family to rush to India along with him so that Kajol can immediately be married off to her fiancé in India. Shah Rukh follows her lady-love down to a small village of Punjab where the celebrations for the wedding along with the usual gaiety and upbeat mood of the Punjabis provide another setting in a different time and space, which easily stirs the nostalgia among the diasporic audience.

Amrish Puri is shown feeding the birds in his village as well as in London. There is a sense of relating immediately to the two cultures; one culture is preserved in the heart and the other one is a lived experience. There is a different homecoming in the film: the father forces the family to shift to the village in Punjab as he is hurt and feels insecure by the behaviour of the Indian youth in the UK. He fears losing grip on his values and traditions that hold his family intact, and believes that a physical transfer from India to the UK or the UK to India can actually make a difference. Shah Rukh's character explicates the notion just opposite to Amrish Puri's opinion as he doesn't want to elope with Kajol even at the behest of her mother who fears that her daughter will suffer suppression and discrimination for being a woman. The character of Shah Rukh was hugely popular among the diasporic audiences as he portrayed that élan which the diaspora wishes their generations to possess so that they may nurture the Indianness in their hearts with a perfect match with the progressive attitude of the West. Shah Rukh, with his sweet nature and caring attitude, wins everybody's heart in the family but not enough to get a nod for Kajol's and his liaison. At the end of the film the things fall in place as they do in almost all Bollywood films. The bride is then taken away by the bridegroom. The homecoming is in a way distributed in the film as Amrish Puri comes home to Punjab whereas his daughter and Shah Rukh come home to the UK. Home is shown to be not just the physical affinity to the homeland but home is where the people are at peace with their existence. Thus living in the foreign land is not shown as the reason to lose one's roots in the film; rather the protagonists in the film depict the new upbeat diaspora that manages to strike out a balance between the home and the exile. The film has been made with an attention to the desires of the Indian diaspora that doesn't want to come back finally but definitely cherishes a dream to return and therefore enjoys a momentary gratification of this dream through this film.

Subhash Ghai's *Pardes* was a big hit in India and was one of the early films which were made eyeing the diasporic bunches as the potential territories for the successful business overseas. The film's plot runs around a matrimonial entangle that comprises two young Indians of affluent origins from the US and a young girl of conventional origin from India. The girl (Mahima Choudhary) is engaged to the son (played by Apoorva Agnihotri) of her father's old friend settled in the US. The problem comes up when the girl comes to terms with the reality after going to America with her fiancé's family, that her fiancé is not a true Indian at heart and has imbibed most of the Americanism in his behaviour. She drifts away from him only to get closer to her fiancé's friend and confidante, Shah Rukh Khan, who is opposite to Apoorva Agnihotri. He values Mahima's Indianness. Both find themselves in love with each other, and the love triangle gets complex enough to bring both the families to India where the issue is resolved with a little violence but more or less with typical non-violent amicability. Even Apoorva Agnihotri's family members uphold that their son has been found wanting in the test of Indianess. The film is shot with the picturesque backdrop of the canonic structures of the two cultures: from the Brooklyn Bridge, Times Square, Manhattan City to the Taj Mahal, Buland Darwaza, Fatehpur Sikri and the green farmlands of Indian villages, all provide an eyeful of camaraderie between the obvious geographical identities and the oblique imports of familiarity for the diasporic audience who are close to both the lands. The film was a bigger hit overseas for the reason that the film does not propagate homecoming in the traditional sense, but rather is close to the desires of the diaspora about relentless relating "personally or vicariously, to that [India sic.] homeland in one way or another, and their ethno cultural consciousness and solidarity are importantly defined by the existence of such a relationship", (Safran, 1991, 83-4). The family of Apoorva Agnihotri manages to live up to this expectation consciously reasserting the solidarity of such a relationship with their homeland by upholding the virtuous behaviour of Shahrukh Khan as a quality desirous of a groom for Mahima Chowdhary. The popularity of *Pardes* can also be attributed to the fact that the upper middle class and affluent Indian diaspora are at leisure and comfort now, to look beyond for their options of entertainment and cultural interactions. In countries like the US and the UK the Indian diaspora (also the South Asian diaspora) is living in big communities where the Bollywood not only acts as common mode of entertainment but also as a representation of moral values and cultural identities. For the first generation diasporic audiences *Pardes* is one of those Bollywood films which they consider as a 'fortress' and agents of authority for generating and enforcing ideas of a 'paradisiacal homeland' and notions of an authentic culture (Brosius, 2005, 215).

Karan Johar's *Kabhi Khushi Kabhi Ghum* (*KKKG*) also runs into different countries with a story line that depicts a father–son conflict, a sibling love, two love stories and above all a conflict between tradition and modernity. Hrithik Roshan plays the younger brother and Shah Rukh Khan plays the elder one. Contrary to the unification and final meeting that take place in the homeland in the previous Bollywood films, in this film the family reunites in the foreign land; traditions are upheld, modernity is embraced and multi-culturalism is celebrated.

Besides these thematic aspects there are various graphics and audiovisual aspects interpolated in the recent films in Bollywood in order to provide a treat to the diasporic audience. There are songs and instances in *KKKG* that frame the central part of the audiovisual treat to the diasporic audience. Jaya Bachchan, who plays Shah Rukh's mother, explains on phone the significance of Karwa Chauth (a festival on which the married Hindu ladies observe fast for a day to seek long life for their husbands) to Kajol, who plays Shah Rukh's wife, without knowing that she is actually talking to her estranged daughter-in-law. There is a celebration on this festival where the couples (Shahrukh –Kajol and Hrithik-Kareena) dance to the tunes that sing of seven lives' commitment while flaunting designer Indian clothes with ethnic accessories. Although the Indian diaspora live in the big communities in the US and the UK yet still they don't get much of the chance to attend various ceremonies and rituals enough to let their younger generations know the exact thing. Therefore such portrayals in the films tend to draw a big attention of the diasporic audience. Such similar celebrations are there in *DDLJ* too where the Mehendi song is being danced to by the whole family besides a Karwa Chauth sequence. The technique is quite obvious as the new film-makers realise the significance of these songs, festivals etc. and spend huge part of the film budget in order to make them the ultimate selling points of their films among the diasporic audience. *Pardes* too has a song 'Yeh mera India ..I love my India' which echoes in the backdrop like an anthem.

In another recent film, *Ramji London Waaley*, the protagonist Ramji (played by Madhavan) goes to London. He is a chef by profession and tries his luck in the foreign land. After a series of events the film reaches the climax which is a prolonged depiction of the dilemma of Ramji—whether he should come back. The film revolves around this dilemma but does not portray the foreign land in the bad light. For Ramji, going to London means: acquiring a new set of experiences and a new identity which empowers him to settle down in his own country with a new vigour. The title of the film is the most peculiar feature as the term 'London Waaley' (habitant of London) is a typical coinage of the colloquial Hindi language where the name of the native place is suffixed with one's name in order to have an identification and sense of belonging to one's native land. The title thus hints at the dichotomisation of a sensibility as although Ramji comes back to India but he has now become a 'London Waala'. This merging of the two diverse notions foregrounds the effort of the film-maker in order to reach a point of harmony between the two cultures so that the film may have a popular viewing among the diasporic audiences.

Film-makers have been trying to reach out the diasporic audience of the whole of the South Asia. In many films Pakistanis and Indians are shown to have a good understanding between them. Their camaraderie is often portrayed in the films. Recently made *Namaste London*, the leading lady's (played by Katrina Kaif) parents have a close familial relation with a Pakistani family whose son (played by Upen Patel) is a close confidante of Katrina Kaif. Interestingly, both the families suffer from the similar cultural problems with regard to their young children, as shown in the films. This film also shows a homecoming when Akshaye Kumar brings Katrina to India as his wife. In the film *Naam* too the protagonist Sanjay Dutt has a closer relationship with a Pakistani family that also decided to finally come back to their homeland after getting sincerely touched by the melancholic lyricism of the then famous number 'chiththi aayee hai...' rendered by Pankaj Udhas in the film. The fact that the subcontinent's people can understand Hindi films and most of them can even speak Hindi creates new 'geographies of identities' in the distant lands where the culture and language are completely alien. Therefore, this cross-cultural interaction is reached out through the films by the film-makers who definitely aim to project what is liked by the rich diasporic audience in such films.

Conclusion

A study of the pre-1990s and the post-1990s separately leads to conclusion that the changes which have taken place over the decades in the lives of the diasporic settlers, which are more or less positive changes, have provided new vistas of film-making for the Bollywood film-makers. The economic affluence, multiculturalism and a perennial 'homing desire' combine to embolden the Bollywood film-makers to interpolate more and more diasporic sensitivities in the films.

References

Bose, Derek. *Brand Bollywood*. 2006, Sage Publications: New Delhi, Thousand Oaks, London.

Brosius, Christiane. "Bollyworld through the Diasporic Lens", in *Bollyworld,* Raminder Kaur and Ajay J. Sinha, eds., 2005, Sage Publications: New Delhi.

Brah, Avtar. *Cartographies of Diaspora: Contesting Identities.* 1996, Routledge: London and New York.

Lavie, Smadar and Ted Swedenburg (eds). *Displacement, Diaspora and Geography of Identity.* 1996, Durham and London: Duke University Press.

Safran, William.. 'Diasporas in Modern Societies: Myths of Homeland and Return', *Diaspora,* 1, 1, 1991, 83-99.

21

Shifting Continents in Kiran Desai's *The Inheritance of Loss*

— *Priyanka Tripathi*

Whitman states, "India is a vast and complex country; it contains multitudes." and English expresses that diversity better than any Indian language precisely because it is not ingrained in any one region rather phenomenal in the upcoming global scenario. In the wake of steady expansion and more recent explosion of Anglo-Indian and Indo-Anglican writing, the literature of Indian diaspora has become the object of close attention. In the same context observation of Kiran Desai's *The Inheritance of Loss (2006)* is not only inheritance of loss but also loss of inheritance. It is a refined, intensely pertinent assessment of globalisation and the Indian diaspora. Migration is a sword with sharp blades on both sides. The sentiment of deficit is intensive and awful when one leaves one's birthplace. Every person handles with such situations in one's own way. "Could fulfillment ever be felt as deeply as loss?"[1] She asks in the beginning pages of the novel and keeps on pondering over the same throughout. *The Inheritance of Loss* contemplates on loss as an emotional location, a sentiment shared by a gamut of characters continually torn and split by their meets with the modern world.

Kiran Desai was born in India, did her schooling in Delhi and Kalimpong in the Himalyas. She then moved to United States and did her graduation from Columbia University. In this novel she flashes back and forth between Kalimpong and New York throughout. The beginning of the novel truly reflects the longing and belongingness of the novelist to India:

All day, the colors had been those of dusk, mist moving like a water creature across the great flanks of mountains possessed of ocean shadows and depths. Briefly visible above the vapour, Kanchenjunga was a far peak whittled out of ice, gathering the last of the light, a plume of snow blown high by the storms as its summit.[2]

This picturesque description of the Himalayas is not hypothetical that Desai would have heard of or read in magazines. They were the reminiscences of the ten years she had spent in the eastern Himalayan town of Kalimpong.

Not only the craft but also the emotional content of the plot ties itself to more than one country. This also is a familiar landscape to her. Her mother, the well-known novelist Anita Desai, is half German and half Indian. Her grandmother never returned to Germany after the war. Her paternal grandfather left India to study in England. In her early teens, Desai's parents divorced and her mother first took her to stay in Kalimpong, then later immigrated with her to England. At 15, she moved again, this time to Boston, where her mother got a teaching assignment in a college. "We went through the immigrant experience together," she says and also adds, "As an immigrant you tell yourself a story that you'd like to believe and you keep reinventing yourself through a process that involves many stories."

The novel, which covers the India of 1980's India and America, opens in the town of Kalimpong located on the Indian region of the Himalayas, where Sai has come to reside with her grandfather, a retired, Western-educated judge, JemuBhai Popatlal Patel. The novelist says:

> In Kalimpong, high in the northeastern Himalayas where they lived—the retired judge and his cook, Sai and Mutt—there was a report of new dissatisfaction in the hills, gathering insurgency, men and guns. It was the Indian-Nepalese this time, fed up with being treated like the minority in a place where they were majority. They wanted their own country, or at least their own state, in which to manage their own affairs.[3]

Orphaned at a young age, Sai has grown up in isolation but is taking her first tentative steps towards love by being amorously involved with her math tutor, Gyan, the inheritor of a Nepali Gurkha mercenary. But the social and economic gulf divides them in due course, and it becomes too clear, causing him to withdraw and fall in with a group of ethnic Nepalese insurgents in the name of colonial modernity. Their neighbours are an odd assortment from Uncle Potty who loves his tipple, and Aunt Noni and Lola who between them take care of Sai's sketchy education.

In a parallel narrative, we are shown the life of Biju, the son of Sai's grandfather's cook, who belongs to the "shadow class" of illegitimate immigrants in New York, and who spends much of his time escaping from the authorities, moving from one ill-paid job to another. But the cook considers him 'the luckiest boy in the world' who was granted an American visa and is making a new life in New York. His hopes and dreams are entirely focused on him, and he keeps boasting about him with everybody every now and then but the real condition is in contrast with the boasted situation or the situation depicted by his son in his letters. Desai writes when she describes one of the Indian restaurants Biju works at:

> In the Gandhi café, the lights were kept low, the better to hide the stains. It was a long journey from here to the fusion trend, the goat cheese and basil samosa, the mango margarita. This was the real thing, generic Indian, and it could be ordered complete, one stop on the subway line or even on the phone: gilt and red chairs, plastic roses on the table with synthetic dewdrops, cloth paintings portraying.[4]

What bind these apparently dissimilar characters is a shared historical legacy and a common experience of impotence and humiliation. "Certain moves made long ago had produced all of them," Desai writes, referring to centuries of subjection by the economic and cultural power of the West. But the initial stages of an evidently even field in a late-twentieth-century global economy serve simply to scratch those wounds rather than heal them.

The judge's story, which comprised cruelly concealed memoirs, emerges intermittently, and together these incongruent sagas craft an asymmetrical but gripping description. This is a structure which she considers as emotional parallels or pattern. In the novel, the judge's journey to racist England as a student follows the agonising process by which he becomes alien even to himself. To quote from the text: "Eventually he felt barely human at all, leaped when touched on the arm as if from an unbearable intimacy, dreaded and agonised over even a "How –do-you-do-lovely –day" with a fat woman dressed in friendly pinks who ran the corner store".[5] On his return to India, he finds himself spurning his culture, family and wife. He states, "An Indian girl could never be as beautiful as an English one".[6] In due course he unconsciously makes an attempt to "colonise" his backward wife.

"'Take those absurd trinkets off,' he instructed her, annoyed by the tinkle-tonk of her bangles. 'Why do you have to dress in such a gaudy manner? Yellow and pink? Are you mad?' He threw the hair oil bottles away and her long hairs escaped no matter how tidily she made her bun". [7]

In this manner, Desai cautiously gears the private and personal into a wider political framework. The hostility between a husband and wife becomes globally proportioned: "They belonged to this emotion more than to themselves, experienced anger with enough muscle in it for entire nations coupled in hate".[8] It shows, without judgement, what happens to those who abandon the old for a new life. In fact, the reason why he accepts Sai so willingly is because she is a lot like him, a Westernised Indian, an "estranged Indian living in India." She tries to trace the pattern of the loss.

Longing is perhaps the thing that the characters in this novel do best. They long for home, they long for love, and they long for acceptance — yet rarely are they skilled at locating any of the above. That's not to say that the lives in this story don't include tenderness and occasional moments of cozy pleasure. They do. But perhaps Gyan, the young tutor, says it best when he glimpses - after failing to find a sense of purpose in history and politics, that "happiness has a smaller location."[9] Desai endeavours to illuminate the consequences of colonialism and global conflicts of religion, race, and nationalism. Through Jemu, we experience the postcolonial era in all the cruelty of its old, ingrained hatred and prejudices, and through Sai we experience the precarious present. Her characters are so alive, the places so vivid, that the reader is always inside their lives. The antagonisms and tremor of the larger world — the collision of races, classes, cultures, and generations—

are filtered through the characters. Desai is not representing India rather presenting India with a Western perspective. What Pankaj Mishra comments is not devoid of truth: "Although it focuses on the fate of a few powerless individuals, Kiran Desai's extraordinary new novel manages to explore, with intimacy and insight, just about every contemporary international issue: globalisation, multiculturalism, economic inequality, fundamentalism and terrorist violence".

Thus, we find that Desai's novel is full of shifts, be it geographical, physical or even emotional, and thus it very much can be read as a work bordering on the recurrent theme of majority of diasporic literature.

References

1. Desai, Kiran. *The Inheritance of Loss*. London: Penguin Books. 2006. p. 2.
2. Ibid, p. 01.
3. Ibid, p. 09.
4. Ibid, p.145.
5. Ibid, p. 40.
6. Ibid, p. 168.
7. Ibid, p. 172.
8. Ibid, p. 173.
9. Kehe Marjorie. *Hearts in Search of Home: A review of "The Inheritance of Loss."*

22

The Diasporic Poetry of G.S. Sharat Chandra

— *Basavaraj Naikar*

G.S. Sharat Chandra (1945-2000) was a poet of Indian diaspora living in America. He has published five collections of poetry namely, *April in Nanjangud* (1971), *Once or Twice* (1974), *Heirloom* (1978) *Immigrants of Loss* (1993) and *Family of Mirrors* (1993). Recently he has also published a short story collection entitled *Sari of the Gods* (1998).

He hails from Nanjangud in Mysore district of Karnataka State, India. After his education in Law at Pune (India) he went to Canada and received another law degree from Osgoode Law School in Toronto. There he felt that "lawyers were pompous asses...There was racism in Canada then and no one would hire me. I left Canada and went to Iowa City." [1] It was there that Chandra began to realise an ambition cherished since his days as a teenager – to become a poet. This was his greatest achievement. Later he became a Professor of Creative Writing in the University of Missouri, Kansas State, USA and practised the genre of poetry, fiction, and short fiction.

In the early seventies, he published interesting translations of a few *vachanas* of Sarvajna in *London Magazine*. A brief look at his career is enough to show how he was compelled by the contingencies of his life and quirks of fate to leave his motherland and settle in America in search of better material comforts and recognition. Obviously, he was destined to be an expatriate poet who was to oscillate between two cultures, i.e., native Hindu culture and American culture at least in the initial stage of his migration. In the later stage, he was slowly absorbed by the American culture, which diminished his attraction for the native culture and nostalgic attachment.

As the poet's vista of experience grew wider, his perceptions of life grew sharper and his dilemmas also might have multiplied. A migratory bird has to keep on adjusting itself to ever-new atmosphere without losing its basic identity. "We are all, he seems to say, immigrants in the land of imagination."[2] He believes that "It is human to miss something that was there before – country, town, place, street, wives, husbands."[3] Thus we may trace an evolution in Sharat Chandra's poetic career, which begins with native experience, passes through immigrant experience and ends up with American experience.

Sharat Chandra's early experience in his native land may be seen in his early collections of poetry. In his interview with Mary Vasudeva and Deepika Bahri, Sharat Chandra clarifies his views about his native place and childhood experience as follows:

> No neglect or abandonment by family, as Bruce King erroneously speculates in his book Modern Indian Poets in English. I had a wonderful childhood in a large family. But the sense of being lost is a quest for answers not simply for myself, but for understanding the conflicting psychological selves we possess.[4]

In the present article an effort has been made to understand the major themes articulated in *Heirloom* and *Once or Twice.* The poems in this collection show not only his native and homely experience in India especially in Karnataka, but also his separation from his motherland and the consequent nostalgia. Like many globetrotting poets, he also has the advantage of adopting a contrastive mode of perception, i.e., East-West encounter. Familial relations happen to be the dominant themes in the poems in *Heirloom*. Family, therefore, becomes a dominant metaphor controlling the poetic perception of Sharat Chandra. While in India he prepares himself to go to America and while in America, he nostalgically remembers India and corresponds with his father and other relatives:

"I feel terribly nostalgic and miss everything that was part of my life. But it is important that this sort of nostalgia shouldn't overwhelm the sense of universal aesthetics. Poetry is art and art doesn't accommodate sentimentality".[5]

Biff Russ observes:

> Chandra's particular hell, like Dante's, is centred in his sense of displacement..Dante himself, banished from his beloved city of Florence, demonstrated that one of the essential qualities of all damnation is homesickness. Chandra, in his updated way, knows exactly what he means.[6]

Most of the poems in *Heirloom*[7] and *Once or Twice*[8] deal with Indian, especially South Indian, more especially South Karnatakian life — like painting, sculpture, beggary, bureaucracy, funerals, holy shrines, fishermen, farmers and other details of cultural environment. Family or familial relationships happen to be the dominant metaphors in his Indian poems. The relationship between father and son in its various manifestations is an important motif in some of his poems.

In "Poems for My Father", the poet recounts the last moments of his father and his attachment with the latter and the former's expectations about the latter. The first stanza describes the illness of his father and how the entire family is silently worried about it:

> In the kitchen my father
> squats as usual,
> the family gathers around
> to discuss his last illness,
> my father looks well,
> he scoops up the rice and curry
> eats it calmly,
> he too is talking of his illness.

Then he describes how his father's disease was not diagnosed properly, how it was malaria and not cancer, which enervated him and how he appeared to be recovering. The poems, obviously, articulate the poet's nostalgic memory about his father, the concern of the members of his family for the father's health and their anxiety about his imminent death. The poet, who has been living in America thousands of miles away from his motherland, feels a special bondage to his family and the head of the family, i.e., father. What is admirable in the poet is that in spite of being in America and enjoying a very comfortable life there, he cannot afford to forget his father as the Indians, especially Hindus attach a great deal of importance to the father because father and mother happen to be gods for the children.

But when the poet goes away from India to America he receives a letter from his mother that the father has started bleeding. The poet is unable to reconcile himself to the harsh reality and has a wishful dream. He suffers from deep anxiety about his father. Again the father appears to be temporarily better and wants to wait for the poet's publication of his book of poems named after his native place, i.e., Nanjangud, for a hearing aid and a little port wine. But before the father's expectations are fulfilled he is overtaken by death. After his death in Mysore, he appears to the poet in America (i.e., Mount Pleasant) and seems to talk with him telepathically.

The expatriate or diasporic experience consists in one's going away from one's country and coming back to it nostalgically and to notice the change that has been brought about in the native country by Time. It is this experience, which has been recounted in the "Return" section of the poem. When the poet lands in India, perhaps at Bangalore or Bombay, he feels the torrid heat of the tropical country, which provides a sharp contrast to the cool climate of America:

> At the airport
> The family Fiat
> crackles in the heat,
> the doors are hot
> as the underside
> of an electric iron.

The backwardness of the village, hence of the country stares hard in the poet's face:

> The roads to home
> are scant bound as ever
> coolies move along the potholes
> with gravel pans on their head
> bullock carts trundle
> in and out the car's wheel-span.

The effect of Time on life may be felt conspicuously. His mother has become old and looks as frail as a sparrow. His father is dead and cremated according to the customs of his caste:

> My father
> cremated by the river's bend
> then transferred in a basket
> skull pelvis femur
> lies under the mango tree
> free of caste and skin.

Life continues and modernity has crept into the town. The rich have bought air-conditioners and the poor are reconciled to their lot. The poet plans to go for a pilgrimage. The mother is reconciled to her widowhood and loneliness. The idea of the father's death makes the poet aware of the possibility of reincarnation, which is part of Hindu faith.

In the poem entitled "Consistently Ignored," the poet shows the boy's curiosity, seriousness and the maternal humour and myth-making capacity. In the villages of Karnataka and also perhaps in India, the mothers tease their children by saying that they bought them from some beggar or caught them from the sky. It is this collective myth that the poet tries to deconstruct in the present poem:

> Consistently ignored in a family of ten
> I asked mother, 'Am I your real son?'
> She paused from grinding spice,
> 'No, I bought you from a beggar
> For a bushel of rice'
> From behind sisters giggled.

The boy (i.e., the poet), unable to distinguish between humorous myth and reality, takes it very seriously and begins to search for the beggars from whom he might have been bought:

> I matched features, spied on beggars
> Roamed the backyard thinking
> Of distant huts, certain
> My mother sat busy in one
> Scheming to trade another son
> For fish to add to that bushel.

The boy's inability to understand the parental humour is itself quite humorous and throws light upon the working of a boy's psyche.

The metaphor of the family is conspicuous in "Brothers." The brothers, who are brought up together and grow together, are separated by the contingencies of life like marriage and jobs at different places. Perhaps the separation is part of one's growth in life. The poet deplores that:

> My brothers come visiting less and less
> they come
> leaving their wives and children
> in sleep.

The poet wants to be close with them once again and longs for the bliss of childhood marked by fraternal affinity and cordiality:

> I hold their hands
> we are children once again
> this is the dream I understand
> which takes me
> to places where I would stay
> places
> I would not want to leave.

The poet longs to recover the lost affinity and cordiality:

> We should go on this way
> forever
> I tell them they listen they listen
> they promise to be closer.

In this poem Sharat Chandra obviously shows the universal experience of man in very simple terms. He has shown how the process of growth in life involves the loss of childhood, paradise and the distancing from the close relatives and how a sensitive soul longs for the recovery of that paradise. The poem remotely brings to our mind the poems of similar themes by Wordsworth.

In *Heirloom*, there are a few poems, which are autobiographical in nature and give expression to his thoughts about his personal predicament and dilemmas. In "My Thirty Third

Morning", Sharat Chandra offers an autobiographical picture about himself. He turns thirty-three on a grey morning and dreams of a song, of a crow, of ducks with silent squawks and thrushes with suspended whistles and imagines himself to be a crow being scared of squawking ducks. His thirty-third birthday is marked by a sort of fear and mechanical living without any grand or colourful dimension to it:

> The crow crows at the break of light
> Who would say it has inclinations
> Scares easily of squawking ducks
> Head-on thrush collisions,
> It's none of these but myself
> Turning thirty-three on a grey morning.

"My Thirty-Fifth Birthday" is a nostalgic evocation of the poet's childhood in Karnataka, India and also shows a contrast between the Indian past and the American present. He, for example, remembers his vernacular medium of instruction and his slips in the recitation of Sanskrit hymns from the *Vedas* for which he is disliked by his high school teacher. Likewise, he remembers his chaste aunt, who used to sniff a brand of snuff named after a goddess. Similarly, he remembers the old gramophone records of military hotels blaring with their sound and chasing his car. He also remembers Mahatma Gandhi, who taught him the lesson of native life:

> Inside a touring talkies
> Gandhi himself pointed
> his fingers at me from a slide
> which read
> 'Be worthy of your mother country.'

The irony may be in the contrast between the past days spent in India and the present stay of the poet in America:

> All this
> just because
> until late in the night
> in this American town
> I drank scotch
> and cursed in English.

In "Buckled to My Waist," Sharat Chandra recounts his close relationship with his father and the importance of paternal advice. He seems to request his seven-year-dead father to forgive his mistakes as well as his longing for perfection. He confesses that it took him fifteen years to realise the truth of his father's advice:

> It has taken me fifteen years to learn
> the wisdom of your last whisper,
> fifteen years of dragging a makeshift
> bridge of words buckled to my waist.

The poet seems to be disillusioned with poetry, which has become a commercial affair, 'a chase of ordeals without hoof.' Although the eyes travel freely, the mind cannot do so as it is anchored to its bone. Similarly, the poet may be engaged in the free exercise of his imagination, but he cannot soar in the sky, as he is earth-bound. The over-all vision of the poems seems to be the striking contrast between the harsh reality and the unshackled play of imagination.

In the epistolary series of poems entitled "*Letters from My Father*" Sharat Chandra offers details of his family background in Nanjangud, the Government of Karnataka, their problems and concerns and socio-religious problems, etc. In the first letter, the father writes about the three ministers or politicians, who wear the Gandhi-cap and control the Government and debate over the use of English language. Then he writes about his poverty:

> Today we had no rice
> so we ate green beans and curd
> the milkman is out looking for a patch of grass,
> it has not rained since 1973

Then the father writes to the son about the failure of rains in Karnataka and the effort of the Government to get some artificial rains with the American help:

> our government has proclaimed
> they'll make rain
> the eldest son of our chief
> is already in America
> to ask the President for some clouds.

The ironical contrast between the scientific method of attracting the clouds and the religious especially superstitious method of conducting some ritual to attract the rains is suggested in a very subtle fashion by the poet. The hunger of the people is described in a very ironical tone by the nephew of the poet:

> Your nephew says
> if the government cordoned off
> the hungry millions together
> over a parched field of wheat
> *they'd cry enough to make bread.*

In the second letter, the father informs the son about the effect of political life upon the civilian life. The poet's doctor-sister is transferred to some other place simply because she made the Deputy Minister's wife wait for some time. In the third letter, the father informs the son about the geographical and social changes, which have affected them adversely. The heat is terrible hence 'sacrificial.' The effect of Time on human age is described by the father: "This afternoon my skin hangs heavy on my back".

The economic poverty has brought about a lot of change, almost degeneration in the society of Karnataka. It is indirectly described by the poet:

> The washerman's donkey hops
> round and round in the alley
> it isn't convinced
> the garbage pail is empty of dinner leaves.

This description is followed by an ironical one:

> No one eats with leaves any more
> it's faster from hand to mouth
> if there's enough to hand
> to mouth...

The fourth letter recounts the father's mystic experience so common in old age among the Hindus:

> I have a strange feeling
> someone sits in the front-room

fanning the heat from his face:
do you think it is Him?
Perhaps he took a shortcut by draught...

The mystic experience is accompanied by a philosophical reflection in a Hindu's life. The father asks such a philosophical question:

Isn't the body a wrap within a wrap
folds of goatskin
hiding the dark it hides from
the dark it'll accompany?

In the fifth and last letter, the father writes about the poet's mother. It easily shows the mother's religiosity, concern and affection for the son:

Your mother sends dried camphor
from the feet of the Lord:
her eyes still light up at your letters
though she fails on her feet.

The father further advises him to go to the third country for better prospects and nobler ways of living. The last section looks like an anti-climax on account of its note of practical suggestion:

If you don't hear from me
do not be pensive
it only means
I've run out of ink...

The lengthy epistolary poem, thus, offers a varied picture of the Hindu family, socio-political, financial and mystical aspects of life. All these details are part of the poet's diasporic nostalgia for his motherland, and his desire to keep in touch with his roots lest he should forget or lose them as he is overwhelmed by the American culture.

"The Black Deity" depicts the superstitions of the Hindus in an objective fashion. When the poet watches the black idol of a goddess on the *Mylapur* hill of Madras, he notices the hot afternoon and the drying trees. The horrid summer of India creates the problem of water and food for the natives. The villagers, who cannot understand the irregularities of Nature, blindly attribute them to the wrath of a goddess in accordance with their anthropomorphic religious belief:

> At the village men whispered
> Of the black deity's wrath—
> Pestilences or death in the family.
> The priest counselling sacrifice
>
> Kept glancing at the tree
> Where the batu-birds stilt-walked.

The poet, who understands the superstitious belief of the Indians, tries to visualise the scene of people getting ready to offer the sacrifice:

> Now, miles away from the tree,
> I have a vision of a posse
> With lanterns and axes
> Creeping up the hill.

"Vendor of Fish" offers a beautiful picture of the life of a fisherman marked by hard labour and hope of security and comfort so essential for human happiness. The poet describes his diary of hard work in the first stanza:

> All night he waits at the harbour
> his eyes the colour of sea
> the sea the colour of trawlers
> he grabs the finest wipes them
> on his shawl his shawl
> the colour of blood.

One may easily see the unifying bond between the fisherman, the boat, the sea and the fish in the stanza. There is almost a religious devotion in the fisherman for the whole phenomenon of his profession. The fish that the fisherman catches has a practical, especially a commercial value for him. It is inevitable for his survival, i.e., for his food:

> Fish the colour of rupees
> he thinks of the meal he'll buy

the meal of chapatis and kurma
the fish in the smell of kurma
he packs them in the basket with ice
his hands the colour of fire.

It is the dream of a better life that galvanises him and quickens his movements. The dream also enhances his aesthetic sensibility thereby enabling him to appreciate the beauty of the fish. His joy of life expresses itself in the form of a song:

He leaps on the tar road faster
than sweat can print his feet
the distance is the colour of dreams
the fish in the basket shine
sawdust daubs their fins
he sings in praise of their colour.

In "Self-Portrait", Sharat Chandra offers an autobiographical picture. He claims that he has no belief in astrology and does not have a clear picture of his future life:

There are scars instead
of lines on my palm
I've no biography
only remembrance.

He is aware that his life is marked by a sense of emptiness:

I say
leaves have a habit
of giving in to emptiness
like oysters with pearls
missing...

When he encounters an astrologer in a nameless street, who holds a horoscope to his face, he bares his shirt and shows them his bony body and walks away from them.

"Relatives" (*Once or Twice*, p.11) happens to be an imaginary picture about the poet's own future life. When he writes his last poem, his relatives come to him and ransack his body for the last poem and try to arbitrate over his art. The poet seems to be satirising the possessiveness and the greed of the relatives, who want to derive some profit or even reputation from the poet, but alas, without trying to understand his heart:

His manuscripts fly around
like feathers of a shot bird
his love spreading
her long dress her hair.

They try to understand some hidden message in his tears and examine his cheeks. They seem to be in a hurry to understand him:

he examines the cheeks as he wipes them
he stomps his boot with urgency

When they cannot understand the meaning of the live poems, they believe in the afterlife of the same and therefore, seal them in transparent wrappers and send them to lawyers:

He believes in the afterlife of the poem
as silverfish eggs of moth
he seals them in cellophone
he sends them to his lawyers.

Finally, when they cannot understand the meaning of the poem in their lifetime, they leave it to their children to pursue it:

We'll bequeath our search
to our children they say
owning the last poem
will be its own reward they say.

But they feel proud of the physical possession of the poem, though they can never enter its semantic heart.

In "Tirumalai" (*Once or Twice*, p.18), the poet highlights the contrast between religious faith and the harsh and ugly reality in the Hindu context. Venkateswara happens to be the Lord of Seven Hills and attracts thousands of devotees every day. The poet also being a Hindu is naturally inspired to visit the deity:

Lord Vishnu's place
Also known as Lord Venkateswara

He turned stone on the seventh hill
While visiting earth on a curse
He ran into woman trouble.

After explaining the mythical background of Lord Venkateswara's descent to the earth, the poet describes various aspects of the deity's role. He is known as a rich-god in South India:

Since then he's grown famous
As arbiter of disputes
Bribed with rubies and emeralds
By those who can afford such bribes.

Politicians speak well of him too
So do government servants
Wanting promotion or increment
Women wanting child or husband.
Some visit incognito
Others with bare hands
Or faceful of tears.

Thus people have pitched their faith in the Lord of Seven Hills for various reasons. The poet also is made by the circumstances to believe in it:

I, when I was four,
Gave the Lord my head of hair
I was told that would make me rich
My hair prosperous.

But the irony is that the poet's faith is totally nullified by the harsh reality of his experience:

The father who said that is dead.
My mother who held me to the barber
Ails with age and despair
The hills have changed hands
I have grown bald
And owe two payments
On the alimony.

The brief examination of the Indian themes in Sharat Chandra's poems shows how the opposite pulls of longing (for India) and belonging (to America) control his emotions and perception and how he has to strike a balance between physically going away from the native country and emotionally coming home repeatedly. This paradoxical experience of going and coming happens to be an important aspect of diasporic experience.

References

1. Mackle, Lynn, "Features", *University News*, October 7-13, 1996.
2. Russ, Biff, *The Kansas City Star*, Sunday, October 24, 1993.
3. Mackle, Lynn, "Features", *University News*, October 7-13, 1996.
4. "Swallowing for Twenty Years/the American Mind and Body: An Interview with G.S. Sharat Chandra" by Mary Vasudeva & Deepika Bahri, *Journal of Commonwealth and Postcolonial Studies*, Vol 5, No.1. Fall 1997, published, April 1998, Georgia Southern University, Statesboro, USA. p. 13.
5. "An Interview with G.S.Sharat Chandra: A Poet of Indian Diaspora," Basavaraj Naikar, *Literary Vision*, New Delhi: Sarup & Sons, 2005, p.116.
6. Russ, Biff, "The Kansas City Star", *Sunday*, January 15, 1995.
7. Sharat Chandra, G.S. *Heirloom*, Hippopotamus Press, Surrey, 1978
8. Sharat Chandra, *Once or Twice*, Hippopotamus Press, Surrey, 1974.

Index